What's the Shape
of Narrative Preaching?

EUGENE L. LOWRY

What's the Shape of Narrative Preaching?

Essays in Honor of
Eugene L. Lowry

MIKE GRAVES & DAVID J. SCHLAFER, EDS.

CHALICE
PRESS
ST. LOUIS, MISSOURI

Cover art: © Crosiers
Cover and interior design: Elizabeth Wright

Visit Chalice Press on the World Wide Web at
www.chalicepress.com

10 9 8 7 6 5 4 3 2 1   08 09 10 11 12

Library of Congress Cataloging–in–Publication Data

What's the shape of narrative preaching? / edited by Mike Graves and David J. Schlafer.
   p. cm.
   Includes bibliographical references and index.
   ISBN 978-0-8272-4255-5 (alk. paper)
   1. Narrative preaching. I. Graves, Mike. II. Schlafer, David J., 1944-
III. Title.
   BV4235.S76W43 2008
   251—dc22
2008007541

Printed in the United States of America

Contents

PART III

Prospects: What Fresh Shapes Might Narrative Preaching Take?

Selected Works of Eugene L. Lowry

Books

The Homiletical Plot: The Sermon as Narrative Art Form. Atlanta: John Knox Press, 1980.

Doing Time in the Pulpit: The Relationship between Narrative and Preaching. Nashville: Abingdon Press, 1985.

How to Preach a Parable: Designs for Narrative Sermons. Nashville: Abingdon Press, 1989.

Living with the Lectionary: Preaching through the Revised Common Lectionary. Nashville: Abingdon Press, 1992.

The Sermon: Dancing the Edge of Mystery. Nashville: Abingdon Press, 1997.

The Homiletical Plot: The Sermon as Narrative Art Form. Expanded edition. Louisville: Westminster John Knox Press, 2001.

Articles and Essays in Books

"The Homiletical Bind," *Christian Ministry* (January 1975): 20–22.

"The Narrative Quality of Experience as a Bridge to Preaching," in *Journeys Toward Narrative Preaching*, 67–84. Edited by Wayne Bradley Robinson. New York: Pilgrim Press, 1990.

"Peace and Passion in Preaching," *Pulpit Digest* (September-October 1990): 84–86.

"Preaching or Reciting? Theft in the Pulpit," *Christian Ministry* (March-April 1991): 9–12.

"The Revolution of Sermonic Shape," in *Listening to the Word: Studies in Honor of Fred B. Craddock*, 93–112. Edited by Gail R. O'Day and Thomas G. Long. Nashville: Abingdon Press, 1993.

"Narrative Preaching," in *Concise Encyclopedia of Preaching*, 342–44. Edited by William H. Willimon and Richard Lischer. Louisville: Westminster John Knox Press, 1995.

"Preaching the Great Themes," in *Preaching on the Brink: The Future of Homiletics*, 57–65. Edited by Martha J. Simmons. Nashville: Abingdon Press, 1996.

"Surviving the Sermon Preparation Process," *Journal for Preachers* 24 (Easter 2001): 28–32.

"What Progress!?" in *What's the Matter with Preaching Today?*, 159–69. Edited by Mike Graves. Louisville: Westminster John Knox Press, 2004.

Published Sermons

"Listening to the Dark, (1 Kings 19)," *Pulpit Digest* (July-August, 1990): 11–17.

"The Drink, (John 4:3–19)," in *Best Sermons 3*, 237–46. Edited by James W. Cox. San Francisco: Harper and Row, 1990.

"Cries from the Graveyard, (Mark 5:1–19)," in *Daemonic Imagination*, 27–39. Edited by Robert Detweiler and William G. Doty. Atlanta: Scholars Press, 1990.

"Strangers in the Night, (John 3:1–9)," in *Journeys toward Narrative Preaching*, 78–84. Edited by Wayne Bradley Robinson. New York: Pilgrim Press, 1990.

"Stones and Bones, (Acts 6:1–14; 7:51–60)," in *Best Sermons 7*, 190–95. Edited by James W. Cox. San Francisco: HarperSanFrancisco, 1994.

Introduction

For at least twenty-five years now, the discipline of North American homiletics has been in the throes of an emerging new homiletical paradigm. Many of us mark its beginning with the publication of Fred Craddock's first book on preaching.

Thus Eugene Lowry commences his own volume, *The Sermon: Dancing the Edge of Mystery.* The "new homiletical paradigm" of which Lowry speaks, now more than thirty-five years in the making, has been called a "Copernican revolution" in preaching theory.[1] If Craddock has been Copernicus, showing the preaching world how sermons revolve around listeners as well as texts, then Lowry has been the movement's Galileo. More than anyone else, Gene Lowry has repeatedly engaged the work of Fred Craddock and added his own creative voice.

The connection between these two homiletical luminaries is telling. Lowry fondly remembers how, just three years after he had himself accepted a position at Saint Paul School of Theology, Craddock published *As One Without Authority.*[2] Appearing when it did, the book's influence on Lowry's career was immeasurable.

1

One could argue that many of the questions Craddock asked in his groundbreaking work have shaped Lowry's own contributions to preaching as he has sought answers to Craddock's questions:

- Craddock asked why forms of Greek logic continue to influence sermons more than the literary forms of the Bible. Lowry responded by looking to the parables of Jesus for homiletical guidance.
- Craddock pondered why ministers continue to "serve up monologue in a dialogical world." Lowry highlighted the participatory nature of narrative preaching, with a loop that involved listeners.
- Craddock asked why so many preachers feel compelled to give away their sermons in the first moments, like starting a joke with the punch line. Lowry responded with the suggestion that the beginning of a sermon should "upset the equilibrium" of listeners and create a "homiletical bind" (the originally proposed title for his highly influential work, *The Homiletical Plot*).
- Craddock wondered why preachers so often make plain what is mysterious and ineffable, and why listeners' doubts and questions are ignored. Lowry asserted that ambiguity is the essential characteristic of narrative preaching, that in our preaching we must dare to dance "on the edge of mystery."
- Craddock asked what it would mean for sermons not just to say something but do something. Lowry wrote of the sermon as plot, an evocative event.

Throughout his career, Gene Lowry has maintained the highest respect for the work of Fred Craddock. Nowhere is this more evident than in a story Gene tells on himself in relation to Fred. Gene had gone in for a surgical procedure. In the recovery room as he began to emerge from the anesthesia into a semi-conscious state, the attending nurse asked him, "Who's Fred Craddock?" Gene responded spontaneously, "Who's Fred Craddock? He's the most influential homiletician of the twentieth century!" Then struck with the oddity of the question, Gene added, "Why do you ask?" The nurse informed him that, for the entire time he had been under anesthesia, Gene had mumbled over and over, "Fred Craddock has no peer. Fred Craddock has no peer."

This collection of essays begs to differ with that assessment. While all contemporary teachers of preaching work in the light of Craddock, Lowry's impact has been meteoric as well (evidenced most recently in his selection as Lyman Beecher Lecturer for 2009). Thus, in this volume fourteen contemporary homileticians honor Gene with their own appraisals of narrative preaching. Some engage Lowry's work directly, others tangentially. All wrestle with one issue: the shape of narrative preaching. By "shape," we refer to the *status* of narrative preaching today as well as to the different expressions of narrative sermon *form*. The authors explore a host of questions, such as: Is narrative preaching just a fad? What are the biblical precedents? The historical roots? What has changed since 1980 when Lowry first published *The Homiletical Plot*? What might need to be rethought today? What are the strengths and weaknesses of the narrative approach? What is the role of narrative preaching in a time of rampant biblical illiteracy? How does narrative preaching jive with postmodernism? How does narrative preaching help to shape congregational life?

Although arranging the essays according to Lowry's loop would have been poetic, alas, we focus on three points. The first section, "Wellsprings," explores factors that have given rise to the current narrative preaching movement. Charles Rice surveys recent homiletical history, looking at some of its most influential persons and their approaches. Ron Allen examines four different understandings of narrative preaching and the theology undergirding them. Beverly Zink-Sawyer considers how the rise of narrative preaching and the New Homiletic coincides with increased numbers of female preachers and feminist approaches to the preaching task. Bobby McClain earths the roots of narrative preaching in the rich soil of the African-American pulpit tradition.

In the second section, "Assessments," contributors discuss the current shape of narrative preaching. Dick Eslinger traces the evolution of Lowry's thought, and addresses some of the criticisms it has provoked. From varying but complementary angles—and a seasoned, generation-long perspective—Fred Craddock, David Buttrick, and Tom Long all weigh the implications, culturally and theologically, and the cost and benefits of undertaking the preaching task as a narrative art form. Confronting several sometimes shrill objections to Lowry's method, Robin Meyers belts out a response in resonance with the jazz improvisation that is as much a hallmark of Lowry's homiletic as is his "loop."

Ultimately, students must take the work of their teachers in new directions. Thus, in the final section, "Prospects," Frank Thomas explores possible connections between narrative preaching and the phenomenology of hope. Barbara Lundblad challenges the narrative preaching movement to engage more directly and deeply the narratives of women and other marginalized persons, especially as found (but often ignored) in biblical texts. Mike Graves notes the importance of ambiguity in Lowry's narrative preaching, but wonders what it would be like only to *hint* at resolution in the sermon itself—just as some of Jesus' more radically open-ended parables do. Analyzing New Testament epistles as narratives of moral discernment, David Schlafer asks how preaching might be employed in fostering faith community responses to moral crises and quandaries. Employing musical metaphors, Tom Troeger imagines what narrative preaching might look like in an increasingly globalized world, concluding with a poetic tribute to Lowry and his work.

Gene Lowry's contribution to homiletics calls for a collection like this to be published, and we are grateful to Chalice Press for supporting this project. Normally, graduate students who were nurtured by their master teacher and wish to pay him tribute would take on editing such a collection. In Lowry's many years of teaching at Saint Paul School of Theology, however, he worked primarily with preachers in training for parochial ministry. Gene has mentored the two of us in many formal and informal ways over the years. We consider him not only a mentor but a colleague and friend. Therefore, on behalf of the Academy of Homiletics, we have taken it upon ourselves to compile these essays. The Academy would not be what it has become without the published works of Lowry; neither would the Academy's annual gathering, with Gene at the jazz piano on Saturday nights. Add to that Gene's remarkably gracious wife, Sarah, a fixture at Academy gatherings. (Some of us would rather see her than Gene any time.) It is to the two of them that this work is lovingly dedicated.

Advent 2007
Mike Graves and David J. Schlafer

PART I

Wellsprings

What Gives Shape to
Narrative Preaching?

1

A More-or-Less Historical Account of the Fairly Recent History of Narrative Preaching

CHARLES L. RICE

Narrative preaching is neither new nor novel, especially in the American experience; it has taken many forms in the pulpit. The earliest preachers were eager to tell of the signs of Providence both in nature and in human affairs. A Massachusetts divine declared that "the cow doth calf and the milk doth clabber, and great are the ways of God." When the first settlers came ashore they told their story in a phrase, a narrative that continues to sway the American psyche: "Having been brought safely to this good land..." Believing they were a people whose every trial and achievement revealed divine Providence, they melded their history with the biblical stories. That coalescence of story with Story continues to this day.[1]

In the pulpit, this confident narrative has often taken the form of testimonial. The compelling, sometimes tear-jerking story of conversion has been characteristic of the revival movement. Across the spectrum of denominations and forms of worship, it is the exceptional American preacher who has not turned to the personal illustration to move the congregation. In his history of the United States, Henry Steele Commager concluded that there is nothing Americans like so much as a huckster.[2] The stock-in-trade of the huckster, politician or revivalist, has been the enthralling narrative. Ronald Reagan used vignettes of the war hero and the working mother, touching stories—often illustrated by the presence of the very person—to sway Congress and the public, a technique still in use. Garrison Keillor, on *A Prairie Home Companion*, tells down-home stories about family, small-town life, and religion that have both heart and a political edge. Even on television, among the most popular documentaries are those that tell stories of individuals—from Thomas Edison to Jesse James—or the story of the nation, its tragedies and triumphs.

A powerful influence on the American pulpit in the first half of the twentieth century was Harry Emerson Fosdick, founding pastor of the Riverside Church in New York City and preacher to the nation on the National Radio Pulpit. Fosdick called for a reconsideration of rigidly theological and textual preaching, advocating "life situation" preaching instead.[3] He claimed that those who preach are greatly mistaken if they assume that people come to church with a burning desire "to learn what happened to the Jebusites." Rather, he said, people come with human questions and problems. The preacher, accordingly, should speak to specific human situations. Not only did Fosdick tell biblical stories; he told stories that came his way as he went about the work of a city pastor. He carefully recorded the events and the dialogue of his daily rounds, and this material found its way into the Sunday sermon.[4] The result was preaching Fosdick described as "pastoral counseling writ large," a model that has had lasting influence on the American pulpit.

But in seeking the sources of narrative preaching, we need to go much farther than American culture. Storytelling is a universal and indispensable human means of symbolic communication. Humanity lives by narrative; hearing and telling stories we organize and give meaning to our experience. Our ancestors gathered by the fire to remember and create stories as a way of giving meaning to the present and moving purposefully toward the future.

Frederick Buechner has said that Christians are people who know some stories and tell them to others.[5] This is no less true of those who follow Judaism. The Hebrew Scriptures start with, "In the beginning," and the Christian Bible ends with a vast and colorful drama of the end. Everything in between is steadied and propelled by telling the old stories and connecting them to the daily drama of our unfolding history.

So, what has occurred in the field of homiletics since Amos Wilder published *Early Christian Rhetoric* in 1964 is not so much invention or innovation as rediscovery. Christians and Jews have lived by story from the beginning. What we have seen is a growing body of literature, accompanied by preaching in the churches, exploring the theological underpinnings and homiletic possibilities of preaching as storytelling.[6] The chapters that follow in this book reveal the rich terrain of that exploration and the contribution of one of its leading scouts, Gene Lowry. This chapter will describe the seminal work of representative figures.

Amos Wilder [1895–1993]

Biblical scholar—and brother of playwright Thornton Wilder—Amos Wilder, first in *Early Christian Rhetoric* and later in *Theopoetic*, laid the groundwork for homiletic advance in the last third of the twentieth century. Wilder's interest in rhetoric and literature came to focus on the literary heritage of Judeo-Christian faith. In his effort to allow the Bible and contemporary literature to cast light on one another, he published *The New Voice: Religion, Literature, and Hermeneutics*.[7] Here he shows that among the many literary forms of the Old Testament, the narrative mode is primary: "In Israel an earthy kind of realism came to birth such that its recitals encompass and interweave the whole story of heaven and earth and of man in unique fashion."[8] Narration, Wilder says, creates order: "Indeed, the biblical epic remains as a kind of cable or lifeline across the abyss of time and cultures, because man is here sustained over against anarchy, non-being, nescience. In this sense language is, indeed, a 'house of being.'"[9] Israel lived by narrative, dwelt in a house of narration: the history of a people, the lives of its kings and prophets, the stories of men and women, and the imagined story of the coming messiah and the reign of peace.

Wilder went on to investigate the language of the gospels, asking what rhetorical forms provided the earliest expressions of Christian faith. He was among the first to point toward story as a natural speech-form for the gospel. The anecdote, he says, belongs to the earliest speech of the church and is essential to the community's celebration of the gospel. Wilder gives an example in Jesus' cure of the blind Bartimaeus at the gate of Jericho, calling this story "a small companion piece to the Resurrection-drama."[10] He suggests that the models for preaching as storytelling are in the gospels themselves.

Wilder concludes that the nature of the gospel *per se* shaped the language of the early church as these faith communities relied primarily on various forms of story.

How they expressed themselves, Wilder claims, was formed by *what* they believed, by the gospel itself, just as Jesus' quintessential preaching took its shape—in the parables—from his vision of the reign of God. Wilder writes:

> How Jesus and his followers spoke and wrote cannot be separated from *what* they communicated. It was the novelty of grace and the fundamental renewal of existence which brought forth a new fruit of the lips, new tongues and rhetorical patterns... The language phenomenon which broke into the world with the discourse of Jesus and which continued in the church arose out of a depth of impulse which imposed plastic expression throughout. The early Christian vision and grasp of existence...had a dynamic character...a level of apprehension which the New Testament speaks of as that of the Spirit.[11]

This was new wine, demanding new and supple containers. From the beginning, the gospel demanded imaginative expression. In his later work, Wilder stretches this further:

> In liturgy and festival, but also in prophecy, the divine reality mediates itself through plastic images and metaphors and stories which take hold of our experience. It is only through such a total register that the Gospel can reenact itself anew in our time.[12]

This understanding of biblical language has had a lasting influence on the direction of homiletics into the third millennium.

In his description of the earliest Christian communities, Wilder set forth a dozen ideas that proved seminal for the teaching and practice of preaching:

1. Language is potent, and the word, particularly the spoken word, is central in Christian faith and practice.[13]
2. Expression of the Christian gospel is extempore.[14]
3. There is no commitment to a holy language, a "language of Zion."[15]
4. Christian rhetoric is not verbose, and this economy of expression derives from the nature of revelation.[16]
5. This speech is communal.[17]
6. Our words, following the incarnation of the Word, are prone to the incognito and the understated.[18]
7. This rhetoric is directed toward the heart.[19]
8. This language is artful without being studied, as in the parables of Jesus.[20]
9. The parables of Jesus reveal the organic connection of metaphorical speech and the kingdom of God.[21]
10. Christian communication, more often than not, is story.[22]
11. Poetry is a large part of both the Old and New Testaments, and the poetic should be understood as organic to human life.[23]
12. The New Testament writings are largely works of imagination, as faith reveals itself in the varied and plastic expressions of its various genres.[24]

The gospel has been passed on and interpreted as a continuing narrative. From the early fathers of the church to the present, we see pastors and teachers doing their interpretive and guiding work as storytellers: the narratives of Augustine and the allegories of Origen; the preaching friars, such as Jacque deVitry and his *exempla*; even the windows and sculpture of Europe's cathedrals, telling the Story when preaching had lost touch. Though we might not call the Reformation imaginative, it was a great and vital new story, unfolding in the stories of its leaders and in the vivid telling of examples of faith.

Edmund A. Steimle [1907–1988]

For more than a quarter of a century as a teacher of preaching— at the Lutheran Theological Seminary in Philadelphia and at Union Theological Seminary in New York City—Edmund Steimle, both by his own preaching and through his students, shaped American preaching. He was heard widely on "The Protestant Hour" from 1955 to 1974. Those who listened to his distinctive voice absorbed a distinctive approach and style. His easy, dialogical manner—cultivated especially for radio—trained the ears of preachers and churchgoers alike for sermons in the inviting style of the storyteller.

His preaching was friendly, low-key, down to earth, disarming in its simplicity. In a letter to the Lutheran Department of Press, Radio and Television, an executive of the National Broadcasting Company wrote:

> I thought you would like to know what a favorable impression Dr. Steimle's broadcasts have produced among the professionals in the radio field. I have been out of the country, and not able to hear every broadcast, but my own reaction (and a general one, I think) is that he is exceptionally pleasing and compelling. There is about his voice and manner an informality that is at once expressive and intimate. In my view, this is far and away the best manner such a speaker could have, for radio is a very personal medium, speaking to multitudes, to be sure, but to each one individually.[25]

A person hearing Steimle for the first time would have been puzzled: he did not sound like a preacher. His sermons were given in the context of conventional Lutheran liturgy, but he called these addresses "conversations."

Steimle was the son and grandson of clergy, for whom the question of language was a major issue. So strongly did his grandfather believe that the Lutheran liturgy should be said in German that he withdrew seven congregations from the Northeast Synod of the Lutheran Church to form the German-speaking "Steimle Synod." Young Edmund was steeped in this ethnic tradition, but he also loved being an American. Rather than going to a Lutheran college, he enrolled at Princeton, where he studied English. Every sermon he wrote reflected this love of the language. Thus Steimle prepared the way for the growth of the "New Homiletic," and for a new emphasis on preaching as narrative. Employing the most exacting discipline in exegesis and in sermon composition, Steimle relaxed the form and style of preaching. Anyone hearing him would have sensed new possibilities for preaching. It was possible simply to speak *with* people, as if talking to someone over a cup of coffee about an issue of mutual importance, trusting the story to carry the message without coming down hard or laboring a point.

In large measure, this was just the sort of person Steimle was. He had a clear theological perspective, however. Steimle's homiletic was shaped by a theology of the Incarnation. As he put it: *God does not blast away; God comes down.* His own contemplation of the meaning of the Incarnation led Steimle to speak in such a way as to give preachers permission to tell the Story in the form of ordinary story.

In 1980, Steimle—along with Morris Niedenthal and Charles Rice—published *Preaching the Story*. In the introduction, Steimle wrote: "We have chosen to concentrate our focus...on that one insight, or perspective, which the three of us regard as of high importance: preaching as storytelling and the preacher as raconteur."[26] This book sets preaching in its threefold context: the Story, as found primarily in the Bible; a community's particular story; and the story of the preacher. The sermon is organically connected to the ongoing life of the Church, to the present experience of a congregation in its unique cultural and social context, and to the life of the preacher herself or himself. The authors write:

> Anyone who has experienced preaching, whether in pulpit or pew, knows that it is an event—a moment, a meeting, a sudden seeing—in which the preacher, listener, the message, and the impinging social environment all come together. Can we find a word for that event, a paradigm which will recognize all the elements and in doing so tell us what preaching is, and how it is done when it is done well?... Let us consider the storyteller.[27]

The paradigm pervading the book is *shared story*. Christian faith is hearing, telling, and living a story. Accordingly, given the nature of the Bible and of the daily life of the listeners and their ordained speaker, it is inevitable that preaching will be at its heart narrative.

Steimle was influenced by the work of H.H. Farmer—he assigned Farmer's *The Servant of the Word*[28] to most of his classes—who stressed the personal nature of preaching. Farmer made much of the human voice itself, and of the intimacy of speaking and hearing. Human beings like nothing more than a good story, especially when it is told person-to-person. Thus, in every culture we find the circle of storytelling:

> Picture, then, the storyteller—a listener, a host...in the middle of a circle of people; by the lake or around the fire; at the supper table on the evening of the funeral, over food gone cold and dishes unwashed; one to one, as the story comes out for the first, the healing time; over breakfast, with the newspaper open, remembering a little girl or boy; on the Fourth of July at a picnic, or at home on a snowy day with your grandparents; in a foxhole or a bar, or at the family reunion or around the communion table. The opening line is liturgical, a call to enter in and let something happen: "Once upon a time..." or "Do you remember when...?" or "I've never told you this, but..." or "A certain man had two sons..." Whenever it happens and whatever the form, we recognize it immediately, and we begin, as W.B. Gallie has said, to *follow*, to go with the story and the storyteller, whether the story is unfamiliar or one we have heard a thousand times.[29]

In the fall of 1970, at the annual meeting of the Academy of Homiletics in Princeton, Morris Niedenthal and Charles Rice presented papers solicited by Steimle, who served that year as president of the Academy. Niedenthal's paper appears in *Preaching the Story* as "The Irony and Grammar of the Gospel." Concerned for prophetic preaching, and trying to avoid sermons as "bad news," Niedenthal proposed a less heroic and more positive approach. The ironic mode "goes straight to our denial of ourselves as human beings in the concrete actuality of each: a mixture of weakness and strength, cowardice and courage, sin and faith."[30] Preaching in the ironic mode calls for telling the real stories of human life. In the second part of his paper, Niedenthal reminded readers that preaching is not in the subjunctive, conditional mode: "If you do this, then..." Rather, the gospel is in the indicative, telling the story of God's "mighty acts." Preaching brings together the real human story and the account, in the indicative mode, of God's Story.

Rice's paper on "The Expressive Style in Preaching" also called for a more unapologetically human approach. He compared a more mature and experienced preacher in introductory preaching to a novice, a woman. The man gave a sermon on "Do Not Be

Afraid,"—it was Advent—three points with illustrations from the lives of Lord Admiral Nelson on the burning deck and the brave wartime nurse Edith Cavell. The woman, by contrast, told the story of her daughter's struggle with depression during the Christmas season, a simple account of conversation in their kitchen and the effort to celebrate, or at least to go through the motions of the holiday. Rice called for a more personal homiletic relying on narration of ordinary human experience.[31] Both papers, sparked by Steimle's preaching and pedagogy, were seeking a way toward a freer homiletic confident in telling stories to communicate the Story.[32]

Rice expanded on his paper in a longer article in 1976, "The Preacher as Storyteller."[33] There he brings the work of Harvey Cox to bear on the growing interest in a narrative homiletic:

> Harvey Cox argues [that] what we need, from religion especially, is more personal ways of communicating which will make room for the eccentric, the particular, the concrete—for the quiddities and graces of human personality. We are too prone, says Cox, to live by "signals," those unambiguous and impersonal means of communication which allow society, or even a highly organized church, to hold together. What we need today, Cox thinks, are more provincial and personal ways of communicating— autobiography, "corporate autobiography," testimony— which help individuals and groups of people to identify themselves as persons with roots in the past and a place in the present.[34]

Edmund Steimle and those he influenced were seeking something like that. As wary as Steimle would have been of words like "autobiography" and "testimony," he saw the need for a more personal and story-like homiletic.[35]

Frederick Buechner [1926–]

Along with the works of Wilder, Farmer, John Fry (*Fire and Blackstone*) and B.D. Napier (*Come Sweet Death*), Steimle had most of his students reading Frederick Buechner's *The Magnificent Defeat*, published in 1966. On the last page of the book Buechner ends the sermon with a call to see the miracle at hand, the presence of God in our ordinary existence. It is a sermon on the parable of the good Samaritan, and the miracle is one person seeing another and stopping to help. He tells the story in his characteristic way, with imagination and freedom. He concludes:

> As surely as a sailing ship is made to sail with the wind, so are you and I and everybody else in this wide world over made to live bound to each other as a brother bound to a brother, giving and receiving mercy, binding up each other's wound, taking care of each other. If we only look at our own lives, seeing not what we expect them to be, but what they are, we cannot help seeing that. It can be imagined otherwise. We might have been made to live on self-interest or solitude or pure reason. Yet it is so…We kiss the flower that bows its head to us, open our arms, our lives, to the deepest miracle of reality itself and call it by its proper name, which is King of kings and Lord of lords, or call it by any name we want, or call it nothing, but live our lives open to the fierce and transforming joy of it.[36]

In his sermon on the annunciation he summarizes the point of view that shaped both his preaching and his work as a novelist and essayist:

> "In the sixth month the angel Gabriel was sent from God to a city of Galilee named Nazareth, to a virgin betrothed to a man whose name was Joseph, of the house of David; and the virgin's name was Mary," and that is the beginning of a story—a time, a place, a set of characters, and the implied promise, which is common to all stories, that something is coming, something interesting or significant or exciting is about to happen. And I would like to start by reminding my reader that in essence this is what Christianity is. If we whittle away long enough, it is a story that we come to at last. And if we take even the fanciest and most metaphysical kind of theologian or preacher and keep on questioning him far enough—Why is this so? All right, but why is *that* so? Yes, but how do we know that it's so—even he is forced finally to take off his spectacles and push his books off to one side and say, "Once upon a time there was…," and then everybody leans forward a little and starts to listen.[37]

This meant for Buechner that the preacher's stock-in-trade was the commonplace and earthy. In his sermon on the walk to Emmaus he says that the disciples saw Jesus and heard the word "not in a blaze of unearthly light, not in the midst of a sermon, not in the throes of some kind of religious daydream, but...at supper time, or walking along a road."[38] About the time this book was published, the movement that came to be known as the "New Hermeneutic" was asserting that the word of God was an *event*, and that this saving moment was inseparable from what Ernst Fuchs called simply "daily life."[39]

Not only Buechner's sermons but also his autobiographical, theological, and fictional writing have influenced homiletics. His gift lies in a light touch in bringing together the biblical and human stories, so that one illumines the other. This juxtaposition is seen in his description of waking up one morning: "Darkness was upon the face of the deep, and God said, 'Let there by light.' Darkness laps at my sleeping face like a tide, and God says, 'Let there be Buechner.'"[40] Here story meets Story, and—as Paul Scott Wilson says—the spark that we call the preached word jumps between them.[41]

Buechner offered preachers new possibilities for learning from other storytellers. Homiletical literature having to do with fiction and cinema began to appear. The eleventh volume of The Preacher's Paperback Library, titled *Interpretation and Imagination*, appeared in 1970,[42] which attempted to point preachers to novels, plays, poetry, and films as avenues for interpreting the gospel. The author relied especially on the cultural theology of Paul Tillich[43] and the historico-ontological hermeneutic of Frederick Herzog[44] as a way to bring contemporary experience into genuine dialogue with Christian tradition:

> The historico-ontological method, then, enables us to hold together religion in the limited sense—holy history and the tradition stemming from it—and religion in the broad sense, the whole range of man's concerned experience. Any serious preacher who does not know it already will eventually discover that he of all people must *live* that method, or, better put, that he holds together in his person holy history and ontological concern. Great preaching appears where a man lives by faith in the

world. The homiletical task is hermeneutical: the preacher is intent upon coming to and sharing understanding. Hermeneutics is finally a way of being in the world. That way of being in the world is homiletical: the specific place where the Christian tradition meets present experience is the sermon…It was the homiletical task which led me to think that contemporary literature might provide a place of meeting where faith sees itself more clearly and is, accordingly, able to make itself more visible.[45]

Edmund Steimle once said: "The sermon that starts in the Bible and stays in the Bible is not biblical."[46] The Bible in its reliance upon storytelling and its interest in human affairs—the history of a people, economics and politics, domestic life, nature and agriculture—calls on the preacher to consider the text in a living context.[47] *Interpretation and Imagination* seeks to open the preacher toward a larger, more worldly use of narrative by incorporating five sermons, each of which brings together a story from popular arts and a text from scripture.

Fred B. Craddock [1928–]

In 1971, out of Oklahoma came a slender volume that was to open even wider vistas. As Professor of New Testament and Preaching at Phillips University, Fred Craddock wrote with a recognition that "Homiletics was hanging by its nails on the edge of most seminary catalogues."[48] He described the apparent decline in regard for, and in the effectiveness of, preaching. There was, Craddock claimed, something essential missing, having, in part, to do with form:

> [T]he sermons of our time have, with few exceptions, kept the same form. What message does such constancy of method convey? Either the preacher has access to a world that is neat, orderly, and unified which gives his sermon its form, or he is out of date and out of touch with the way it is. In either case, he does not communicate.[49]

Craddock sought for preaching that could transform the listener: "We will know power has returned to the pulpit when and where preaching effects transformation in the lives of men and in the structures of society. There is reason to believe that this transformation is not far away."[50]

Craddock was careful to say that there is no one way to preach. Echoing Wilder, he believed that "the forms of preaching should be as varied as the forms of rhetoric in the New Testament, or the purposes of preaching or as the situations of those who listen."[51] At the same time, he introduced a method that became a guideline to a variety of sermons. This methodology was primarily a matter of *movement*. Does the sermon move and in what direction? Movement is of fundamental importance not simply because the speaker wants to get somewhere in his presentation but because the movement itself is to be an experience of the community in sharing the Word.[52]

The conventional form of homiletical movement receives a fair hearing—preachers have used deductive method with undeniable success, yet: "Simply stated, deductive movement is from the general truth to the particular application or experience while induction is the reverse."[53] Craddock argued that deductive movement is more formal than actual, more a succession of points than a series of movements that mirror experience. Craddock made his case for inductive method in preaching—not only is inductive method closer to the way human beings think and live; it reflects the actual sequence of the preacher's preparation: "In most sermons, if there is any induction it is in the minister's study where he arrives at a conclusion, and that conclusion is his beginning point on Sunday morning. Why not on Sunday morning retrace the inductive trip he took earlier and see if his hearers come to that same conclusion?"[54]

If this is done well, Craddock said, it will not be necessary for the preacher to make the applications of the conclusion to the lives of the hearers: "If they have made the trip, then it is their conclusion, and the implication for their own situation is not only clear but inescapable."[55]

Such language echoes Jesus' estimate of his parables to carry their own meaning, and his reluctance to explain them: "The one who has ears to hear, let him hear." Craddock's method has equal confidence in the capacity of human experience to carry the meaning, and in the ability of human beings to move with the preacher on this inductive journey.

Craddock stressed two matters essential to inductive movement: concrete experience and respect for the hearer. Human experience participates actively in the event of the word of God.

The closer the preacher stays to the human story, the better chance there is of achieving transformation through preaching. And—as with all storytelling—the teller, the preacher, must trust not only the story but the listener.

This language resonates with anyone interested in preaching as narrative: movement, participation, taking a trip, concreteness, leaving much to the hearer. Himself a master storyteller, Craddock can spin out a tale the length of an entire sermon. He can also use narrative in the most succinct way. For example, in showing the difference between the deductive and the inductive: "The minister says 'all men are mortal' and meets drowsy agreement; he announces that 'Mr. Brown's son is dying' and the church becomes the church."[56] In his recovery of the orality of preaching and its communal character, its concreteness and movement, Fred Craddock advanced narrative preaching far down the road toward lively and life-changing speech. A very specific way of accomplishing this appeared in 1980 in Eugene Lowry's *The Homiletical Plot.*

Barbara Brown Taylor [1951–]

In 1986, Barbara Brown Taylor published a collection of seventeen sermons, *Mixed Blessings.*[57] We are not likely to see a more accomplished set of narrative sermons, so lean and earthy, crafted by one who loves words and the Word. She owes much to Buechner and Craddock, as she acknowledges. We could also say that, in this frank and disarming way of telling stories, she owes something simply to being a woman. If we ask how we got to the place we have reached in narrative preaching, we must consider that women have tapped the deeper possibilities of storytelling in the pulpit.

In that first seminary class at Drew, where my student shared in her sermon what was going on in her family in a troubled Advent, it appeared that women were bringing something new to homiletics. At Duke Divinity School, as a graduate teaching assistant, I had taught only men—most of them still wet behind the ears—learning exegesis, textual-expository form, and something of an academic style. In my first female student I met a mature person willing to bring a real human story to the service of the gospel.

The economical homilies of *Mixed Blessings* bring the human story to preaching in a way that only a woman could have managed in the early 1980s. Looking back on that time some of us will remember women in seminary trying to imitate men in the pulpit. Had that effort succeeded, we would all have been the poorer. Who but a woman would take us to a mud bath in California's wine country to lead us to holy baptism? And who but a woman would end the sermon as she does, pointing to Jesus and his baptism?

> He has always led us from within our midst, joining us in the water, in the mud, in the skin to show us how it is done. If he had not been baptized, now *that* would have been sin for him—if he had chosen to separate himself from us as he had every right to do. But he did not. He took the plunge right along with the rest of us and so it came to pass the he who was without sin was baptized in the river Jordan to avoid the sin of standing apart from us. He is our servant and our Lord, and he never asks us to go anywhere he has not been first. From dust to dust and ashes to ashes, from the cradle through the waters of baptism to the grave he knows what we are up against and has showed us how to live so life never ends: choosing whatever will bring us closer together, and above all choosing the things of earth—doves, water, mud, skin, love—to carry out the purposes of heaven.[58]

Following the lead of Barbara Brown Taylor, women preachers have tended toward storytelling, and shown freedom and vulnerability in the art. In recent years we have seen this taking the form of careful reflection on preaching as local and communal, in the work of Lucy Atkinson Rose,[59] Leonora Tubbs Tisdale,[60] and Jana Childers—who has taken this to the level of dramatic performance.[61] As a consequence, we have also seen greater freedom among both men and women to tell and trust the story, however earthy, to embody the Word.

Martin Luther King Jr. [1919–1968]

The sixteen sermons published as *The Strength to Love* in 1963[62] are the merest approximation of what actually happened when Martin Luther King Jr. stood among his people to tell their story and—in a style that made the two inseparable—to preach the gospel.[63] As Henry Mitchell has shown, African American preaching is distinguished by its orality, spontaneity, and evocative power.

> African-American preaching is…imaginative, narrative, and prone to generate experiential encounter. This is in opposition to the Euro-American tradition of cognitive, essay-type sermons, designed to inform and convince by means of logic and reason. In white tradition, the implicit goal has been more intellectual assent than impact on life….A contemporary trend among academically prominent homileticians moves toward the *experience of the Word,* and in recent years this has brought greatly increased fruitfulness to the dialogue between African-American and Euro-American scholars.[64]

As an African American preacher, Martin Luther King could bring a whole congregation—even a vast audience filling the mall at the Lincoln Memorial—to tell its story, and to merge that story with the story of salvation. Even those who got no closer to Martin Luther King Jr. than the television screen have seen this.

We might not immediately identify the preaching of Martin Luther King Jr., or that of African American preachers generally, as narration. These sermons are not so likely to include the vignette or the extended narrative in the familiar pattern of an unfolding story: beginning, middle, and end. But if it is kept in mind that the African American preacher is more concerned with the story of a *people,* then the sermons of King and many others are clearly narration. The story that they and their people hold in common merges, in their preaching, with the story of Israel and with the gospel.

The image of the passionate preacher, who has deeply internalized the story of his people, and whose imagination is furnished with the biblical story, has become part of our homiletical legacy. Is it too much to say that every storyteller in the pulpit, every preacher who finds spontaneity and freedom by being caught up in a narrative, is indebted to the African American preacher? Henry Mitchell speaks of the "recovery of a powerful art."[65] That recovery has, in one expression or another, moved far beyond the African American pulpit.

Eugene L. Lowry [1933–]

Most would agree that Eugene Lowry's work, from *The Homiletical Plot* to the present, is about freedom in the pulpit. Lowry's ironic language in what may be his most memorable phrase—"doing time in the pulpit"—suggests both the bondage to formal outlines and static essays, and the possibilities of preaching as *an event in time*. This idea, which he exemplifies in theory and practice, continues to stir up those who work at preaching.

Lowry's writing has implications for virtually every aspect of homiletics. How do we approach the biblical text, from the first move toward listening to the scriptures? Are we aware, at each stage, of the situation of those who will hear this sermon, whose real lives question and implore the text, even complicate hearing it? How do we go about mapping out the short trip through the changing terrain that will be the sermon? What vehicle for communication— manuscript, notes, memorization, and so forth—could we use to be present at this event in time? How is the sermon related to the liturgical movement that surrounds it and to the time—Sunday to Sunday—that follows it?

Some would say that Lowry's method is itself too tight, that a congregation going through the loop every Sunday could eventually find it as old hat as the three-points-and-a-poem sermon. Others are not sure that sermons should always come to the satisfying resolution that we hear in Gene Lowry's jazz piano. Still others wonder if the method takes us back to the gospel's appearing as a kind of "tag line," the bad-news-good-news-let's-go-have-brunch Sunday morning.

Anyone willing to consider the vast and amorphous discussion of narrative preaching and to propose a specific way of doing it is bound to get both our gratitude and questions. Lowry has both. He has shown us something that is of the essence of preaching, used his experience and personal gifts to show us how that might work out in a challenging approach to preaching, and has been ready to entertain our questions. His own work has experienced the loop—the moments of complication—and we have all benefited that he has not yet reached, as Richard Eslinger puts it—"final homiletical rest."[66]

Where should we seek the sources of Eugene Lowry's work? It is clear that he shares the concerns—biblical, hermeneutical, homiletical, ecclesial, and social—of those named in this chapter. He has participated actively in the life of the Academy, both as a teacher and a colleague. But who can overlook his love of music, especially jazz, in his development as a thinker and writer?

John Knox, the great biblical scholar, delivered the James A. Gray lectures at Duke in 1956, on biblical preaching. He said:

> The Bible is the most realistic, profound, and moving account of man which man has produced. But preaching is also profoundly, radically, concerned with man, his need and his redemption, and it is no more effective, or even more genuine, than the preacher's understanding of the human situation is deep, and sure, and true.[67]

This is a point many have made, but none has considered so carefully as Lowry the implications of this for the *way* we preach. Preaching, not unlike soulful music, partakes of the human condition. As Lowry tells us in describing the sermon as a "plot," this is the way people experience life. That reality gives jazz its shape, as it opens the scriptures to the interpreter, illuminates doctrine,[68] and, as in Lowry's method, gives preaching its form. We must preach, someone said, from the soles of our feet. That is jazz, and that is the soul of Lowry's homiletic.

Knox went on to describe truly biblical preaching, beginning with a radical statement:

> The difference between biblical and unbiblical preaching has little to do with the structure of the sermon and whether it is topical or expository in form. The difference lies deeper than that. If it is possible to…to preach a quite unbiblical sermon on a biblical text, it is also quite possible to preach a quite biblical sermon on no text at all.[69]

Biblical preaching, Knox says, has four characteristics: (1) it stays close to the essential biblical ideas; (2) it is "centrally concerned with the central biblical event, the event of Christ"; (3) it "answers to and nourishes the essential life of the church"; and (4)

> True preaching is itself an event—and an event of a particular kind. In it the revelation of God in Christ is actually recurring. The eschatological event, which began in the coming of Christ and will end with the final judgment on, and the fulfillment of, history, is taking place recurrently,

or if you prefer, continuously, in the sacraments and preaching of the church. If this is not true, neither the sacraments nor the preaching matters much. Indeed, if that is not true, sacraments and preaching, in any authentic sense, do not exist at all.[70]

In one way of seeing it, Lowry's contribution is his own particular and original exhibit of preaching as an event in time. Congregations who celebrate the eucharist following every sermon may have easier access to this understanding, and less need for resolution within the sermon itself. That would be, for some, the place at which Lowry provokes the persistent question: Is it not the whole of the church's worship, its weekly liturgical loop, in which human questioning and longing, sin and need find the peace that passes all understanding?

2

Theology Undergirding Narrative Preaching

RONALD J. ALLEN

Preachers and scholars of preaching use the phrase "narrative preaching" to designate four related but often different approaches to the preaching task.

1. For some ministers, narrative preaching refers to sermons that are actual stories containing little if any explanatory material.[1] From start to finish, the preacher employs setting, plot, and characters to tell a story. This telling, without commentary, is how the sermon communicates its message. The preacher may simply retell a tale from the Bible or Christian history. Sometimes such story-sermons are created from the preacher's imagination; at other times, a pastor will tell stories from movies, novels, or short stories, from the lives of the congregation or from the preacher's own life. Or ministers base such a message on their personal experience, but disguise that element by telling the story as though it were about someone else. Occasionally, preachers tell two or more stories together.

2. Narrative preaching can signal the conviction that a sermon as a whole should move in a way that is similar to a story, though the content of the sermon is not a single, extended narrative.

This is Gene Lowry's own position.[2] The content may contain conventional biblical exegesis, questions raised by the biblical text and life, quotes from authorities such as theologians or social scientists, critical analysis (e.g., theological, social, political, and economic), and anecdotes from the news and the lives of the congregation and the preacher. While such sermons may contain propositions, syllogisms, and other conventional modes of communication and argument, the preacher arranges the pieces of the sermon to work together so that hearing the sermon is similar to the experience of hearing a story.

3. Narrative preaching is occasionally associated with doing theology by telling stories and reflecting on them. This informal and variegated movement is sometimes called "story theology." Sometimes these theologians and preachers let the stories do their own work; sometimes preachers reflect upon the stories.[3]

4. In a more technical sense, "narrative theology" refers to a theological approach, associated with the contemporary movement of postliberalism, the central conviction of which is that the work of the theologian and the preacher is to retell the biblical story(ies) so as to clarify their claim upon the contemporary world.[4] Many narrative theologians eschew attempts to ground epistemology, revelation, truth, and other concerns in philosophy (or in any mode of reflection outside the Bible or Christian discourse) or to interpret the Bible and Christian doctrine in, or correlate them with contemporary categories of thought. Instead, these theologians typically assume that the narratives of the Bible are trustworthy guides to the meaning of life (even if they are not always scientifically accurate), and they seek to elucidate the story of the Bible on its own terms. The narrative preacher thus seeks not to interpret, but to narrate the congregation into the larger and ongoing biblical story.

While these four approaches to narrative preaching have different nuances and sometimes move in different directions, they are undergirded by common themes. In this chapter, I summarize the key elements, beginning with the "narrative quality of experience." The Bible itself and the core of Christian doctrine have an overarching narrative character. I consider what happens when we hear a story or follow material conjoined in a plot. In the latter part of the chapter, I critically reflect on narrative preaching. Along the way, I mention some points at which these four approaches to narrative preaching intersect with those critical concerns.

Recognizing that interpretation always reflects aspects of the interpreter's predispositions, biblical and homiletical scholars increasingly reveal their own social locations. Believing this trend to be beneficial, I note that while I cut my preaching teeth on the second approach to narrative preaching (the whole sermon moving in a way similar to how stories move), and still deeply respect and practice that approach to preaching, I am a process (relational) theologian, practicing mutual critical correlation, rather than a narrative theologian in the technical (fourth) sense. Nevertheless, I aim to represent that viewpoint sympathetically if sometimes critically.[5]

"The Narrative Quality of Experience"

Long ago, Stephen Crites wrote a now famous essay that sets the stage for this discussion: "The Narrative Quality of Experience." Crites makes the crucial point that "the formal quality of experience through time is inherently narrative."[6] Our individual lives, and the lives of the communities of which we are part, inherently have a story character as we go from moment to moment, from day to day, year to year. From the moment we are born to the moment we die, our everyday experiences are individual narratives, and they are caught up in ever-larger narratives of family, community, nation, and world. Our most primal level of perception—before we can even speak—has a narrative quality. Within these narratives we often find ourselves reflecting on the significance of these narratives—smaller and larger—in which we live.

Linguists sometimes speak of two levels of language use, loosely corresponding to the primal experience of life as narrative, and to the secondary mode of reflection.[7] The first level is language that is close to the ways life unfolds in form and feeling. Event follows event, and out of the sequence, moments emerge when we come to perspectives on the purposes of life. Language and patterns of expression that are expressed similarly are often quite powerful, as they are charged with the feeling of primary experience. Narrative is a classic example of first order language, for narrative reproduces the experience of life itself. Narrative language has the quality of the experience it describes.

In the second level of language usage, we speak more abstractly to reflect on the meaning of existence. In this mode of expression we tend to speak in propositions; we name and evaluate experience according to categories, so we can place particular experiences or stories in larger patterns of meaning. This use of language allows us to speak with precision about matters ranging from science and medicine to mathematics and economics as well as feelings and values.[8] Indeed, philosopher of language Susanne K. Langer says, "Bare denotative language is the most excellent instrument of exact reason."[9] Second order reflective language enables us to remove aspects of ambiguity and to articulate clearly important aspects of what we mean, believe, and intend.

This penchant for clarity of propositional expression, however, also presents a difficulty, for life contains elements that are deep, complex, intuitive, and charged with feeling and awareness that cannot always be expressed in propositional discourse. In fact, we cannot always say clearly what we mean in propositional language because such talk may not allow for the larger penumbra of lived complexity within which the talk is taking place. The great strength of this second order function of language is to help us name and evaluate relationships among ideas and other matters, but elements of life experience are often intertwined with one another in ways that second order language cannot easily or satisfactorily negotiate. Often an experience or an encounter with an idea contains something "more" than can be clinically described.[10] The experience of hearing a narrative often evokes awareness of the "more," although we cannot describe it in a scientific way; when we hear a good story, we typically feel the presence of the "more."

Narratives not only *express* experience but also can *form* experience in those who receive the story. Hearing a story is very much like living through event(s) that the story tells. As Crites observes, "Stories give substance to the form of experience because [experience] is itself an incipient story."[11] In this regard Langer comments, "The 'livingness' of a story is really much surer and often much greater, than that of actual experience."[12] Why? Because the storyteller omits distracting detail (such as "my son is using a chainsaw outside my study as I write this") so that we can focus entirely upon the story itself.

Though Crites does not write about preaching per se, his comment about sacred stories extends to sermons that create a sense of "self and world." Such stories and sermons "orient the life of people through time, their life-time, their individual and corporate existence and their sense of style, to the great powers that establish the reality of their world."[13] People then live out of such narratives.

Preaching that directly tells a story filled with the depths and complexities of life thus creates in the congregation an experience that comes alive through the story-sermon (the first understanding of narrative preaching mentioned at the outset of this article). For Langer, the hearing of the story may be even better than being present at the event narrated in the story, for the congregation can be more fully attentive to the story. The story that is the sermon becomes a part of the experience of the congregation. Sermons function similarly when they use a narrative genre for the overall movement of the message, even when the sermon does not tell a story (the second understanding of narrative preaching), for the narrative movement of the sermon corresponds to the movement of life. Although such a sermon may not tell a conventional story with setting, plot, and characters, the act of reflecting on a biblical text (or on a doctrine, a practice, or a personal or social issue) in a narrative movement creates an imaginative experience of life itself.

These perspectives are illuminating as we consider that the Bible—the most important presence in forming Christian consciousness and community—both contains stories and has an overarching narrative character. While the connection between Christian doctrine and narrative is less obvious, doctrine (including systematic theology) also partakes of narrative qualities.

The Bible Tells a Narrative

Narrative theologians make the point that in order to understand a person as fully as possible, we need to hear and understand that person's life story, for this story reveals character, values, commitments, and feelings. We learn who people are, and what we can trust them to be and do, by hearing what they say, following how they act, paying attention to where they invest time and energy, noticing whether they live with integrity and keep commitments, learning why they change, discovering what decisions they make under stress, and so forth. Such stories have dynamic qualities and can incorporate unexpected developments that take place along the way. Even when our primary reference point for a person is a particular saying or a particular action, we understand that person more fully when we can place that saying or action in his or her larger life story. By following the larger patterns of what the person does and says, we learn who he or she is. The same thing is true of communities. To understand a community (such as a congregation or a movement) as fully as possible, we need to understand that community's story.

This phenomenon is particularly true when it comes to Christian community. The foundation of narrative preaching lies in the idea that Christian identity is essentially the story of God (and the world) moving from creation and fall through redemption to new creation. To be Christian is to be part of this story that begins with creation and continues until God's purposes completely shape every individual person, relationship, and event.[14] As Richard Lischer says:

> We tell stories because God's involvement with a historical people generated a story. The point is not to tell bunches of substitute stories for their inspirational value or to recount meaningful experiences that are vaguely analogous to divine truths but to tell one story as creatively and powerfully as possible and to allow that one story to probe our world.[15]

Philosophers of language, literary critics, and rhetoricians have long made the point that the meaning of a text is organically connected to the form of the text. A text is not simply a container for an idea in the same way that a cup is a container for a fruit smoothie. The meaning of a text is related to its form in the same way that a person is related to that person's body.[16] As the ancient Israelites taught, a person does not *have* a body but *is* a body. To change the form of a text is to change the meaning of the text. To preach in a narrative mode is to maintain organic continuity between the primary narrative quality of Christian experience and the sermon. To be sure, preachers and congregations often need to reflect critically on particular aspects of the larger Christian story, but these reflections—even when propositional in nature—are simply moments in the larger narrative framework of life.

The Bible plays a key role in the process of forming Christian identity as it tells the story of God and the world, and in so doing unfolds the character of God, the world, and the purposes of life, as interpreted by the biblical authors.[17] The Bible begins with the creation of the world, the entry of sin into the world and its consequences for humankind and nature, and the primeval history (Gen. 1—11), then focuses on the promises of God to the whole human family that are modeled through God's relationship with the family of Sarah and Abraham. Beginning with Genesis 12 and continuing through Joshua, the Bible tells the epic journey of that family from Ur through its journey to Egypt and enslavement and liberation, to the entry into the promised land. The story follows the judges (Judges), the rise of the monarchy and its division, the exile into Babylon (1 Samuel–2 Chronicles, some of the prophets), and return to the holy land where they live as a colony of occupying powers, including Persia, Greece, and Rome. Within this shaping narrative, the Christian Bible sets the story of Jesus Christ (Matthew, Mark, Luke, John) and points to the church as a confirmation of God's promises to the Gentiles, the great reunion of the human family, and the coming apocalypse (Paul, Acts, some other writings). The Bible climaxes with the apocalyptic book of Revelation and the hope that God will replace the current world (fractured as it is by idolatry, injustice, exploitation, and violence) with a new, unending realm of peace, justice, and love. The community that wants to know who God is, what God offers and expects, who we are, and what we are to do needs to hear this story.

Biblical scholars make the point that the Bible is not actually a single narrative (on the order of a contemporary novel that tells a single ongoing story from start to finish) but is more like a library, a collection of materials that tell or imply a set of ongoing stories. Scholars of form criticism and literary criticism help us recognize that the Bible contains many different kinds of narratives, such as sagas, call stories, parables, and miracle stories. Beyond that, many parts of the Bible are expressed in genres other than narrative ones, such as commandments, proverbs, oracles of judgment and salvation, letters, catalogues of virtues and vices, and apocalyptic visions. The Bible is not only diverse in literary and rhetorical forms but is also diverse in theological viewpoint. Biblical interpreters identify at least the following different theological viewpoints embedded in the biblical narrative: Elohist, Yahwist, deuteronomic, priestly, wisdom, apocalyptic, and Hellenistic Judaism. Of course, within these streams of thought, individual biblical authors and schools often articulate their own distinctive ideas. Indeed, some of these schools of thought offer not only different but conflicting, even competing, interpretations. However, while the biblical materials are diverse in literary genre and in theological worldview, they are, fundamentally, part of the ongoing story of trying to come to as clear and compelling an interpretation as possible.

To be sure, Christian identity involves more than listening to the biblical story. This identity emerges as the congregation interacts with the Bible, Christian tradition and doctrine, and the movement of the Holy Spirit—and as preacher and congregation reflect on the significance of these things for today. Even the narrative theologians do more than simply retell the biblical story; like other theologians, they reflect on the possible meanings of the biblical story and on the wider Christian story beyond the Bible in discursive and propositional modes.[18] However, the process of reflection—even when analytical and propositional—is itself a chapter in the ongoing story.

The Narrative Context of Christian Doctrine

Christian history from the time of the Bible until today is also narrative in character. One way to understand Christian history is to think of it as events following one another in which people living after the Bible attempt to come to adequate interpretations of the Bible and the implications of biblical interpretation for subsequent generations. These later generations attempt to correlate aspects of their own historical and theological settings with the biblical witnesses. From era to era, Christians respond to philosophical elements, social and political conditions, and other factors. Church historians attempt to tell the story of how particular communities in particular places came to particular understandings and embodiments of Christian faith.

Within the biblical period itself, and increasingly afterwards, occasional preachers and communities begin to outline the core of Christian faith in creeds and to explain Christian faith in other propositional modes of expression.[19] The Apostles' Creed (second century C.E.), for instance, is a series of sentences that summarize some leading Christian ideas about God, Christ, the Holy Spirit, the church, and the life everlasting. However, the historic creeds are informed by a narrative element in that they tend to follow the broad outline of the Bible moving from creation ("creator of heaven and earth") through God's activity in Jesus Christ (often summarized from birth through death and resurrection) to the climactic destiny of human life and the world ("the life everlasting"). Indeed, elements of the creeds often invoke aspects of the biblical narrative. Furthermore, the creeds arise from specific historical circumstances. The creeds are not disembodied sets of assertions but are records of living expressions of human stories to understand God in the midst of dynamics of particular moments in history.

We could say something of the same about many other writings through Christian history.[20] Even when preachers and theologians such as Augustine, Aquinas, Luther, Calvin, and Wesley seek to explain aspects of Christian faith in propositional discourse, they presume the biblical narrative. Moreover, they typically write in response to the stories of their times—particular conditions or events. For instance, when the Visigoths had sacked Rome and many people were in a state of despair, Augustine described the city of God. Although Christianity had become the official religion of the Emperor, some Romans believed that the former deities were punishing the Empire for turning away from pagan worship. Augustine wrote *The City of God* to encourage people to live in hope that the God of the Bible would replace the sin and chaos of the human city with the city of God.

Since the Enlightenment, many theologians have developed a propositional genre of summarizing elements of Christian faith and showing their relationship to one another—usually called systematic theology (or dogmatic theology). Systematic theologians often write in basic categories that are logically related: revelation and how we know God; basic beliefs about God, Jesus Christ, the Holy Spirit, the church, and the world. Systematic theologians typically deal with a wide range of concerns in the Christian community, such as providence, evil, ethics, prayer, baptism and the sacred meal, mission, and eschatology. Although systematic theologians typically write in an analytical style (and seldom in pure narrative), their work not only presupposes the stories of their times but is often their attempt to show how the biblical stories (and their interpretations) intertwine with contemporary stories. A particular systematic theology typically presumes the particular narrative of contemporary experience that the theology addresses. Liberation theologies, for instance, arise from a background of repression—e.g., ethnic, racial, gender, political, economic, and social.

While doctrine is often formulated in the form of propositions, doctrinal ideas typically receive their fullest and most evocative content from their place in the larger narrative framework of creation-fall-redemption-new creation, and from the specific biblical content associated with them. For example, the proposition that "God is love" is one on which almost all theologians, preachers, and Christians would agree. But the stories of God redeeming Israel from slavery, restoring the community after the exile, and raising Jesus from the dead as the sign of the new creation specify, deepen, and give much more emotional content and contact to this idea.

We might think of a statement of doctrine as the precipitate of a story of reflection on the Bible, previous theology, and experience that is intended to sum up the best of a theologian's or church's thinking for a particular moment of history. A statement of doctrine is a snapshot of what the church, at its best, believed at a special moment of history. Later generations may lose sight of the story of the historical circumstances and reflection that led to the statement of doctrine, so that today's congregation finds the affirmation distant, disembodied, cold, and even arbitrary.

A narrative approach to preaching can help the congregation develop a sense of the narrative context of Christian doctrine by leading the congregation to recover the story that gave rise to the doctrine and by helping the congregation discover how the doctrine can help shape the narratives of the congregation's life in the coming days and weeks. As I comment elsewhere, the preacher can give the doctrine a face.[21]

Critical Reflection on Narrative and Preaching

Like any movements in preaching, concern with narrative brings some cautions.[22] None of these concerns are inherently problematic, but all are serious enough for preachers to cultivate a critical eye regarding the practice of narrative preaching.

Perhaps the simplest matter has to do with sermons that are actually stories (the first approach above). Clifford Geertz, a leading anthropologist, urges people who attempt to analyze and understand communities to work toward "thick" descriptions—descriptions of the communities that go below the surface of what can be easily seen to the emotional, intellectual, relational, ritual, and ethical complexity or thickness of real life.[23] The same should be true of the story sermon, but preachers sometimes tell stories that are trite, neat, formulaic, or that otherwise do not adequately embody the struggles of human life. Those who would preach in this mode need to tell real stories about real people in real situations with which the congregation can resonate in depth.

Some ministers make excessive claims about the universality of the appeal of narrative preaching. Some who preach sermons as extended stories (first approach), who practice story theology (third approach), and who preach sermons that are narrative in structure though not in actual content (second approach) do not directly state the conclusion, claim, lesson, or moral of those sermons. They feel that the congregation itself needs to draw its own implications or conclusion. Some ministers shun sermon structures that are linear, that unfold as logical arguments, or are organized around points. These preachers assume that adults can draw conclusions and make their own applications from messages that are indirect or inductive in style. This assumption neglects an important insight into how human beings think and process communications. Research shows that the mental operations vary greatly from person to person. Many people—a majority in some congregations—are not hard-wired (so to speak) to draw their own conclusions from sermons.[24] Their patterns of thinking are less attuned to narrative and more to conventional, logical reasoning. In order to feel like they have heard a sermon, they need to hear a point, and often they need to understand the logic by which the preacher got to the point. These qualities are not functions of intelligence but of thinking style. Even those who naturally think in narrative and intuition must sometimes think through problems or issues in ways that follow patterns of conventional logic. Thus, pastors who preach only stories or who consistently leave members of the listening community to arrive at their own conclusions will not fully communicate with linear thinkers, and will leave them frustrated. Preachers need to be able to communicate in a variety of sermon styles.

Narrative approaches to preaching do not always take account of the full range of types of biblical literature. Although the Bible itself may have an overarching narrative structure, within the Bible are a multitude of genres of literature such as commandments, proverbs, riddles, oracles of judgment and salvation, letters, codes of virtues and vices, and apocalyptic visions. As noted previously, philosophers of language, rhetoricians, and linguists note that the form or genre of a text is a part and parcel of the meaning of the text. To change the form of communication of a text is to change meaning. Indeed, different kinds of biblical narratives have very different purposes—e.g., sagas, etiologies, parables, miracle stories, and conflict stories. As noted above, sometimes a preacher can use a narrative structure (especially of the second type) to help the congregation encounter texts in biblical forms other than narratives. But based on the insight that form and function are organically interrelated, a popular movement in preaching emphasizes that preaching from a particular genre of text often honors that text best when the form and function of the sermon follow the form and function of the text.[25] A proverb, for instance, may call for a sermon that is proverbial.

Occasions sometimes arise in the life of the congregation or the wider culture that call for a more direct approach than is sometimes typical of the first three modes of narrative preaching. I am thinking particularly of occasions when an issue is immediately on the surface of the congregation's consciousness about which it has questions. Natural disasters (e.g., hurricane or tornado), the outbreak of war between countries, an assassination, an uprising in a particular part of the city, the collapse in the stock market, the close of a local major employer, an act of vandalism on the church property or a conflict within the congregation regarding whether to relocate, the discovery of some form of sexual impropriety or abuse, the death of a beloved member—such events often evoke such an immediate awareness that the congregation is hungry to get directly to the heart of a straightforward theological explanation. "How is God related to this situation?" From time to time, less urgent occasions may also call for plainspoken propositional interpretation. For example, during the season of raising support for the church budget, the preacher may simply want to explain the theological rationale for such support, and how the budget puts that rationale into practice through the life and witness of the congregation. I know many congregations who would benefit from such sermons regarding the meaning of baptism and of the taking of the bread and the cup. Many years ago, Ernest T. Campbell preached a sermon entitled "Every Battle Isn't Armageddon."[26] In a similar way, preachers need to remember that not every sermon has to come across with the fire and power of Peter's sermon on Pentecost (Acts 2).

Narrative theologians and preachers in the fourth category sometimes have difficulty dealing with biblical texts or theological doctrines or practices that are problematic because their working assumption is that the purpose of preaching is to narrate the congregation into the biblical story. However, this movement faces some questions. For one, the Bible does not voice one unified theological narrative or viewpoint, but contains diverse (and sometimes quite different) theological perspectives. One cannot speak simply of *the* biblical story but needs to speak in more nuanced ways of the aspects of the biblical narrative at work in a particular sermon and how these motifs interact with those of other theological families.

For another challenge, the biblical story contains elements that are horrific—e.g., slavery, repression of women, divine approval of violence and killing. The four gospels, in different ways and to different degrees, devalue certain Jewish leaders, institutions, and practices, thus contributing to anti-Judaism and ultimately to anti-Semitism. To be sure, narrative theologians try to ameliorate the effect of such materials by, e.g., finding new exegetical interpretations that are friendlier to the contemporary ethos, or bringing the difficult passages into dialogue with other parts of the Bible that do not endorse such viewpoints. Nevertheless, narrative theologians do not have a clear and consistent set of norms by which to gauge the theological and ethical appropriateness of differing and difficult theological claims within the Bible (and in larger Christian tradition).[27]

Under the influence of the electronic media culture, many people in North America increasingly arrive at life values and make decisions on the basis of images and other elements of electronic culture. The capacity for clear-minded critical thinking is waning. On the one hand, narrative preaching in all forms above is well-suited to the imagistic and intuitive ways of assuming an identity and charting a life course for people in our time. On the other hand, Arthur Van Seters points out that narrative approaches to preaching can be complicit in the breakdown of critical thinking so commonplace in our time when they attempt to form a congregation's consciousness by giving the congregation images out of which to live without also helping the congregation recognize why those images are theologically appropriate.[28] Indeed, in a time when the church is increasingly exhorted to be a countercultural presence, some aspects of narrative preaching seem to reflect the culture. From time to time, at least, sermons should help the congregation reflect critically on the degree to which it thinks and acts on the basis of genuinely critical thinking.

Narrative approaches to preaching have played a significant role in revitalizing preaching in the last thirty years, in no small part because the theological undergirding of this movement is so closely connected to the Bible, Christian doctrine, and the tasks of preaching. Indeed, narrative is a way of doing theology in the pulpit. However, narrative will not be the singular approach to preaching in the future, for some texts and occasions call for different forms of preaching. Indeed, the emerging postmodern world prizes diversity and pluralism. Nevertheless, narrative modes of preaching will continue to play a vital role in helping the gospel come alive in congregations as part of a larger network of approaches.

3

A Match Made in Heaven

The Intersection of Gender and Narrative Preaching

BEVERLY ZINK-SAWYER

A decade ago, in *The Sermon: Dancing the Edge of Mystery*, Eugene Lowry reviewed "The Current Shape of the New Homiletic." He named strands that together had woven a new, rich tapestry of gospel proclamation. Starting with the mid-twentieth century, preaching had partnered with contemporary disciplines to engage the needs of a rapidly changing church. The result was a wealth of fresh ideas. From Fred Craddock's theory of inductive preaching and David Buttrick's phenomenological approach to Lowry's own emphasis on narrative movement to the participatory, conversational styles of African American and feminist preaching, the New Homiletic introduced sermon styles appropriate for a new era of listeners. Patterns of preaching that had served the church for nearly two thousand years would not be adequate for most twenty-first–century ears. "However one defines the issues that have brought us here—and they are many," Lowry declared, "we have come to a new day, a new paradigm in preaching."[1]

While this revolution in homiletics was taking place, another was taking place on a parallel track: an exponential increase in the numbers of female clergy and preachers. According to the United States census of 1970, approximately 3 percent of American clergy were women. By 1990 that number had risen to about 10 percent.[2] Today, while the statistics vary, most mainline Protestant churches report that women comprise 20 to 30 percent of their ordained clergy, with a couple of traditions approaching 50 percent. At seminaries representing those denominations, it is not unusual to find more than half of those studying for ministry to be women. A significant number of women preachers, can be found today even in traditions that do not ordain women (such as the Roman Catholic Church) and in denominations that do not officially endorse women pastors and preachers (such as the Southern Baptist Convention).

With this notable increase in the past thirty years, it is hard to believe that women have not had some kind of impact on the practice of preaching. Throughout church history, homiletics has been shaped by the interplay of preachers, listeners, and changes in the worlds where they live. What, then, can we say about the preaching of these women, and how that has shaped preaching in general? More specifically, how has women's preaching influenced, and been influenced by, the narrative movement of the past few decades? Would the shape of narrative preaching today be what it is without the contributions of women preachers?

The Great Gender Debate

Before considering these matters, however, we need to address the prior questions. Is there such a thing as "women's preaching"? If so, what does it look like? Is it different from "men's preaching"—whatever *that* looks like? No doubt these questions have been discussed as long as women have *been* preaching—a long time, for women have been proclaiming the gospel since the resurrection. The debate did not take shape, however, until women entered pulpits in significant numbers. By the mid-1980s, the numbers of women preaching in congregations, studying in seminaries, and teaching homiletics in schools of theology had increased dramatically, leading women preachers themselves, as well as those who listened to them, to make observations about the particular qualities and characteristics women bring to the vocation. In a 1982 essay on "Gender and Preaching," Maxine Walaskay of Colgate Rochester Divinity School concluded:

> There is something quite unique and undefinable about one's first experience with a woman in the pulpit.... We subjectively know the uniqueness without words or without comprehension of what the differences might be. The experience itself may be pleasant or not; the sermon may be marvelous and powerful. It is different.[3]

This realization prompted homiletical observers to begin positing what those gender differences might be and from whence they might come. In 1984, Edwina Hunter, then professor of preaching at Pacific School of Religion, did one of the first intentional studies of women's preaching. She interviewed thirteen homiletics professors at ten seminaries, asking them about the work of their female students in classes, and whether they observed differences between the preaching styles of men and women. These professors agreed that, as the numbers of women in preaching classes increased, so did observable differences between gender styles. In the early to mid-1970s when few women were in seminary, there were few observable preaching-style differences between men and women, because women were still imitating male models. However, as more women registered for theological studies—specifically master of divinity programs—they became more comfortable in this new role and with their male colleagues. Soon they began to preach differently.[4]

Women's sermons, the surveyed professors noted, "became more creative, more woven. They dared to tell more personal stories, to use more images and to use hermeneutics growing out of their own experiences." The professors observed that their women students seemed "to be able to 'concretize' and 'get right to the heart of the issues' found in the biblical text."[5]

Several years after Hunter's study, Christine Smith took a deeper look at women's preaching, using four collections of women's sermons published during the mid-1980s. Smith's study confirmed Hunter's findings and interpreted them through the lens of the feminist metaphor of "weaving," a metaphor that, Smith maintained, described "the gathering of distinctive qualities" of women's preaching.[6] Summarizing those qualities, she said:

> The sermons in all four collections are rich in imagery, poetic language, and personal illustrations from women's lives. In many of these sermons there is an interwoven quality that integrates personal story, creative and imaginative language, and imagery rooted in female experience. There is a pervasive indicative mode, an increased sensitivity to inclusive language and God imagery, and many explicit illustrations from female experience in the world. Themes of oppression, suffering, and pain are also points of strong emphasis through these volumes.[7]

Smith found the uniqueness of women's preaching to be rooted in their life experience as women. Whether attributed to nature or nurture, education or acculturation, social scientists continue to affirm gender differences in how women and men perceive and relate to the world. The experiential dimension seems to be the one place where gender theorists and their critics alike agree that differences arise. Since all preaching is rooted in experience—the experience of one's encounter with the gospel and its claims upon one's life—there cannot help but be gender differences in preaching.

"The human experience of the preacher is central both in terms of how one understands the Gospel and how one touches the human experience of others, that is, how one communicates the mystery of salvation as a living reality," Mary Catherine Hilkert reminds us. Women's experience "of sexuality and life, the relation of woman to body, nature, the childbearing and nurturing processes and the historical experience of marginalization, exclusion and subordination within society and the church, constitute a different framework for perceiving reality from that of men."[8] Elaine J. Lawless, who has studied women's preaching in both Pentecostal and mainline traditions, comes to a similar conclusion. In an essay on women's sermons, she pauses to raise the obvious question. "What does that mean, 'women's sermons'? For me it means sermons that are grounded in female experiences." Lawless goes on to challenge her own theory:

> Could I always identify a sermon preached by a woman versus a sermon preached by a man? I am not certain I

could. But in all of the sermons that I have heard delivered by women, I find characteristics that clearly identify the sermons as stemming from and alluding to a female life.[9]

This inextricable connection between preaching and life—or, more accurately, between the preacher and her or his life—seem granted in the debate over gender differences in preaching. Hilkert acknowledges that women's preaching "is more relational, more rooted in experience, more in a narrative style, more collaborative, and so on than is the preaching of men." However, she allows it was "simply not always the case." Nevertheless, she states, "Without being able to spell out the dimensions of gender differences, I would still claim that women bring a different experience of life to the hearing and preaching of the Gospel."[10] Edwina Hunter puts it this way: "Certainly there are considerable differences in the experiences men and women bring to their interpretation of biblical texts. Similar to "people of other races and cultures," women "bring hermeneutical riches to preaching which we have not yet fully realized."[11] Ten years after her initial work, Hunter again raised the question about gender differences in preaching and concluded: "I continue trying to provide an atmosphere in which men and women can discover for themselves their own individual preaching voices; yet I cannot help being aware of how many differences there are between the acculturation of women and of men, as well as psychological and physiological differences."[12] When Hunter faced her own question about gender differences, she concluded she could not answer it, but

> I only know that something deep inside me demands a speaking out: *If there are no gender differences in preaching, then there should be!*...I have come to believe that the One in whose name we preach has a purpose beyond our imagining. Why call so many women to a preaching vocation if women are not going to be different from men in their preaching? Why call so many women if they are not going to say things that men have not said or do not say? Why call women to preach if they do not speak in ways strangely yet surely integral to the wholeness of being women?[13]

Hunter calls for what she termed "incarnational preaching," the kind of preaching that emerges from being "in close relationship, simultaneously, with ourselves and with the One who called us. In this way, she maintains, "We embody the Word. We let the gospel live through us and in us. Our bodies come alive and we tell the story we preach with our whole beings, from the tops of our heads through the soles of our feet."[14]

As others have done, Hunter roots gender differences in preaching in the life experience of being female or male rather than in stereotypical styles or behaviors. The danger in making unequivocal statements about the preaching of women or men is that as soon as a sweeping generalization has left our lips, someone points to an exception to the rule. The challenge of defining "women's preaching" is akin to the struggle described by Cleophus J. LaRue when asked to discuss the characteristics of black preaching. He notes "a very powerful and settled school of thought among black preachers that says there is no such thing as black preaching *per se,* with its own specific characteristics and distinctive traits. Those who maintain this view say there are black preachers who preach, but they don't preach black, they simply preach the Gospel."[15] Nevertheless, LaRue concludes, there *are* preaching characteristics that, while not necessarily unique to black preaching or representative of all black preachers, "when taken together they come to the fore with such clarity and presence that one would not err in saying that these are some of the things you find repeatedly in the best of black preaching."[16] The same can be said for women's preaching. There are characteristics that can be found repeatedly in the best of women's preaching.

Nowhere is the difficulty of identifying women's preaching more evident than when we are discussing narrative preaching. Pondering this essay, I could not escape a sense of irony—the person honored in this volume is a male who has done more to define narrative homiletics than anyone. Eugene Lowry himself notes this irony when listing models of the new homiletic in *The Sermon*. He describes the "conversational-episodal" sermon identified in the works of Lucy Rose and Carol Norén, both of whom link that sermon form (although not exclusively) to women preachers. After noting that connection, however, Lowry states, "I think it obvious that this kind of preaching is not practiced only by women." He goes on to cite the sermons of Tex Sample and Fred Craddock as examples of male preachers who are more comfortable with conversational-episodal sermon forms than more traditional, linear forms.[17] Each of us could add our own examples.

Most theorists who have shaped narrative homiletics have been male. When we think of narrative, we think of Eugene Lowry, Thomas Troeger, Edmund Steimle, Charles Rice, Morris Niedenthal, Richard Jensen, and others. Part of this may be due to the fact that women have come only recently to homiletics as teachers and theorists. What role they might have played in the early days of defining the field of narrative preaching is impossible to ascertain.

Finding a Homiletical Home

What, then, *can* we say about gender and narrative preaching? At least this: narrative preaching styles have helped women find their preaching voice, their "homiletical home." The increase in the numbers of women preaching concurrent with the increasingly popular narrative preaching movement has resulted in "a match made in heaven," providing many women with a homiletical style that fits comfortably with their natural preaching instincts. At the same time, women preachers have helped to popularize and refine narrative techniques. Certainly the narrative movement would have developed with or without the simultaneous influx of women into pulpits. It has roots in new understandings of how we apprehend information, the rise of narrative biblical hermeneutics, the embrace of traditional narrative styles such as African American preaching, new theological approaches, and a rediscovery of the significance of story in human experience. The presence of women seeking preaching voices and finding an affinity with narrative styles, however, caused an evolution to become a formidable movement.

How have women found their "homiletical home" in narrative designs and content? Many women preachers embrace more creative, dialogical, open-ended sermon styles—that is, characteristically narrative designs—eschewing the linear, monological, authoritarian sermons preached through much of Christian history. This affinity for narrative styles, theorists suggest, has to do with gender preferences as demonstrated by studies of women's psycho-social development and their unique ways of communicating. Studies by gender theorists such as Carol Gilligan, Mary Belenky, and Deborah Tannen have identified patterns of female socialization that give rise to the distinctive ways in which women tend to communicate.[18] Women's tendency to keep a "constant eye to maintaining relational order and connection," as Gilligan puts it, defines their style of communication. "It was concern about relationship that made women's voices sound 'different,'" Gilligan reflects in her study of women's psychological development, "within a world that was preoccupied with separation and obsessed with creating and maintaining boundaries between people."

Homiletical theorists similarly have identified the relational quality of women's behavior discerned by social scientists. In her study of women's preaching, Christine Smith notes: "rather than tell people what to do, women invite persons to reflect upon their lives and the nature of their faith commitments."[19] Carol Norén calls the connectedness between women preachers and their listeners "intuitive communication" based on meanings "already shared between preacher and listeners." It is "a conscious reflection of what [women] believe preaching is—and what it is not," she contends. "Persuasion to a particular point of view and/or transmission of religious truths are not the preacher's goals. Instead, preaching is a profound act of human connection and intimacy."[20] Such an understanding is manifested in women's pulpit practices, some of which challenge homiletical tradition. In a recent study of gender and rhetorical space in preaching, Roxanne Mountford defines women's pulpit practices as "feminizing sacred space." Women preach "in the context of long-standing traditions that have excluded women," challenging them to develop "spatial strategies" including "storytelling, dialogue, and personal disclosure as well as leaving behind the safety and authority of the pulpit" to walk down the aisle on Sunday mornings. Such "ritual transgression[s] of sacred space,"[21] space that has been "gendered" for centuries as male and circumscribed by particular styles and practices, have enabled women to engage in new styles of preaching that reflect their concern for human connection and intimacy.

The understanding of preaching as "a profound act of human connection and intimacy" leads to what I believe to be the most significant intersection between gender and narrative homiletics. Among other gifts, women have brought a recognition of the legitimacy of the narrative quality of experience, one of the marks of the New Homiletic. Women's affinity for narrative—particularly in terms of story but also in terms of a narrative understanding of theology and sermonic movement—is the one gender characteristic that is mentioned repeatedly in the debate over gendered preaching styles. Perhaps that is because narrative has served as the primary way in which women have "feminized sacred space" and claimed their right to the authority of the pulpit. Certainly men have always used story effectively in preaching; but men and women, theorists observe, use narrative *differently*. With ready access to the pulpit throughout Christian history, men have not had to rely on narrative to legitimate their right to proclaim the word. They stand in pulpits with the assumed authority of twenty centuries of Christian proclamation. Women preachers have not had such access to the pulpit, nor been granted immediate legitimacy as proclaimers of the Word. The way women claim the authority to be heard is by means of authentic witness to the truth of the gospel, witness best conveyed through story. Preaching women say, in essence, "We, also, have seen and experienced the good news and we, too, have testimony worth hearing." The God-given authority to proclaim the gospel is the same for men and women, but the human path to that authority is often different for women. Pondering why women seem to tell stories so well, Charles Hackett, in the introduction to a collection of sermons by Anglican women, concludes that their storytelling ability is related to the female experience, the reality that "[t]hroughout history, the story has belonged to the disenfranchised and powerless." Hackett raises this "provocative idea":

> [W]omen have been excluded from access to traditional ecclesiastical authority but they have been a crucial part of the *story* from the beginning. Their authority, like the authority of the story-form itself, has had to come from an intuitive ability to empathize and to speak the indicative word about the human situation in such a way that those who heard recognized their own being and their own dreams.[22]

In a similar way, Christine Smith connects women's authority with the pervasive "story" quality in the sermons she has studied. "Women's authority is rooted in the very act of naming and speaking words of faith and hope from the perspective of being female," she observes. "This perspective has never been fully voiced before in the history of the church or world. This kind of authority has little to do with outside structures, or rights, or privileges; rather it has to do with a quality of naming and witnessing that is born from within the lives and souls of faithful women."[23] Smith realizes that "for women, story and narrative theology are more than a means of effective theologizing or a type of imaginative communication. Story and narrative theology represent a powerful and important way of naming reality for women,"[24] a reality that was not always valued or even heard. This way of naming reality, Elaine Lawless discovered, results in "a different kind of sermon creation and delivery, a sermon based on women's ways of trusting what they know. And what they know comes from their own experiences." In the public forum of the American pulpit, we find "women speaking and telling their own stories within the traditional Christian story in order to frame a message of integration and connection."[25] Experience for women preachers serves "as an authentic avenue for acquiring knowledge of God… Experience, theirs and others, is hermeneutical."[26] It is the result of women "hearing one another to speech," as Nelle Morton phrased it in the early days of the modern women's movement.

> Every liberation movement rises out of its bondage with a new speech on its lips. This has been so with women coming together, seeking to get in touch with their own stories and experiences which they have discovered welling up from within, from underneath, from out of their past, from out of their traditions rather than down from above…Through hearing and speaking, women sense the possibility of theologizing out of their own experiences.[27]

More often than not, the validating stories of women that theorists have observed are *personal* stories. After listening for many years to the ways in which men and women tell stories from the pulpit, Lawless concludes: "The major differences I see in the storytelling is the way in which the women utilize personal experience stories in their sermons to validate their theology and their spirituality." Since women have gained access to the pulpit, she notes, "they have claimed it as their own and used that context intentionally and fully as a place to tell their stories—stories that connect the religious message with the stories of their own lives."[28]

Authority and legitimacy—"voice," as it is sometimes defined—for women preachers is most often rooted in their own experiences of faith. For this reason, *personal* story has been noted as characteristic of the preaching of many women. Those women resist centuries of homiletical wisdom advising against self-disclosure in the pulpit. While there are good reasons to beware the use (and, especially, overuse) of personal stories in sermons, such stories have provided women with both an expression of authority and a point of connection with their listeners. "Through the telling of their own stories," concludes Leonora Tisdale in a discussion of women's ways of preaching, "women keep the gospel close to the ground, making very local connections between the biblical story and our lived lives."[29] This is not to suggest that women preachers *always* or *only* use personal story to convey the gospel message, but to suggest that personal story used as testimony has provided a way for women to validate their own experiences of faith, to legitimate their calls to proclaim the gospel, and to find a connection between their listeners and the theological constructs of the biblical text. Personal witness and story have validated the proclamation of women through the centuries of American religious history,[30] and they continue to shape the preaching of women today. "Through their first-person stories, women's stories," Lawless observes,

> the women were providing a new validation for the connection between women's lives and their personal, intimate relationship with the sacred. However, a woman's stance *as a woman*, relating her experiences to her audience and relating her own experiences to her perception of God in her life, was not an exclusive stance. The stories of the women authenticate the immediacy of an immanent God prepared and willing to enter into relationship with them and with all other humans, in mutual and collective connection *in spite of differences*.[31]

Where in the (Homiletical) World Are We?

Given the abundance of women in pulpits today, and the increasing openness to the leadership of women in church and society, what can we say about women's preaching three decades after the first significant influx of women into seminaries and ministerial positions? Are judgments regarding a "women's preaching style" still valid? And how have women helped to shape homiletical styles, especially in narrative preaching?

Those who observe preaching styles today probably would conclude that we have come full-circle from the observations made about women's preaching a few decades ago. As mentioned above, the professors surveyed in Edwina Hunter's early study noted that their first women preaching students seemed eager to imitate traditional "male" models of preaching in order to be accepted as preachers, creating "few observable preaching-style differences between men and women."[32] Over time, however, as the number of women in seminaries increased, women discovered a "safe space" in the classroom that enabled them to find their own voices. In a similar way, women have claimed the safe space of the sanctuary and imprinted it with their own faithful mark. They have brought new images, personal stories, daring sermon designs, first-person monologues, and even a reconfiguring of the worship space itself, testifying to women's recently discovered sense of freedom as called and gifted children of God. Women preachers "make no excuses for this," as Elaine Lawless notes:

> They do not try to tell men's stories. They do not try to mimic men's sermon styles, narratives, jokes, mannerisms, or dramatic presentations. They stand as women and tell stories about women's experiences; they weave sermons that are clearly *grounded in female experiences*—experiences that inform content, structure, presentation, and style.[33]

While not imitating male styles, however, women certainly have *influenced* them. Just as women for decades were shaped by the preaching of their male colleagues, a homiletical reversal has occurred as men have been shaped—whether they realize it or not—by the women preachers with whom they learn and minister. As a result, once again it has become increasingly difficult to discern gender differences in preaching—not because women are imitating traditional male homiletical models, but because women and men are learning from each other. Women preachers have contributed to a return to blended gender styles, but this time around, those styles are as varied and plentiful as the preachers practicing them. This is good news, witnessing to the increased numbers of women preachers, seminary students, and homiletics professors, which enables women and men more easily to learn from each other and discover the freedom to employ ever more faithful ways to proclaim the gospel.

There is in this trend, however, a bit of less-than-good news: the danger that any distinctive voice women once brought to the pulpit might disappear. Once again I am reminded of Hunter's conclusion: "If there are no gender differences in preaching, then there should be!" If all of us are called to preach, as Hunter claims, "relationally and incarnationally," then there remains a place for preaching that reflects gender and other personal characteristics. Indeed, as Mary Catherine Hilkert puts it, "What is most basic here is that because women both hear and speak the Gospel 'in a different voice' the whole community is impoverished if we hear the word of God only as interpreted in and through the male... experience of life." The story of God's grace in Jesus Christ is "inexhaustible," Hilkert reminds us. "The richness of the mystery which we proclaim is diminished and distorted when we fail to hear the Good News as reflected through women's stories."[34] In and through the voices of women, the church is blessed to receive the gift of experiences of faith long ignored. It is only in the fullness and diversity of all God's children that human words have any hope of bearing witness to the word of God Incarnate.

As we seek those ever more faithful ways to proclaim the gospel, women preachers stand in pulpits with hearts full of gratitude for the gift given to us by Eugene Lowry and other male colleagues who have pioneered the narrative preaching movement. We have been blessed with the means to find our voices as preachers at a critical and exciting time in homiletical history. Women in turn advance the narrative movement as we respond to God's call to bear authentic witness to the gospel. This intersection of gender and narrative results in "a match made in heaven," a match that, we hope and pray, will continue to thrive in our common efforts to tell the Story.

4

African American Contexts of Narrative Preaching

The Audacity of Hope

WILLIAM B. MCCLAIN

In his recent book *The Audacity of Hope,* the junior senator from Illinois, Barack Obama, reaffirms the rich heritage and powerful preaching tradition of the historic African American church as he recounts his own experience of that tradition, and shares his personal testimony of faith:

> I was drawn to the power of the African American religious tradition to spur social change. Out of necessity, the black church had to minister to the whole person. Out of necessity, the black church rarely had the luxury of separating individual salvation from collective salvation... [I]t understood the biblical call to feed the hungry and clothe the naked and challenge powers and principalities. In the history of these struggles, I was able to see faith as more than just a comfort to the weary or a hedge against death; rather it was an active, palpable agent in the world.

Long before it became fashionable among television evangelists, the typical black sermon freely acknowledged that all Christians (including the pastors) could expect to still experience the same greed, resentment, lust and anger that everyone else experienced....the lines between sinner and saved were more fluid; you needed to come to church and to embrace Christ precisely because you had sins to wash away—because you were human and needed an ally in your difficult journey, to make the peaks and valleys smooth and render all those crooked paths straight. It was because of these newfound understandings—that religious commitment did not require me to suspend critical thinking and social justice, or otherwise retreat from the world that I knew and loved—that I was finally able to walk down the aisle of Trinity United Church of Christ one day and be baptized.[1]

The tradition of narrative preaching Senator Obama heard in Trinity United Church of Christ in Chicago from The Rev. Dr. Jeremiah Wright has been central in the history of the African American church in the United States. Some would say there is no Black preaching that is not narrative and biblical, and that it has always been so. While that can be debated, there is more than a kernel of truth in this bold assertion.

African American preaching is an art involving serious retelling and interpretation of the biblical message with native oratory, storytelling, graphic portrayals, word-picture painting, the use of an "anointed or 'sanctified' imagination," a wholistic involvement of both preacher and pew, warmth and spontaneity in preacher and congregation, and a clear call for social justice.

For many years, and in many quarters, there have been two test questions asked after a sermon is delivered in an African American church: First, "*Can* the preacher tell the story?" and second, "*Did* the preacher do so?" Other questions pointing to the same expected result are: "Did the preacher make it plain?" "Did the preacher stand on the wall?" "Did the preacher stand where John stood?" In their own peculiar African American church idiom (that crosses all denominational lines) these and other questions have been employed as ways of evaluating both preaching and preachers. These questions are designed to ascertain whether or not the preacher has proclaimed the gospel story with such passion and vivid imagination that all could hear, follow, understand, and believe. No other event or task is more important in the African American church than preaching. There is a common saying in the African American church: "The people will forgive the pastor for almost anything, except *not* preaching!" When people leave, can they say, "YES, we *had* church!"?

If the answer to the first pivotal question is in the affirmative, then the preacher passes many tests: (1) "having been called"; (2) being "anointed"; (3) being an authentic representative of "the Black preaching tradition"; and (4) being "a good preacher." However, if the answer to the first question is "yes" and the answer to the second question is "no," then that preacher is condemned as lazy, trifling—as having "flunked."

The Black Folk Preacher

There are roots of the African American church tradition of "telling the story" reaching back to pre-slavery African gurus and practices. What was half-forgotten was also half-remembered by the recently arrived Africans. I marvel still at the creative genius of the African American slave preacher's ability to create a bicultural synthesis bringing together that rich and colorful African background with so many "sensitivities to subtleties of signal and substance"[2] and the culture and faith of the evangelical "Magnolia Missions," as C. Eric Lincoln used to call the effort at Christianizing the slaves by the Society of the Propagation of the Faith in Foreign Parts, which continued with the Second Awakening and the Camp Meetings.[3] These newly converted African American Christians identified with the oppressed Hebrew children, the prophets, and the Crucified One. They heard the stories and the oracles of the prophets, particularly the eighth-century prophets of the Old Testament—their condemnation of social injustice and their prophecies of a new social order where justice would reign. Their identification took on a kind of immediacy and intensity in their setting of slavery. Howard Thurman was right in his assertions about *Jesus and the Disinherited*.[4] These African Americans identified with the poor, nail-driving, Jewish carpenter of whom Nathanael asked: "Can anything good come out of Nazareth?" (Jn. 1:46).

Their interpretation of the Bible was controlled, not by the *literal* words of the texts—in many cases, if not most, they could not even read the text. With vivid imagination, identification, and creativity, they gave meaning to the passages they heard read. They reached out through space and time to appropriate and apply the meaning to their lives: climbing Jacob's ladder; Moses crossing the Red Sea to be free of the oppressive Pharaoh in Egypt land; Joshua fighting the battle of Jericho till the walls came tumbling down; Deborah giving charismatic leadership and uniting the tribe against the enemy; Ezekiel in the valley of dry and disconnected bones that were connected and brought to life again because of the word of the Lord; Daniel defeating the lion in its own den; the faithful widow of Sidon helping the prophet to carry out a God-ordained transaction; Job "waiting for his change to come;" little harp-playing David, a shepherd-boy, beating a giant with a sling shot and five smooth stones; the Hebrew boys in the fiery furnace being delivered by "the fourth man in the fire." And all of this leading up to the birth of "Mary's little darling baby," "Sweet Little Jesus Boy," the one who was born in a manger low with no place to lay his head, but who becomes the liberating Master and King Jesus, who rode into the city to be whipped up a hill, lynched on a cross, buried in a borrowed grave; and who conquered sin, death, and the grave in resurrection, who declared victory and claimed the keys to the kingdom.

All of this they saw as ways a mighty God delivers struggling people when they are in danger of being overtaken by their enemies, or when trouble was getting them down. And so they sang of their greatest, most powerful Friend who could do anything but fail. They preached and sang of the One who stood where there was nowhere to stand, "when there was neither a whither or a where," and a "God who could draw straight with crooked lines." They preached and sang:

> God is a God! God don't never change!
> God is a God! And He always will be God.

And it was this powerful, ever-present, always winning Friend they referred to when they moaned to themselves in a hushed and down low song:

> I'm gonna tell God how you treat me.
> I'm gonna tell God how you treat me…
> Some of these days or
> When I get home.

A Strange Silence of the Hebrew Bible or a Romance with It

John C. Holbert has complained that the Hebrew Bible is being neglected in preaching:

> I am a trained scholar of the Hebrew Bible who attempts to teach Christian seminary students something about what it means to preach from the scriptural text. Having read the literature of the field of homiletics and listened to sermons in many churches over many years, I recognize this fact: There remains a strange silence of the Hebrew Bible in the church. One can go for more than a few Sundays in many churches without ever hearing any news from the books of our scripture that precede the New Testament.[5]

I think John Holbert is right. But I also know that he was certainly not attending many African American churches (or those who stand in the African American preaching tradition) when he lodged this complaint. I believe that the romance between the African American church and the Old Testament that has lasted more than two centuries is still alive—although it is jeopardized by some who trivialize the tradition in right wing ideology that masquerades as orthodox theology, marketplace theology that makes of the church vendors of "cheap grace" and escapism, and prosperity theology that simplistically identifies material things as evidence of God's grace.

There has been an enduring romance between the Black church, its preaching tradition, and the Old Testament. In a society of people a long way from home, struggling to find the story of their lives, the Old Testament and the life of Jesus have provided rooting and meaning. This has been the experience of a people in a "strange land," but who somehow tied the voice of God they heard about in America under the magnolia tree to the sighing and the whispering of the wind they had heard in the African forest and the bush country back home. They have been a people with an audacity of hope. The Israelites' story became their story. The God who delivered Daniel could and would deliver them. The strong God of the Hebrew Bible was the One they needed. No weak God would do. They needed, prayed to, glorified in song, preached about, and praised a Mighty God, a God whose strength was demonstrated over and over—the One who never loses a battle. This Sovereign God was omnipotent, omniscient, and omnipresent. As Benjamin Elijah Mays, a nationally recognized African American preacher and president of Morehouse College, wrote in his signal work, *The Negro's God*:

> In both Heaven and earth God is sovereign. He is a just God—just to the point of cruelty…God is a warrior and He fights the battles of His chosen people….God takes care of His own…He will also see to it that the righteous are vindicated and the heavy laden are given rest from the troubles of this world… God is near. God understands. Even when no human understands or sympathizes, I can tell God all of my troubles.[6]

Classical Black Preaching and Classical Sermons

James Weldon Johnson, in *God's Trombones*, attempts to capture the God-ideas and the style of African American folk preaching in verse form. Johnson says about the classical black sermons, "[they] passed with only slight modification from preacher to preacher and from locality to locality." His description of the Black preacher at the beginning of the last century is a moving and classic passage:

> He strode the pulpit up and down in what was actually a very rhythmic voice, a voice—what shall I say?—not of an organ or a trumpet, but rather of a trombone, the instrument possessing above all others the power to express the wide and varied range of emotion encompassed by the human voice—and with greater amplitude. He intoned, he moaned, he pleaded—he blared, he crashed, he thundered… The emotional effect upon me was irresistible.[7]

Most people are only familiar with "The Creation" sermon in that collection. But several others, including a funeral sermon, and also the prayer, "Listen, Lord," are still pretty much a standard form of prayer in the Black church. Variations of this model have developed, small changes are made in terms of order, and a few images are added or left out, but the norm is well set.

Of this prayer I once wrote, "even though we know what is to follow and could repeat the lines before they are uttered, our hearts still wait to hear them." From Mississippi to Michigan, from California to the Carolinas, from Atlanta to Atlantic City, the form of this prayer is heard, known, and understood. It is a model prayer that belongs to the African American community and is not Baptist or Methodist, Pentecostal or Presbyterian, although it may be heard more often in traditional African American churches. I experimented recently with this notion in a group with approximately twelve to fifteen African Americans present from a variety of denominations. I would give part of the line, and invariably they were able to finish it. It is an African American liturgical possession of which the Black church has been the careful custodian. It begins:

> Almighty! And all-wise God our heavenly Father! 'tis once more again that a few of your humble children come knee-bent and body-bowed before your throne of grace to call upon your holy and righteous name. We come as empty pitchers before a full fountain...
>
> We thank you that you watched over us all night long while we slumbered and slept. We thank you that the bed we slept on was not our cooling board. We thank you that the sheet we slept on was not our winding cloth.
>
> We thank you that the blood was still running warm in our veins. We were able to get up this morning clothed in our right mind. We thank you that you have allowed our golden moments to roll on a little longer...

Somewhere in the prayer we will hear the petition about the preacher and the preaching:

> And Lord! One more kind favor I ask you. Remember the one who is to stand in John's shoes to declare your word between the living and the dead. Your word is sharper than any two-edged sword... Strengthen him where he is weak and build him up where he is torn down. O let him down in the deep treasures of your word...[8]

As there has been this classic prayer form, there have also been the classical sermons and sermon texts in the African American preaching tradition. If we can take as a definition of classic, "any work that is considered worth attention beyond its time,"[9] then there are some classical texts and sermons in the historical African American preaching tradition in the Black church. But before I cite them, let me relate two experiences that led me to explore the notion that there is such a tradition.

When I finished Boston University School of Theology, I was assigned to Haven Chapel Methodist Church in Anniston, Alabama. After I had been there a few months, one of the old sainted members of that congregation, Sister Irene Berry, sent word that she wanted her pastor to make a call at her home. Never mind that she was in church last Sunday—as she was every Sunday, in good health, and her mind was still just fine—although I guess she was then into her late eighties, if not nineties. Sister Berry had something important to discuss with her young pastor. After the usual genteel Southern conversation exchange and a glass of "sweet tea with lemon," she got down to business: "Reverend, when are you going to preach the sermon on 'The Eagle Stirs Her Nest'?"

The second experience occurred at Emory University a few years ago during the time of the burning of black churches in the South. They invited me to preach in the chapel for a special service around that issue and to raise funds to assist in the rebuilding of those churches. Several Black pastors from the city came, including some faculty from local seminaries. After the service they had a sit down meal and Don Saliers of the Candler School of Theology faculty, who had served as the organist for the service, joined a group. As is so often the case with Black clergy, we started talking about preaching and sermons we remembered. Saliers was astonished at the collective memories of particular sermons and texts preached by various African American preachers from several denominations. He said to me afterward, "Bob, you should write some of those down before that is all lost to another generation." It had never occurred to me that this was not a common experience among all other preachers.

Let me list a few of these classic texts, themes, and titles. You will note that they lean overwhelmingly and strongly toward the Old Testament:

- Moses and the Burning Bush
- Moses and the Crossing of the Red Sea
- The Children of Israel Wanting to Go Back to Egypt
- Joshua Crossing the Jordan
- Joshua and the Children of Israel into Canaan
- Samson and the Philistines
- Job

- David and Goliath
- The Twenty-third Psalm
- David Confronted by Nathan
- Isaiah in the Temple the Year Uzziah Died
- The Eagle Stirs Her Nest
- Naaman the Leper Dipping in the River
- Ezekiel and the Valley of Dry Bones
- The Hebrew Boys and the Fiery Furnace
- Daniel and the Lion's Den
- John the Baptist and Jesus
- The Good Samaritan
- The Prodigal Son
- The Crucifixion
- John on the Isle of Patmos

Of course there is a pattern of narratives, but also there is a clear notion that God is a powerful God, who cannot fail, and will always be present. But this same God is also a God of grace and love, a God of mercy and forgiveness, a God who cares like a mother eagle who teaches her young to fly, but does not let them fall in the process, but swoops down when they are floundering and bears them up on her wings. This is the Mighty God whose greatness, mercy, justice, love, and holiness are transparently revealed through the life and work of God's earthly son, Jesus, who becomes the Christ of our faith and the source of our salvation.

The great social historian and classical scholar of the history of Black people in America captured the role and importance of the slave preacher and the power of the art of preaching. W.E.B. DuBois, in his work *The Souls of Black Folk,* says of the Black preacher: "The Preacher is the most unique personality developed by the Negro on American soil. A leader, a politician, an orator."[10] Again, DuBois points out that the slave preacher who appeared on the slave plantation was both African and slave, free in spirit (though bound by law and custom), "interpreter of the unknown," and "the one who rudely and picturesquely expressed the longing, disappointment, and resentment of a stolen and oppressed people."[11] It was through the art of preaching that the people understood, appreciated, and responded to a story that was at once imaginative and creative, freeing and binding, a "sledgehammer of truth," and a "rock in a weary land." In the words of Gayraud

Wilmore, in *Black Religion and Black Radicalism*, "The slave preachers were agents of protests and change while simultaneously providing a unifying message to those in bondage."[12]

The slave preachers' sermons were filled with vivid images, picture painting, dramatic delivery, and biblical interpretation. As described by one observer: "Some of the most vivid reproductions of Scripture narrative I have ever listened to were from the lips of such men, who might with proper training been orators." One missionary to Georgia commented, "What wonderful preachers these blacks are!" Then she attempted to illustrate with an attempt at a reproduction of the sermon:

> I listened to a remarkable sermon or talk a few evenings since. The preacher spoke of the need of atonement of sin. "Bullocks c'dn't do it, heifers c'dn't do it, de blood of doves c'dn't do it—but up in heaven, for thousands and thousand of years, the Son was saying To the Father, 'Put up a soul, put up a soul. Prepare me a body an' I will go down and meet Justice on Calvary's Brow!…'" [Describing the crucifixion:] I see the sun when she turned herself black. I see the stars a fallin' from the sky, and then old Herods comin' out of their graves and goin' about the city, an' they knew 'twas the Lord of Glory![13]

African American Preaching and the Homileticians

For many years, African American preachers in this narrative preaching tradition and those who followed told their story in various forms without any notice of the professional homileticians or those who criticized, formed theories of homiletics, or taught courses in preaching. The African American preachers practiced their craft and preached to, and borrowed from, each other. The people celebrated and life went on as it always had until a few homileticians started to look and listen to what these African American preachers were doing and began talking about narrative preaching. Then the African American preachers and teachers of preaching said: "What? You mean you are just getting around to looking at this as the form of holy speech?"

Henry Heywood Mitchell, who published *Black Preaching* in the C. Eric Lincoln Series in Black Religion in 1970, called attention to the African American preaching enterprise in the heyday of Black Power and Black Theology. Years later his work was noticed by the white homileticians, acknowledged, and appreciated, especially by members of the Academy of Homiletics, such as Eugene Lowry, Fred Craddock, Ron Allen, David Buttrick, and others. Gene Lowry and I have had many exchanges and conversations about Black preaching over the years, and about two of my heroes of this tradition: Howard Thurman and the Dean of African American preaching, the erudite preacher and astute eighty-eight-year-old homiletician, the Rev. Dr. Gardner C. Taylor.

And others of us who are African American teachers of homiletics and practitioner/scholars make formal contributions to the academic enterprise of homiletics. But Mitchell is right in his assessment: "Much of what is taught even today is designed only to reach the levels of biblical clarity and dramatic power which these earliest Black preachers developed almost immediately."[14]

Evans E. Crawford, Dean Emeritus of Rankin Chapel of Howard University in Washington, D.C., a former president of the Academy of Homiletics, longtime homiletics professor, and internationally recognized African American preacher, said in a lecture at Howard University Divinity School that we need to "attempt to complement Eugene Lowry's narrative concern in *The Homiletical Plot* with 'homiletical pitch.'" Here Crawford is suggesting that, "in the Black tradition there is a musical sensitivity in preaching which can turn the command to 'count off' into 'sound off,' and we can speak not only of 'sound off' but also 'sound on' as well. I suggest that we think of this as musical calls and response."[15] Crawford's suggestion is in keeping with the contribution he made to homiletics in his book *The Hum: Call and Response in African American Preaching*.[16] There he calls for "participant proclamation," urging that the congregation be a part of the proclaiming of the gospel.

Maybe that is the basis for an "audacity of hope" Senator Obama has: that the whole church can benefit from the creative genius of narrative preaching that has so long been a part of the African American preaching tradition, and can connect that to telling the story of grace and mercy, love and forgiveness, the cross and the resurrection, to new riffs from "God's Trombones," and thereby to join in the battle for economic and social justice, to feed the hungry, clothe the naked, house the homeless, eradicate poverty, preserve our fragile planet, promote peace, to lay down our sword and shield, to "Study war no more."

Obama said that the preaching in the African American tradition led him to have the "audacity to hope" and "to kneel beneath that cross on the South Side of Chicago." He said, "I felt God's spirit beckoning me. I submitted myself to His will, and dedicated myself to discovering His truth."[17]

I believe that if we do not trivialize the gospel, but boldly proclaim law and grace, the prophetic and the redemptive, "the whole counsel of God," there shall be many who will have "an audacity of hope," and all flesh can have it together in a world where we can all walk together and not get weary.

PART II

Assessments

*What Shape Is
Narrative Preaching
in Today?*

5

Tracking the Homiletical Plot

RICHARD L. ESLINGER

The Dynamics of the Narrative Sermon

What does Eugene Lowry have to teach preachers? His funda-mental insights can be succinctly summarized: the sermon as narrative art form embodies a common, ubiquitous shape even as particular sermons vary from week to week; the narrative constants include the mobility of the affair—this is, after all, an "event in time"; the sermon will proceed with some kind of episodic sequence, a "this" leading to a "that";[1] and, finally, any narrative sermon will embody a sudden shift that opens up for listeners a new sense of the ending. Sermonic journeys proceed from distinctive places of origination, moving along through a plotted sequence, to an unexpected outcome: "Please understand, the principle is firm that the sermon is a bridging event in time, moving from itch to scratch, from issue to answer, from conflict to resolution, from ambiguity to closure born of the gospel."[2]

Lowry is adamant regarding this basic movement of a homi-letical plot. To turn the sequence on its head, beginning with answers, is to lose the congregation's interest at the outset. Such sermons begin, Lowry insists, where they should conclude. "When sermons begin with answers, they become resolutions without issues, truths without experiential context."[3] Answers do not come first.

The sermon's movement cannot be reduced simply to these two "bookends." If we leave out critical steps interior to the opening itch and closing scratch, we are left with the old therapeutic problem-solution sermon, an unacceptable strategy. By avoiding any in-depth analysis of the opening problem, the preacher typically adopts "some form of an ethic of obedience: 'Have faith...do better...' (or even worse: 'Do better and then find faith')."[4] The gospel is distorted into a moralizing answer to some presented problem.

Moreover, the nature of the presented problem itself is crucial for the integrity of preaching. Simplistic "challenges to self-esteem" or other equally superficial problems to be solved are not adequate starting points for a homiletical plot. The listener's equilibrium is not sufficiently upset by issues so light as not even to earn their way into a "Dear Abby" column.

The "itch," as in itch-to-scratch methodology, first must be transformed into an issue of profound importance. "The worst-case abuse of issue-resolution sermonic shape occurs when the preacher defines the issue superficially, avoids any in-depth escalation of the matter, and thus triumphantly announces the resolution."[5]

The originating problem will not be resolved in a too-rapid move to a solution; and this opening problem will be of a gravity sufficient to disturb the equilibrium of the congregation to some considerable degree.

This is the heart of what Lowry has taught a generation of preachers. What are they (and we) to make of it all from a critical distance? I propose to explore each stage of his "narrative plot," first with an interest in some internal frustrations one might meet along the way. Then, having made the journey through the shape of the homiletical plot, we will turn to distinctive voices opposing the Lowry project. As Lowry has instructed, we begin at the beginning of the narrative.

The Narrative Sermon: Frustrations along the Way

There are two main versions of the homiletical plot as Lowry depicts it: one containing five stages, another four.[6] A further complication is that in the "Afterword" to the "expanded edition" of *The Homiletical Plot,* Lowry repents of several terms for the original five-stage "loop" and provides an updated drawing of the loop itself.[7] He has consistently allowed for infrequent adjustments in the loop's *ordo*; at times, the stages may be shifted to some degree. Reflecting on the original five-stage model, Lowry notes that "there are some possible variations of movement—particularly as related to stages 3 (*aha*—disclosing the clue to resolution) and 4 (*whee*—experiencing the good news)."[8] Given these variations on the narrative theme, the following chart may be helpful in relating the versions of the plot:

Lowry's Stages of the Narrative Sermon

Homiletical Plot (1980)	*The Sermon* (1997)	*Homiletical Plot,* expanded ed. (2001)
1. Upsetting the Equilibrium	1. Conflict	1. Conflict
2. Analyzing the Discrepancy	2. Complication	2. Complication
3. Disclosing the Clue to Resolution	3. Sudden Shift	3. Sudden Shift
4. Experiencing the Gospel	4. Unfolding	4. Good News[9]
5. Anticipating the Consequences		5. Unfolding

In considering the stages and the frustrations afflicting each along the plotted journey, we will follow the sequence Lowry provides in *The Sermon.*[10]

1. Conflict

A sense of this initial issue is achieved by way of a season of preparation in which the preacher becomes immersed in the biblical text. This is not the time for commentaries or Internet homilies. "Dive in the deep end of the biblical pool," Lowry encourages (92)—both alone *and* with parish study groups and colleagues in pastoral ministry. Read the text aloud and beware of taking it over by imposing prior conclusions as to its meaning. Lowry adds, "We need to operate with an ideology of suspicion— aimed directly at ourselves. We know too much, you know"(92).

During this initial immersion Lowry admonishes interpreters by way of several exercises to "go sideways." Rather than a search for the main idea of the text, the preacher looks for things out of place, for dissonance, for what seems odd or weird. Those called to preach need "a kind of thirst for chaos" (64) in undertaking this textual immersion. Lowry suggests a variety of techniques to tease the trouble out of the text and to get the preacher out of the way. Assembled within a section titled, "Positioning Oneself to Be Surprised" (95–100), these tactics include (1) noticing what we have not highlighted after we have underlined the important passages, (2) shifting perspective within the text and changing one's point of identification, and (3) engaging in "imaginative word-association exercises" (97). Lowry also encourages preachers to allow "preparation timing" (98). Leaving the text at a point of closure would leave us "with nothing to ruminate about while [we] were busy doing other forms of ministry, engaging in family activities, and even sleeping." The lesson: leave the text temporarily at a place of quandary or *"felt difficulty"* (100). In all these techniques, the preacher is intentionally setting out to be surprised.

This immersion does not necessarily or immediately produce the opening conflict that is the first stage in a homiletical plot. Some texts will yield this conflict with ease—the text *is* the itch. At other times, the text's conflict is difficult to discern. Lowry claims that those who provided the church with the three-year lectionary shied away from texts of conflict, delighting instead "in summary resolution texts, while often avoiding any issues that might be raised by the text."[11] Confronted by such lections, the preacher may want to search around the biblical passage for prior or subsequent passages containing a more sideways edge. Or preachers may adopt a strategy favored by Fred Craddock—"find another text that will ask tough questions of the first passage" (63). Finally, this essential immersion in the text may well bring into focus some specific conflict within our contemporary ecclesial or secular context.

What remains constant between *The Homiletical Plot* (1980) and *The Sermon* (1997) is the narrative quality of this first stage. It presents the "itch," the bind, the conflict. In the 1980 publication, however, opening conflicts seemed to be derived primarily from ambiguity and chaos in the contemporary world, or from latent issues in a biblical text. The central purpose of this opening sermon stage "is to trigger ambiguity in the listeners' minds."[12] By the time *The Sermon* was published, a more nuanced framing of this opening conflict seems to have jelled. Yes, the opening conflict could be some aspect of the contemporary human situation, but that perceived conflict emerges in the course of the immersion in the text. Lowry quotes with approval Barth's dictum that the congregation will not even know what questions are worthy of asking until the word of God in Scripture is heard (65). Hence, "the connection between pew and pulpit is never that of a 'want-say' relation" (66).

It is not surprising that a number of challenges arise that can frustrate this project. Texts of Scripture embodying a "doxological purpose" are resistant to a sermonic plot begun in conflict. While Lowry chastises the ecumenical lectionary for favoring such "summary resolution texts,"[13] they do appear in Scripture and challenge the narrative plotting preacher from time to time, whether or not the lectionary is involved in their selection. Clearly, Lowry is happier with conflict-laden texts such as the parables and other types of biblical narrative. David Buttrick observes with regard to his phenomenological method that some texts do not lend themselves to a moves-and-structures sermon: "They may not be within a 'homiletical canon.'"[14] Perhaps Lowry might make a similar disclaimer regarding such summary resolution texts.

2. Complication

The initial problem or conflict does not settle at once into an easy resolution. The plot thickens. "Whatever the particular form of the new homiletic sermon, once conflict happens, things always get worse—and in such diverse ways" (66). In 1980, Lowry labeled this stage "Analyzing the Discrepancy," and involved both preacher and listener in the hard work of diagnosis. The complication is propelled by one word: "Why?" Within the boundaries of this second stage, the most extensive of all five according to Lowry,[15] it is the task of the preacher to undertake the task of diagnosis and analysis, whose outcome may be complications far beyond the imagined problems set forth in the opening stage. How? "Simply, it is to ask why and not be content with your answers. As you continue to reject each answer with another why you will find increasing depth in your analysis, until you come across a reason underneath which you cannot go."[16] Usually, this depth-level answer deals with human motivation rather than surface behavior, and the answer will have sufficient importance to evoke a gospel response.

In *The Sermon*, however, Lowry reconsidered the dynamics of this critical stage, in addition to changing its name from "Analyzing the Discrepancy." He discovered several presuppositions underlying his strategy for deepening the plot. First, this repetitive use of "Why?" revealed that "we obviously were in the context of a fairly discursive left-brain homiletical style" (70). Between 1980 and 1997 theoreticians reflected on the various roles played by aesthetic and discursive modes of thought. Both come into play within the narrative sermon.

A second assumption emerges as Lowry ruminates on his 1980 work. He was still working a left-brain model of interpretation, looking for a "presolutional" theme derived from biblical text or contemporary life (70). Applying the analytical "Why?" to such issues did not always produce much depth of complication. Other strategies are needed, varying according to the genre of the text, the distinctive mode of the narrative sermon, and the congregational context.[17] "Whatever the forms of complication in whatever sermonic types, the critical key is the *move to fluidity* where matters are not indefinite, but yet clearly are indeterminate. The movement at this stage of the plot must be movement toward the actually irresolute, the truly dilemmic, the really bound." (72)

The strategies are no longer restricted to a repetitive "Why?" The outcome and the quality of the analysis, however, remains rooted in narrative dynamics.

Given the essential importance of this stage of complication, Lowry observes a widespread resistance among preachers to engaging in this task. Why do preachers have such difficulty pressing deeply into an issue, especially when that exploration leads to greater ambiguity and a "truly dilemmic" quandary? Several answers are proposed. First, the cultural context for congregation and preacher is one wherein ambiguity abounds. Perhaps because of its pervasiveness, there is a felt need to find a quick fix. We are formed by a widespread "instrumentalism of problem solving" (68) that avoids deepened conflict in favor of straight moves toward nifty solutions. Moreover, Lowry adds, we have within us "this natural reluctance to really break things open" (68).

Little wonder that very shortly after identifying the text's field of concern, articulating the issue, naming the presenting conflict, often we move quickly to close it down, stop the bleeding, and relieve the pain. It sometimes feels like the pastoral thing to do because life can be tough, after all. But such premature closure turns out to be a Band-Aid on life's tragedy, a momentary diversion from the pain—perhaps even an immunity against hearing the good news (68).

Analysis that remains superficial will probably lead to inadequate or even falsified solutions; and since the gospel is never superficial, a homiletical quick fix to any presenting problem may render us immune to good news. Nevertheless, tactics abound in contemporary preaching that serve to "close the case" before deepened complication can be engaged.

Deploy a "mega-story" in place of the hard work of analysis.[18]

Here, a clear trend has been developing for some time. Story illustrations are growing longer, more involved, and more sentimental. Perhaps this is a function of the frequency with which such stories pop up in the preacher's e-mail. Such mega-stories cannot serve to deepen analysis or drive an opening problem to deepened complication. On the contrary, because of their size and pathos, they tend to displace the biblical text, substituting their own story, too, for the narrative of the homiletical plot. In his "Introduction" to Lowry's expanded edition of *The Homiletical Plot*, Fred Craddock comments:

> Either through failure to appreciate the vital importance of diagnosis in a sermon or through the inability to perform it, many preachers arrive at the point of diagnosis and offer an illustration instead. Usually illustrations are interesting, but nothing in the message is more interesting than an analysis of what is really going on, in a biblical text, in a story, in a life. Contrary to popular opinion, illustrations do not cover a multitude of sins.[19]

Substitute a film clip for analysis.

Here, the problem is similar to deploying a story illustration in place of complicating analysis, but with some other "complications" of its own. One such attempt, for example, involved a "theme" of anger, complete with spaces in the bulletin to be filled in as the "message" progressed. After an opening section in the sermon that spoke about anger, the congregation was shown a cutting from the film, *Crimson Tide*. The nuclear submarine captain (played by Gene Hackman) and the executive officer (Denzel Washington) engaged in a brutal exchange with each other about launching their missiles. Anger was certainly illustrated by the actors, but the film clip did nothing to complicate the issue in the sermon. Instead, the complication now before the congregation was whether or not the missiles would be launched. (The clip did not extend to deal with a resolution of that complication and the congregation was left in cinematic ambiguity. It is doubtful if many left the sub and reentered the sermon.) A further "complication" attended this deployment of the film clip by way of illustrating anger. In a conversation overheard after the worship service, the discussion centered on the relative merits of the two actors—Hackman and Washington. Whatever else was accomplished, the preacher did not complicate the sermon's focus on anger.

Attempt complication by telling a first person story related to the problem.

Here the issues relate both to the effectiveness of first person pulpit illustrations and to their use at this stage in the homiletical plot. Most preachers do not have sufficient representative identity for first person stories. Within most African American church settings, the preacher retains such a role representative of the community and will wisely select first person stories that will rapidly be owned by the congregation as "our story." In the majority of church contexts, however, this representative force has long since been lost (or squandered). The opening conflict will likely not "thicken"; rather, the preacher's story will only illustrate the preacher. Regarding the second issue—the use of first person story in the complication stage of the homiletical plot, if narrowly drawn, the story may depict the preacher in a victim role. If the first person story moves on toward a positive outcome, the story has crept out of its complication stage and preempted resolution.[20]

3. Sudden Shift

The sermon will not even have a narrative plot without this third stage. The previous stage of deepening complication has established a downward trajectory into a condition that is "actually irresolute." However, at some intentional delayed location in the homiletical plot, there is a "sudden shift" toward a new and radically different outcome born of the gospel. Initially Lowry spoke of this shift as *the principle of reversal*.[21] There is a clue to resolution that "reverses the train of diagnostic thought."[22] This turn in the direction of the plot was interpreted as a reversal of the situation—as in an Aristotelian *peripeteia*. Occurring about three-fourths of the way through the sermon, there is a decisive turn in plot direction with no possibility of return to the *status quo ante*. Lowry continued to view this crucial stage as one of sudden reversal in *The Sermon*, and in *Doing Time in the Pulpit*. Here, the location in the sermonic plot is reached where "by means of reversal, a new profound simplicity overtakes the confusion."[23] However, Eugene Lowry's thinking on this critical turn in the sermonic plot itself shifted in *The Sermon*: "several adjustments appear now in order" (75). Primary among these is a significant widening of the arc of the homiletical plot's change in direction. The sudden shift can remain one of reversal, a turn of 180°. (So, for example, in the parables of reversal—especially clear-cut in the double reversal of the good Samaritan—a sermon shaped like the plot of the text will encounter a radical reversal at stage three. Lowry also notes that the extended story of the Man Born Blind in John 9 concludes with such a dramatic reversal [76].) However, the Lowry of 1997 sees a much wider range of possible shifts in the sermonic plot at this decisive stage. Many biblical narratives contain a dramatic turn in plot without reversal. What is important, Lowry says, "is that the turn be so decisive that there is no way to go back to the previous view" (77).

The next adjustment in this stage in the plot relates to the now multiple ways in which the gospel can serve this sudden shift. "Where does the good news show up?" Lowry asks (81). He recalls that in *The Homiletical Plot*, 1980, the good news falls into place immediately upon the experiencing of reversal, of "disclosing the clue to resolution." And, it remains the case that any number of sermonic plots may still find the good news erupting just after such a reversal has occurred. On the other hand, "not all texts and topics in preaching work this way" (83). In some texts, the good news itself provides the torque for the plot's sudden shift. A third option is more subtle. Here, as seen in the story of Blind Bartimaeus, the good news takes place subsequent to the complication, but prior to the sudden shift. (Bartimaeus is simply healed.) Sudden shift? It is in Bartimaeus's turn to join Jesus along the way rather than in a returning to his home. (See 83–84.)

The business about relating the good news and the sudden shift is not as complicated as it may seem at this moment. What is important is the preacher's concentration in preparation, not on the final naming of the good news, but on the search for the sudden shift. Once found, it will by its nature "tell" the preacher whether it should come before, at, or after the good news (84).

A further adjustment relates to the timing of the sudden shift within the movement of the narrative homiletical plot. In his previous considerations of the timing of the sudden shift ("reversal" in those writings), Lowry notes that he had set the decisive turn's appearance at about three-fourths of the way through the sermon. Upon further rumination, though, Lowry now adjusts the timing of the turn: "Perhaps five-sixths is better." He adds that on "rare occasions it may happen on the last line" (78). This intentional delay in resolving ambiguity and proclaiming the gospel has not met with universal acclaim in the homiletics community, however. Paul Scott Wilson insists that such a delay "seems less than desirable."[24] "When God suddenly comes into focus at the end of a sermon the gospel is not brought home and applied to the listener's life or the world. Considerable sermon time is needed to make the gospel concrete and to allow people to experience what God is accomplishing in and through them and others."[25]

This question is engaging and important. On one hand, Wilson has lauded Lowry for his imaginative depiction of a sermon as a loop, "like the *icthus* fish symbol turned on its nose."[26] The Lowry homiletical narrative plot, for Wilson, is a rich insight, including the "identification of the midway point as a reversal."[27] On the other hand, the problem for Wilson is that Lowry will not grant him this reversal at the sermon's "midway point." Lowry's word back is firm:

> I disagree with Paul Scott Wilson who wants us to divide the sermon into two halves—with "a fifty-fifty balance between law and gospel."[28] I certainly understand his concern that people carry with them from the worship

service the resolution born of grace. But quantity of words is not the appropriate measure. The quality of impact, the suddenness of perception, and the power of decisive insight are central. (78)

It would seem, then, that we have a bit of a standoff. If the sermon is to retain its quality as a narrative event in time, Lowry might say, then any attempt to locate the plot's sudden shift at the halfway point is folly. Stories do not work that way. Wilson's response is equally adamant. By delaying the sudden shift until such a late point in the sermon, Lowry "gives priority to dramatic surprise instead of to the theological urgency of listeners meeting God and discerning God in the world around them."[29] Perhaps the only resolution of this conflict is by way of a word to the preacher: "If you find the need to balance your sermon in a fifty-fifty split between law and gospel, then Wilson's *Four Pages of the Sermon* model will serve you well. If, on the other hand, you find the text and your context best served through the use of a narrative homiletical plot, then overcome any resistance and delay this turn/sudden shift until quite late in the sermon."

Apart from this "plot-pages" standoff between Lowry and Wilson, the most serious challenge to the performance of this third stage of the homiletical plot concerns the challenges to preachers when it is time to "name grace" or speak gospel.[30] Recall that the preacher will need to articulate the claims of the gospel in some close alignment with the sudden shift of the sermon—whether just prior to it, at the shift itself, or subsequent to the shift. The problem is the challenge to "name grace." For whatever reasons, many who are called to preach in the North American context have been formed and informed how to name all that is negative with great facility. The same cannot be said with regard to matters of the gospel. In both my introduction to preaching classes and in continuing education contexts, when the question of concretion is at hand, I ask the group to image two Buttrick-style moves based loosely on the prologue to John's Gospel: (I) "The world is a world of darkness," and (II) "But Jesus is the light of the world." Both seminarians and experienced pastors prove eager and expert in imaging the first move. They are expert at providing vivid examples of darkness in our world.[31] When the issue turns to the second move, however, few examples of vivid imagery and bright example are suggested. Rather than "speaking of," what is heard is a "talking about" grace and gospel. The rhetoric is discursive, lacking in imagistic concretion, remaining at some distance. So while the methodological task of relating the good news and sudden shift "is not as complicated as it may seem at this moment" (84), speaking of the good news is a huge challenge for many preachers. Perhaps *Naming the Good News* could be the title of Eugene Lowry's next book.

4. Unfolding

With the advent of the sudden shift and the experiencing of the gospel, a brief portion of the sermon remains in which, according to *Homiletical Plot*, 1980, the listeners "anticipate the consequences." Here again, Lowry has undertaken some revision in terminology and content. Commenting on the connotation of the term, Lowry now reflects, "I have no idea what prompted me to label stage 5 (yeah) as 'anticipating the consequences'!"[32] The term "consequences," Lowry muses, has negative associations. His intention, better expressed by the new term, "unfolding," was to speak of a final stage that "always *anticipates the future*, made new by the good news."[33] Not much sermon time remains, but the dramatic, even radical shift brought through the experience of the gospel invites consideration of the new future now offered in Christ. This unfolding stage will have certain characteristics to it, including a "powerful economy with words" (86). "As tension subsides, the listeners will not abide lots of new material. Rather, this is the time to name quickly and powerfully the consequences of our being claimed by the gospel's prophetic and poetic anticipation of "new possibility in the listening assembly."[34]

Utilizing this economy of words, the preacher invites the assembly to the "imagined effect" of the gospel, the "unexpected blossoming" of a new future (87). Without some attention to this unfolding, the sermon is not complete. The good news changes things; the word of God goes forth and does not return empty. In this brief stage, the preacher invites the listeners to share in some of the consequential effect of this sudden shift. The goal of this event-in-time is *evocation*.

When reflecting on some of the challenges to the performance of this fourth and final stage of the homiletical plot, we may recall those preachers who lack sufficient discipline to employ the word economy or power needed for evocation. A related issue involves some preaching traditions in which the payoff of every sermon, based on whatever biblical text, will need to end with the same "call" or rhetorical epic. Not all Scripture intends a first-time call to faith in Jesus Christ, yet some preachers repeat a stereotyped ending to almost every sermon as if they are never preaching to the baptized.[35] In the African American narrative preaching tradition, this unfolding will most likely turn to celebration. The preacher will now move to close the sermon with a joy-filled climax. The challenge here is to discern the appropriate celebration of the good news rather than depending on "tried-and-true celebrative standbys, such as a story of conversion or deathbed healing, or 'taking people to the cross' (the Calvary-Easter narrative)."[36] The unfolding will emerge with Spirit-filled intensity from the specific sudden shift of the sermon as shaped by the distinctive force of the good news.

The Narrative Sermon: External Challenges

Our review and assessment of the four stages of Lowry's homiletical plot have constituted an examination of frustrations internal to the sequence. We turn now to consider external challenges to Lowry's narrative homiletic.

1. The "Preaching as Instruction" Crisis

Lowry himself identifies this challenge. "At stake in this crisis," Lowry remarks, "is a growing reduction of proclamation to that of instruction."[37] Particularly as modeled in some mega-churches, the signs and symbols of the faith have not only been removed from the building and grounds, but from preaching as well. "Moreover," he adds, "in such environs the sermon often is not much more than a few helpful hints about how to still feel good on Tuesday."[38] However, even this low standard for preaching is in some cases set too high: "It is interesting that often in such services even the term 'sermon' is avoided. Terms like 'lesson' and 'message' are preferred. Part of me is glad the title 'sermon' is not used. Whatever minor helpful hints these are, indeed, sermons they are not."[39]

The move toward such "instruction" is celebrated for its prag-matics—"It works!" (Roughly translated: "It brings people back to the church.") Yet this crisis is no cause for despair. Those who entered the church by way of such "messages"—some of them, anyway—will have a spiritual need to go deeper in their faith. As that happens, the helpful hints will not serve; they will be lured deeper to dance the edge of mystery. This crisis may be somewhat generationally based. Recent writing on the "emergent church" points to a spiritual longing by those of a younger generation than the Baby Boomers.[40] Narrative preaching will be welcomed in the emergent church.

2. *The Postliberal Critique*

As Charles Campbell develops the implications of Hans Frei's theology for homiletics, Lowry comes in for repeated analysis and evaluation.[41] Given that both Lowry and Frei draw on narrative models of hermeneutics and that both acknowledge their indebtedness to Karl Barth, it is important for Campbell to highlight the values in Lowry's project, and also, more emphatically, to dismiss Lowry's approach. The positive contributions of narrative homiletics include for Campbell: (1) "a turn to Scripture," (2) the enrichment of the sermonic form, (3) "a new appreciation for the indicative character of the gospel," (4) a recovery of the wholistic dimensions of preaching (to emotions as well as intellect), and (5) the highlighting of "the poetic and metaphorical dimensions of the language of preaching"(121). On the other hand, Campbell's negative critique of Lowry is based in Frei's privileging of character rather than plot within biblical narrative. Campbell affirms with Frei that "the New Testament narratives, with their peculiar ascriptive logic have a specific function, which is to render the unique, unsubstitutable identity of Jesus Christ and to form the community of faith into a 'distant' embodiment of that identity" (55). Both the identity of Jesus Christ and of this "distant" community embodying that identity are unsubstitutable. Moreover, "the key is not the genre of narrative, but the content, logic, and function of the particular narrative of the Christian community—the 'world' of the Bible" (55). If this construal of the function of biblical narrative is correct—the approach held by Frei—then the entire project of liberalism flounders. For Frei "liberal, apologetic theology has consistently had the goal of defending the religious and moral meaningfulness of the Christian faith in relation to general human needs or common human experience" (33). Liberalism's apologetic goal locates Jesus Christ as one regional exemplar of the best of what it means to be human or one whose "good news" answers the most pressing needs and problems of human experience.

Now Campbell turns to his analysis of Lowry's narrative homiletic. In spite of its assets, Campbell finds it seriously deficient, faulting it on several fronts. The experiential character of preaching is emphasized throughout Lowry's work (138). The same "word-event" understanding that weakens the projects of the preaching-as-storytelling homileticians and, especially, the work of Craddock, also afflicts Lowry's efforts. Campbell notes that for Lowry, "The goal is to preach so that 'the experiencing of the word can occur as event.'"[42]

For Campbell, "this experience has a decidedly individualistic orientation, despite Lowry's comments on the importance of story for forming communal identity" (140). Campbell criticizes Lowry for adopting a one-to-one model of preaching based upon the "doctor-patient" or "therapist-client relationship: "he seeks fundamentally to analyze problems in 'interior motivation" and to offer the gospel as a 'cure'" (140). Moreover, this individualistic bias, for Campbell, is disclosed when Lowry turns to an analysis of the biblical characters with the various stages of his plot. What is discovered here is that Lowry, according to Campbell, looks to the inner subjectivity of those characters that provide a linkage with the analogous experience of the individual members of the congregation. For Lowry, Campbell concludes, "an emphasis on the experiential event and an individualistic orientation go together" (140–41).

As detected by Frei, the approach adopted by the narrative homileticians Campbell surveys results in a serious problematic regarding the person and identity of Jesus Christ. "Christology becomes a function of soteriology, which is shaped by an independent analysis of human existence" (164). This symptom of a liberal theology at work is seen most clearly in the decided privilege accorded to the parables by Lowry and the other narrative homileticians Campbell surveys. In a section titled, "If You've Got a Good Parable, You Don't Need Jesus" (173), Campbell argues that Lowry and others have set aside any interest in the character of Jesus the parabler on behalf of a quest for the existential, experiential word-events. The title of Lowry's book, *How to Preach a Parable*, reveals an equating of narrative and parable, Campbell claims. But in this move, the unique identity of Jesus fades away.[43]

It is a remarkable coincidence that Charles Campbell's *Preaching Jesus* and Lowry's *The Sermon* were published in the same year (1997). In the latter, Lowry seems to have anticipated a number of Campbell's critiques. Regarding narrative hermeneutics, Lowry quotes William Placher[44] extensively, at times sounding very much like Frei: "The bottom line for Placher (and for this writing as well) is that 'to the extent that I take the pattern of these stories to be the pattern for my life and of the world, I am committed to believing that the God they describe is not the projection or useful construct of the people in the story.'"[45]

Clearly, Lowry's use of Placher here does not represent the liberal use of biblical narrative as one expression of a ubiquitous narrative anthropology. Rather, Placher—and Lowry—are asserting with Campbell—and Frei—that the stories of Scripture "render or constitute the reality they narrate."[46]

Regarding the individualistic character of Lowry's homiletical approach, here again some interesting resonances occur between the two 1997 publications, *Preaching Jesus* and *The Sermon*. In one summary judgment of narrative homiletics, Campbell concludes: "The problem is that up until now narrative homiletics has provided no resources for thinking carefully about the ways preaching contributes to the upbuilding of the church—the formation of the people of God—*beyond* the individual hearer."[47]

Now, in *The Sermon* (and Lowry's other recent writings), we note a similar insistence on the church as the "middle term" of interpretation between text and preacher. Lowry quotes P.T. Forsyth and agrees that the preacher "is called to preach to the Church," but also must "preach *from* the Church."[48]

In a similar vein, Charles Campbell has chastised Lowry for the latter's problem-solutional liberal approach to preaching (with those "doctor-patient" or "therapist-client" images). In *The Sermon*, however, Lowry confesses, "in *Plot* I often utilized the liberal-sounding terms problem or problem-solution." He adds: "I now tend to utilize such terms as *issue-resolution, conflict to unfolding,* or *tension to closure*. The good news of the gospel, as I have said elsewhere, is not reducible to answering people's every felt need; the good news of the gospel involves a transformation of human experience—its language and practices."[49]

Nevertheless, it is unlikely that Charles Campbell will now invite Eugene Lowry into the postliberal fold. Lowry's word-event approach to preaching is inherently individualistic and Lowry has not at all repented of a homiletical goal of "eventful evocation"[50] (a goal Campbell may well remain convinced is fully experiential/expressive to its core). Even Lowry's clear movement along two decades of plotting sermons from opening problems drawn from current human situations toward opening issues with the scriptural text does not satisfy Campbell. He agrees that in Lowry's recent writings and sermons the biblical text "*both* upsets the hearers' equilibrium at the beginning of the sermon *and* provides the new equilibrium at the end; that is, the biblical text both raises the 'problem' and provides the 'solution.'"[51] Then Campbell adds a glowing compliment: "This approach actually comes close to Frei's position. The biblical text does not simply answer a general human question, but also poses the question itself."[52] Nevertheless, Lowry cannot pass Campbell's test. Even when starting with an issue in Scripture, "Lowry's analysis tends toward the psychological, focusing on the subjectivities and interior motivations of the characters."[53]

In spite of the many commonalities, these two narrative homileticians likely will continue to differ. Even the fact that Charles Campbell also employs the jazz musician image when developing his own constructive homiletic—a perennial appeal for Lowry—does not overcome the perceived incompatibilities.[54] For Campbell, Lowry's homiletical plot remains an example of liberal apologetics with its inherently individualistic bias. Moreover, the selection of plot over character with regard to the interpretation of Scripture condemns Lowry to a general hermeneutic of narrative as human experience. Campbell notes that "once one turns to character one must get specific."[55] Lowry's response to Campbell? Probably it would be to observe that in these critiques, he is now dodging "the slings and arrows of the more radical sort of postliberals."[56] Perhaps the only way out of the standoff is to change the identity of Eugene Lowry's homiletic. Paul Scott Wilson locates Lowry within the on-going tradition of law/gospel preacher—a tradition that centrally includes Karl Barth. Wilson notes, "Eugene Lowry, in a piano presentation at the Academy of Homiletics meeting in 1992, had spoken of the sermon as being like jazz, starting with trouble. Trouble seemed to me like a good word to replace law."[57] The gospel, as noted above, intervenes in the sermonic plot at (or nearby) the stage of sudden shift. What if, Paul Scott Wilson maintains, the Lowry-plotted sermon is one sophisticated version of preaching law and gospel? Perhaps the standoff, then, between Lowry and those "more radical sort of postliberals" could possibly be reframed and thereby renegotiated.

"Happy Plotting"[58]

With this signoff, Eugene Lowry concludes his "Afterword" to the "expanded edition" of *The Homiletical Plot*. It is a greeting that reflects both his gratitude for the enduring interest in his homiletic method over a span of two decades and his encouragement for those who will adopt his narrative sermon plot in the future. Certainly, as Campbell has graciously commented about Lowry's project, "(t)here is no question that many of his insights about the temporal character of preaching and the structure of the sermon can be of immense importance to contemporary preachers."[59] To borrow one of his favorite terms, continuing fluidity has marked Lowry's whole narrative homiletic project. He made bold to propose his homiletical plot in 1980 and, while he has retained the core movement and structure of this loop, Lowry has also been about the continuing work of refining, revising, and even retracting aspects of the narrative sermon. Several generations of seminary students and numerous other preachers now engage the text for Sunday by asking what is strange, usually ignored, or even "sideways." These preacher labor at the hard work of complication, forgoing both a facile problem-solution strategy and the equally superficial deployment of some downloaded mega-story. They return to the text for the gospel that will evoke or accompany the congregation's experience of sudden shift. And they will join all the others for the unfolding.

6

Story, Narrative, and Metanarrative

FRED B. CRADDOCK

Do not let the title of this essay fool you; the subject is narrative—narrative preaching. Not stories. We are not here engaged in swapping stories. Not that such an exercise would be without merit. In fact, I have spent a lifetime telling stories, and it is difficult to imagine that I have been engaged in para-preaching, a game played across the street from the pulpit, sounding like, looking like, but not really being the real thing. Stories can be components of sermons, serious in the service of the message and not simply a recess from the heavy substance of preaching. The old homiletical instruction that a story needs to be inserted every seven minutes of the sermon to allow listeners a break, to let them "come up for air," insults the sermon in all its parts, story and non-story alike. To be sure, some stories may function as illustrations of points being made, points that, without illuminating stories or anecdotes, would remain unclear. Or, a story may function to bring home in concrete terms a point that, without the story, might be clear to the listener's mind, but theoretical or ideational.

However, anyone who has listened to Jesus' stories, the parables, knows that a story may be more than an ingredient of the sermon: it may be the message itself. As such, the story has the density, complexity, and realism of life. To function in this way, the story must be carefully selected, appropriately joined to the sermon, located within the sermon by a good sense of timing, and trusted to carry the freight. So employed, the story may be all that a listener remembers, but it is enough.

All this is to say that the use of stories in preaching is hard work, made even more difficult by the painful necessity of rejecting stories that are interesting, delightful, even moving, but lacking the capacity to contribute to the conversation in a room where the talk is about the reign of God.

Again, the subject here is narrative, narrative preaching, and not about stories that may or may not be components of the sermon. As Gene Lowry has taught us, narrative is a literary form having setting, characters, and plot. Narrative moves from tension to resolution, from ambiguity to clarity, from what seems to be to what is, from guilt to grace, from death to life. Narrative, then, is the shape or movement of the sermon; it is not a piece of the sermon. Narrative describes the whole, not a component.

Narrative, therefore, can be the manner of unfolding matters of utmost seriousness. Narrative does not have to apologize as though it lacked authority, or as though it sacrificed substance to the desire to be interesting. Nor does narrative have to take a back seat to the syllogism in terms of persuasive power. Counselors, sitting before lives shattered and spent, move narratively as a way to inform, to create understanding, and to enable. Theologians offer their readers and their students heavy agendas as narrative. Biblical scholars speak of the narrative of salvation history or of narrative christology, as in Matthew, Mark, Luke, and John. Recent studies of New Testament epistles have explored the narrative worlds of those epistles.[1] There has been a great deal of debate in recent years as to whether or not a narrative about Jesus lay in the background of Paul's preaching and teaching in the churches.[2] In sum, narrative has arrived and is welcomed with respect in classroom and sanctuary, at desk and in pulpit.

But now a new question is addressed to the narrative sermon. It is not a question asked by a listener who brings a rhetorical or literary ear to the sanctuary. Rather, the inquiry is ethical and theological, and may be stated in this way: Does the narrative shape of the sermon mirror reality or does it offer a twenty-minute escape from reality? Mind you, this is not a question of content but of shape. Consider, for example, the novel, also narrative. The novel owes part of its appeal to shape: it leads the reader through clearly defined experiences with clearly defined characters involved in a plot with beginning, middle, and ending. At last, the reader is satisfied with a sense of final resolution, stated or implied. However "real" the novel is, it is unreal in that the reader's own life is not clearly defined in time and space with a sense of movement to resolution. A novel, then, offers the reader a brief respite from a cluttered and disjointed life that seems not to move with purpose to an ending. While engaged with the novel, the reader is allowed to forget the way life really is.

Is this true also for the listener to a narrative sermon? The narrative sermon and the novel have a number of common elements, especially in movement through beginning, middle, and ending. But there is one major difference: the narrative sermon does not claim to offer a brief escape from reality, but claims to hold up a mirror to reality. How so? Because the sermon participates in, assumes, and reveals, whether specifically verbalized or not, a master narrative, a macro-narrative, a metanarrative. The narrative sermon bears witness to this metanarrative not only in its content but in its shape, and dares to claim that the metanarrative is ultimate reality, the divine purpose, now seen, now not seen, which runs through beginning, middle, and ending.

Who is this listener who questions whether the narrative sermon mirrors reality or offers escape from reality? Very likely a postmodern. As the term implies, a postmodern is one who has moved or has been moved by cultural changes past the beliefs that characterized the modern era. The modern age was optimistic, heavily invested in the myth of progress, and in a universal rationality that would bring all of life under the rule of reason. Diseases would be conquered, violence would cease, property would be justly distributed, and the good society would be realized. The postmodern looks around, assesses what has not happened, trashes the modern vision as naïve, and moves into the future with low expectations. There is no sense of purposive movement to life, no sense of a beginning, a middle, an ending. There is no larger picture, there are no universals; everything is relative. So, why not stay in one's own yard and play with one's own toys, which are many, thanks to the economy? If the postmodern affiliates with a church, it makes sense to choose one that is local and free standing, without larger denominational or ecumenical connections. One can thus feel assured that the message and worship will be tailored to neighborhood preferences. Forget the old assumptions that were to undergird the building of larger and larger communities, and accept the obvious: life is full of disconnects and discontinuities.

The postmodern lives in a multicultural, multireligious world. This means being aware of the Other, the person or group unlike me.[3] The Other may be racially different, politically different, religiously different, morally different, culturally different. The Other may have a different sexual orientation. The significant fact is that the Other is no longer in another country or in another part of this country; the Other lives next door. The community-building efforts of the modern era—that is, getting people together in acknowledgment of a common humanity—are abandoned by the postmodern. Fence in the yard, be on the alert, get on the cell phone—not really to communicate, but to avoid communicating with the Other next door.

In the modern era there was a comforting and encouraging carryover from premodern days, the belief in a master narrative, a macro-narrative, or, to use the term now preferred, a metanarrative.[4] Those who trusted in a metanarrative did not always give voice to it, but it was there, perhaps more importantly there because it was assumed. One did not have to verbalize it, perhaps because talking about it seemed to trivialize it or make it somehow appear weak, needing defense or argument or the support of frequent references. A metanarrative is the background for life in the world, the larger context of meaning and purpose in the universe. Background is not really the proper word; a background may be a prop or scenery, providing affect but not integral to the being and doing of life. "Frame of reference" may be more appropriate. To believe in a frame of reference is to believe there is a whole, which gives meaning to the parts. My personal observations, my experiences, my relationships are not all there is. To claim the final authority of personal experience is to deny a metanarrative. Consider embroidery as an analogy. On the underside, the side of our experience, no clear pattern is visible, only threads and what appear to be tangles. However, on the upperside is a pattern clear and meaningful. Only one's faith perceives it, faith nourished now and then by hints and intimations of it.

Some of those who have believed in a metanarrative have been hesitant to claim ultimacy for their larger frame of reference, reluctant to associate it with the divine. For example, some speak in anthropological terms, assuming a common humanity bound together by origin or destiny or aspirations. Others prefer historical categories, finding within and transcending conflicts and regressions, threads of meaningful movement into the future. Yet others may get their bearings from a connection to the universe, a cosmological metanarrative, often intuitive or mystical. Umberto Eco recalled a visit to a planetarium where his host had arranged, thanks to modern technology, to have the sky rotated to show how stars and moons and planets appeared over Alessandria, Italy, the night of January 5–6, 1932. That was the place and time of Umberto's birth. He said his experience was not only of being reunited with his own beginning but also of being willing to die at that moment, bringing to fulfillment a happy life. His life, he thought, was recorded in the "Book of Books."[5]

Many, however, live out their days in a theological context, and they are not hesitant to verbalize it. There are numerous variations. For some it is enough to say, "God is the Alpha and the Omega, the beginning and the end." Others prefer a canonical metanarrative, from Genesis to Revelation, or perhaps from within the canon, the metanarrative of salvation history.

But whatever the shape or name for this assumed world, now brought to the level of conscious reflection, it all amounts to nothing more than nostalgia, a whistling in the dark, says the radically postmodern. All such constructs, all such master narratives, are not to be trusted. Be suspicious of all metanarratives.[6] If yours was a religious one, be satisfied that you have been left with a residue of reverence, even though it is without belief. Life is nonsequential, disconnected, clouded by chaos, and rendered uncertain by the shifting of the ground beneath our feet. Some meaning might be found in a strong social network, but there is none. The pluralism of our time, if taken seriously, means I am the *Other* to you and you are the *Other* to me. We are both dislodged in a world without universals, but filled to the brim with relativities, including moral relativities. You have your truth and I have mine. Who's to say?

You have your right and wrong, and I have mine. Who's to say? There is no referee outside the playing field. Personal experience has triumphed over tradition.

Even so, for some reason these postmoderns continue to come into the sanctuary and sit before the pulpit, perhaps in declining numbers, but they still come. Why? What do they expect to hear? What can the preacher, fully immersed in metanarrative, possibly say?

An honest assessment of most congregations would likely reveal that no preacher speaks to a totally postmodern audience. Premoderns and moderns are present in strong numbers. They love the old songs and the old stories, and their metanarratives are still intact. The truth is, most of us are a mix of premodern, modern, and postmodern. Surveys of "millenials," the generation still in their twenties, indicate a strong gravitation toward the values of the "traditionals"—that is, their grandparents. Maybe they find being postmodern frightening and lonely. Many congregations seem to be satisfied with hearing and seeing on the screen the old metanarratives expressed with the latest technology of the postmodern. This union of premodern metanarrative with postmodern technology is quite common in many mega-churches. Increasing numbers of preachers seem happy to accommodate postmodernism to this extent. And pluralism, another feature of postmodernism, is accommodated by offering a variety of styles of worship. Varieties of church architecture are likewise revealing. But listen carefully to the sermons, and in the background, or even in the foreground, one will recognize the old metanarratives.

If this observation is correct, what is going on here? Are games being played? Are listeners not really postmodern where it counts, but wanting to appear so technologically? Or are preachers offering the illusion of postmodernity, replacing the pipe organ with drums and blue jeans, but never entertaining a simple question about the metanarrative? Perhaps both congregation and preacher are to some extent using smoke and mirrors, but suppose that all of us are more postmodern than we have honestly acknowledged, what would it mean to preach in such a climate? If the central characteristic of postmodern is loss of metanarrative, what can the preacher say?

There is no denying that there are some benefits to a pulpit that looks at life without a master narrative. In the first place, without a metanarrative, what we have is today, here and now. Many believers, including some preachers, have to confess to using the past as a safe place to invest faith. The preacher can read a passage of Scripture and then, as a sermon, offer a review of God's past activity when the sun stood still, enemies were defeated, aged couples had children, the dead were raised, and the Divine voice shook a mountain. Perhaps not intentionally, but celebrating what God once did when enemies were routed was offered as a substitute for facing enemies very much alive. And how helpful the distant future, the eschaton, to right all wrongs, redress grievances, punish the wicked, reward the just, and answer all the "Why" questions. Faith, in effect, could be alternately a beautiful memory and a grand postponement. But, alas, without a metanarrative, the pulpit has to deal with, "In the meantime, back at the church…" Such a challenge would be difficult, but could be fruitful. After all, Jesus regularly deflected questions about "When" and "Where" and gave assignments for "Here" and "Now."

A second benefit to preaching in a climate without a meta-narrative would be sermons more discerning, looking for the presence and activity of God in persons and events all around us. After all, once one can no longer flash on the wide screen in Technicolor the absolutely super extraordinary, one is forced back to basic raw materials on which faith survives; a few verses of Scripture, lines from old hymns, a child's prayer, the words of a stranger, grandmother's lap, and a firm handshake.

Third, there can be gain for the pulpit in jettisoning modernism's myth of progress, its triumph of reason, and the praise of human ingenuity. Triumphalism is replaced by humility appropriate to human endeavors chastened by the failure to conquer disease, end violence, and establish justice in the world. The church now repents of hastily baptizing modernism's arrogant claims, thinly disguising them in religious jargon, and hailing them as the reign of God. The new humility, forced to look at the present, is not simply a sermon topic but a new realism about who we are and what in the world we are doing.

Nearby lies a fourth benefit: having lost a metanarrative, humans no longer march toward the grand finale of their matchless achievements, but rather are brought to a halt before the Great Mystery. Our knowledge has led us, not to certainty, but to mystery. The appropriate posture for the postmodern is awe. In the silence following the admission that there is more than we know, let the loud, strutting, imperialistic sermons with their downward trajectory, claiming to "look at things from God's perspective," quietly slip off stage and go out into the darkness to weep. The preacher, now stripped of master narrative and firm grip on the transcendent, may again be a servant in the community. Even when one cannot connect all the dots, there is much good to be said and done.

Finally, all can welcome the pluralism of a world without a metanarrative. It does not have to silence the pulpit as though pluralism robs one of conviction, taking away a place to stand. On the contrary, pluralism can occasion depth and breadth in the pulpit's thinking and speaking. But let's face it, *pluralism* can be a shadow word, a vague word, a cover for empty sermons and absent convictions. Such preaching deserves no compliment such as "open," "inclusive," or "welcoming." Such a preacher is not ready to enter into dialogue with other faith communities because nothing is brought to the table. Muslim, Jew, and Buddhist come with history, tradition, and conviction. How insulting for the Christian to come empty handed, saying "Whatever." Nothing more honors conversation partners than coming to the table with substance. Allowing content of faith to evaporate in a mist of spirituality serves no one.

Now to the heart of the matter: Does the Christian pulpit offer a metanarrative, sometimes assumed, sometimes stated, sometimes elaborated, regardless of whether the audience is premodern, modern, or postmodern? This is not to say that the worldview of the listeners is unimportant to preaching. Of course not; the preacher exegetes the congregation as carefully as the biblical text. After all, if preaching is the facilitating of a conversation between the text and the people, they must be able to talk to each other, however distant from each other they may seem to be. But in the sincere desire to generate a conversation, does the preacher consider everything negotiable? No, of course not—else why show up at all? We all know some things are negotiable; in fact, some of the material in our sermons could be surgically removed and no blood would be shed. But is metanarrative one of the negotiable items, optional, without which the sermon would still convey the gospel? If it is the task of preaching not only to generate a conversation but also to witness, is a metanarrative integral to that witness?

The position of this essay is Yes; for the gospel to be the gospel, there must be a master narrative, a frame of reference in which life, relationships, Jesus, church, and history are set. Imagine presenting Jesus, or trying to be church, or interpreting events, or engaging the issues in one's world without a context, a larger picture within which to set these activities. To believe in God is immediately to raise questions of whence, whither, and why; to begin to think of God's relation to the world in terms of origin, purpose, and end. If there is no overarching narrative into which personal stories and the human story are set, then, why even speak of a God who does not make a difference anyway? It could be argued that many of the listeners came before the pulpit hoping for a master narrative within which to reflect on the disconnects and contradictions of their lives. But whatever the appetites among the listeners, a metanarrative is good news.

However, the overarching narrative of the sermon needs now to be stated, not simply assumed. In many churches, listeners can come regularly and come away with the sense that the preacher notched every tree, but there still was no path through the forest. Sermons that deal with individual texts and topics may be strong and healthy, but listeners have no frame of reference. Not even disciplined adherence to the lectionary provides it. The lack of a larger picture can in part be attributed to the infrequency of sermons on God. The Christian pulpit does not often enough preach about God. The primary subject of both testaments is God, but many sermons give the impression that everyone already believes in God; our task is to get the listener to believe in Christ, and so "we preach Christ." But what is the frame of reference for Christ? What is Christ's relation to God and to the world? In other words, what is the metanarrative in which Christ makes sense? If the master narrative were to be stated in one word, it would be "God": God as Creator, Provider, and Redeemer; God as Alpha and Omega.

There has been some objection to the idea of a Christian metanarrative on the grounds that it would be exclusive, and the world has had its fill of exclusive and triumphant Christianity. Granted, the story of missions and evangelism has some ugly chapters entitled "Submit or Be Excluded." However, such thinking is not the necessary result of the Christian metanarrative as such, but of certain metanarratives. Just as there can be marriages that are not 50/50 but 100/100, with each person remaining a center of meaning and decision, with neither diminishing or consuming the other, so there can be metanarratives which are welcoming and inclusive. To say this is to say that one's master narrative, one's view of ultimate reality, involves choice. Paul said as much to the Christians in Corinth: "In fact there are many gods and many lords—yet *for us* there is one God, the Father, from whom are all things and for whom we exist, and one Lord, Jesus Christ, through whom are all things and through whom we exist" (1 Cor. 8:5b—6, emphasis added).

To say that the master narrative of one's preaching involves choice is to say that more than one such narrative exists. If the preacher wishes to move the metanarrative from the assumed background of sermons to the articulated foreground (today's listeners would be greatly helped by such a move), arguably the place to begin would be the interpretation of various scriptural formulations of metanarratives ingredient to the Christian faith. One could begin, and not be hesitant to repeat occasionally, by reviewing the history of salvation from Genesis to Revelation. Such a frame would serve well the listener to sermons based on specific texts. The preacher would do well to treat the congregation to Luke's way of presenting the master narrative, tying together law, prophets, writings, historical Jesus, risen Jesus, coming of the Holy Spirit, and preaching to the nations. Nowhere does Luke state his macronarrative more succinctly than in his gospel, 24:44–49. Paul was confident enough of his metanarrative to summarize it as "God's purpose" (Rom. 8:38), which he elaborates in five movements: foreknew, predestined, called, justified, glorified (Rom. 8:29–30). Sometimes he expressed it doxologically: "According to the revelation of the mystery that was kept secret for long ages but is now disclosed, and through the prophetic writings is made known to all the Gentiles, according to the command of the eternal God" (Rom. 16:25b–26). This master narrative informed and encouraged his ministry in spite of the many things he suffered. Without such a frame of reference it is difficult to see how a preacher in any age or circumstance could remain a lifetime in the pulpit. And sometimes Paul set his metanarrative to music:

"For from him and through him and to him are all things. To him be the glory forever. Amen" (Rom. 11:36).

To be true to Scripture the preacher will want to put before the faithful metanarratives that seem contradictory, if for no other reason than that their own lives contain such contradictions. For example, a master narrative running through both testaments maintains that there is direct correlation between obedience or disobedience to God's law and success or failure in life. This theme is often associated with Deuteronomy, but is found in many Psalms, and in the background of such New Testament texts as, "Rabbi, who sinned, this man or his parents, that he was born blind?" (Jn. 9:2). Counter to this metanarrative, however, is another that rejects such a direct correlation (Job), or that points to cases of the wicked prospering and the innocent suffering (Ps. 73), or that insists that God sends sun and rain on the evil and the good, the just and unjust alike (Mt. 5:45). At least one writer is so bold as to say that these competing metanarratives are both enfolded in the character of God. The seer John on the island of Patmos had a vision of God expressed in two images: the throne of power with winged creatures singing praises to the One for whom nothing is impossible, and the Lamb slain from the foundation of the world (Rev. 4—5). Power and vulnerability, justice and mercy: God is both. The preacher whose sermons assume or articulate a metanarrative too small, too simple, too facile may briefly satisfy listeners, but not over the long haul, because life itself will prove to be too much for such a frame of reference. As Father Mapple expressed it in his sermon on Jonah at the beginning of *Moby Dick:* "For what is man that he should live out the lifetime of his God?"

We have thought about story, briefly but positively. We have thought of stories as units or pericopae within a narrative, the sermon. And we have thought of the narrative as assuming or implying or articulating a master narrative, a metanarrative, which is the frame of reference for all the offerings of the pulpit. By this metanarrative all our sermons are informed, encouraged, and sustained. Of this metanarrative all our sermons are linguistic incarnations. Without this metanarrative, all our sermons are but speeches on a variety of unrelated topics, possessing varying degrees of "nice."

Given the discontinuities and discords of postmodern life, we would be well advised to bring our metanarrative out of the silence of assumed background and set it in the foreground, fully articulated. Without a doubt, these master narratives, these claims of meaning and movement and purpose in the world, would be heard, not as supporting the gospel, but as gospel themselves, as welcomed good news.

7

Story and Symbol, the Stuff of Preaching

DAVID BUTTRICK

The year 1980 was big for narrative preaching. In 1980, Edmund Steimle, Morris Niedenthal, and Charles Rice published essays in *Preaching the Story*.[1] In the same year, Eugene Lowry's *The Homiletical Plot: The Sermon as Narrative Art Form* arrived. So did Richard Jensen's *Telling the Story*. Preaching in a narrative form became a live homiletical option. The authors of *Preaching the Story* summed up their purpose with a question, "If asked for a short definition of preaching, could we do better than *shared story*?"

The notion of "shared story" caught on. There was a deluge of books on preaching story sermons in the 1980s and 1990s. Now, in the 2000s, they are still rolling off the press. But Eugene Lowry's work, *The Homiletical Plot, Doing Time in the Pulpit* (1985), *How to Preach a Parable* (1989), as well as his more comprehensive *The Sermon: Dancing the Edge of Mystery* (1997), has been singularly influential with parish preachers, perhaps because his proposal combines narrative form with rhetorical strategy, namely what he has labeled the "loop."

The impact of narrative preaching has been noticeable. If nothing else, preaching has become more interesting, for storytelling is bound to captivate when compared to didactic point-making pulpit productions. At the same time, the notion of narration has stirred up some strange trends. Think of those dreadful "I Nicodemus" sermons, dramatic monologues packed with biblical background and psycho-speculation, but without the mystery of God's complicated presence. Or think again of Craddock wannabes launching a series of personal reminiscences and considering them a sermon. Without the probing genius of Fred Craddock and his theological insight, narrative trivia is still trivia. More usual, but equally disturbing, are sermons that begin with a personal preacher story, a happenstance from the week in between Sundays; the gospel is not a personal moment. Nevertheless, in spite of aberrations, narration is still more interesting than objective point making. At least there is movement of thought.

Deeper still, let's recognize that narrative is built into the nature of human beings. Humans have memory and hope, and they live lives in between. We tell ourselves in stories. Better, we also plot our identity in stories. If we misplot ourselves, no doubt we will mislive ourselves; but we are storied creatures. Human communities also understand themselves by assembling their stories into something we call "history"; thus, communal identity is shaped by narrative. Again, we must note that communities may misassemble their stories. Notice that before 1950, there was a significant absence of blackness to American history, and, not only a lack of black stories but a singular shortage of feminine figures as well. American history was told by stories of white male achievers. As a result, when it came to living in black/white culture, many Americans were socially inept. All of which is to say that narrative is profoundly connected with human beings. We are natural-born storytellers. Thus narrative preaching involved a rediscovery of how people understand themselves.

The Theological Setting for Narrative Preaching

The notion of preaching as telling a shared story was not invented in 1980. No, the idea of narrative theology was being formed in the American mind by the rise of the biblical theology movement in the twentieth century. In earlier ages, there was general revelation gained by reading the sacred mystery of the natural world—the starry wonder of a night sky, the still numen of a forest glade. If the external world did not captivate, there was always an inner world, the unexplored mystery of grace in human beings. In other words, there were available hints of God for those who in faith were willing to see and speculate. Unfortunately, the rise of the sciences relabeled the objective world with tested precision, consigning speculations of faith to the far fringe of fancy. When it came to the depths of human religious experience, we found ourselves living "A.F.," after Freud, where Id, Ego, and Superego appeared to replace Dante's three-story universe. The notion of general revelation was clearly shaken. So, with traditional general revelation stymied, twentieth-century religious thought began to look for revelation beyond the natural world or the interior world of religious affect. Though "history" was a word that seemed to indicate the relativity of dateable human thought, nevertheless, theology in the twentieth century turned to history as the locus of revelation. History as recital: After all, did not psalmists recite mighty acts of God, telling a story from creation to the liberations of the Exodus? And did not apostles such as bold Peter recite kerygma in sermons, a gospel history of Jesus the Christ? So could we not signal "the mighty acts of God" as loci of revelation?[2] Preaching was redefined as recital. Preaching was to rehearse the biblical acts of God concluding with the ultimate act of God in history, namely the arrival of Jesus the Christ.

But please notice that proponents of revelation in history drew a distinction:

> [T]he history to which we point when we speak of revelation is not the succession of events which an uninterested spectator can see from the outside but our own history... When we speak of revelation in the Christian church we refer to *our* history, to the history of selves or to history as it is lived and apprehended from within.[3]

"*Our* history" can be restated simply as *our story*, the story we tell each other in churches, the story that is given us in the scriptures. For the biblical theology movement in the twentieth century, the "the old, old story," a Bible story, was the locus of revelation. Systematic theology, chasing down hints of God in the natural world or in corridors of self, was mere Greek speculation when compared to the God-shaped words of the Bible. Readings of human history could be relative, but communities of faith, shaped by word and sacrament, have always read history as a story of God-with-us. Our story, the biblical story, handed down through the centuries, gives meaning and identity to Christian communities—as long as we still welcome some tenuous link to a wider human history.

Is it any wonder the biblical theology movement spawned narrative theology? Even before Hans Frei wrote his influential *The Eclipse of Biblical Narrative: A Study in Eighteenth and Nineteenth Century Hermeneutics*[4] there were essays on "narrative theology." Yet after his book appeared, narrative theology truly blossomed.[5] But Frei's work was significant particularly for homiletic thought. He argued that for centuries the Bible was read literally and historically. The Bible was a string of stories that sequentially formed a history of human beings under God from creation to eschaton. So people read the Bible as true history and read their own lives within the same storied frame. The Bible was reality. But with the Enlightenment and the rise of objective reason, people began to grasp the rational world as reality. They then attempted to fit the Bible into their real world. Liberals distilled eternal truths from the biblical record while tossing out those embarrassing narratives that stretched credulity. And conservatives were busy trying to defend the facticity of the Bible's literal story in our more modern world; they too lost track of narrative meanings. Frei pleaded for a return to biblical narrative, arguing that once more we must live our lives within the Bible's story. Frei's seminal work fit nicely into Karl Barth's biblical theology. Barth's biblical theology began with his early *Romerbrief*, gathering steam during the century as each volume of his massive *Church Dogmatics* appeared in print. Barthian theology took hold of the mind of American Christianity during the last half of the twentieth century.[6] No wonder that preaching the "shared story" emerged as a homiletical option.

But then, even as it became dominant, the biblical theology movement was shaken. James Barr challenged the notion of biblical uniqueness[7] and, along with Langdon Gilkey, questioned the whole idea of mighty acts of God.[8] Each scholar punched gaping holes in the base assumptions of the biblical theology movement so that in 1970 a leading exponent, Brevard Childs, wrote *Biblical Theology in Crisis,*[9] claiming the movement already had begun to tumble into disarray, although it might survive as "Canonical Criticism." But, in his 1996 Cheney Lecture, Brevard Childs seemed to speak of biblical theology in the past tense. He was nostalgic: for one brief bright historical moment, through the vision of Karl Barth, people discovered true biblical faith, but now the moment was past. Childs seemed to believe that those who criticized the biblical theology movement were no longer willing to affirm the ultimate authority of scripture.[10] If narrative preaching has ebbed as Tom Long suspects,[11] perhaps, in spite of Barthian loyalists, the theological basis has crumbled. Barth himself did not welcome hermeneutic questions, but several critics asked hermeneutic questions, and the biblical theology movement seemed to fragment.

The "Postliberal" Option

Though the biblical theology movement has waned, a postliberal option seems to have survived. But there's a perennial question that slices through the postliberal version of story theology. Hans Frei summed up his own argument succinctly: "Traditionally, the Bible was the means by which the world was perceived. Following the Enlightenment, the world became the means by which the Bible was understood."[12] What's more, Frei proved his thesis as he traced the rise of critical reason from Anthony Collins in the early 1700s to David Strauss in the mid-1900s. He could have looked at sermons from the same periods. Confronted with the story of Jesus stilling the storm, most rationalist preachers grabbed a topic like "Faith for Troubling Times" but then chucked the embarrassing story. Many preachers still do, if they can't find a way to rationalize the story, e.g., "There was a climactic coincidence; the storm ebbed just as Jesus happened to speak." Frei's solution, namely, "Let's go back and live within the biblical story," poses some difficulty. Maybe that's what happens to us in church, where liturgy braced with hymnody can lull the querulous mind. But can we really step back and fold our lives into biblical narrative *per se* without recourse to some fancy theological footwork?[13]

If we have grown up in churches where the Bible is bandied about, and where the liturgy has translated biblical convictions into prayer and preaching, maybe we do operate within a theological structure that, in its origins, may derive from biblical faith. But are we actually going back and living in the Bible? No, we may believe in human ambiguity (we do understand the word *sinner*), and we may also believe in one God who improvises with human "free-blundering" in a graceful way. Also we may have some acquaintance with the Jesus traditions. But the question stands: Does such second-hand faith add up to reentering the biblical world? Can we traverse time, quitting our own socially formed selves, to live within the pages of scripture? We urban children from the North suspect that Southerners may do so once in awhile, but it's a stretch for our own bent and battered souls. But maybe it has always been a stretch. Hans Frei pictures early Christians and Reformation Christians as living inside the biblical world; but did they actually do so? Maybe, as we do, they lived within a kind of symbolic design generated by liturgical custom, but to what extent can liturgy displace the lived social world in consciousness? Our intermittent time in church is not exactly living in a biblical world. The postliberal storytellers have defined a closed linguistic community that is neither church nor a biblical world. If the base problem with "our story" is its isolation from a wider human history, the problem for postliberals is that their "cultural-linguistic" definition of church[14] isolates Christianity from a wider world of conversing human beings.

Story and Metaphor

Yes, we are perfectly willing to credit the idea that narrative is built into human beings. More, we are sure that human communities, large and small, read their identities by assembling a cultic story from history. Narrative is a primary mode of being in the world. But is narrative altogether sufficient for the creation of meaning? There's the question; a question that, once asked, shakes the whole notion of revelation in history. At the beginning of Paul Ricoeur's astonishing three-volume work, *Time and Narrative,* there is an introductory assertion easily overlooked. Ricoeur is writing about his two magisterial works that were published in sequence:

> *The Rule of Metaphor* and *Time and Narrative* form a pair: published one after the other, these works were conceived together. Although metaphor has traditionally belonged to the theory of "tropes" (or figures of discourse) and narrative to the theory of "genres," the meaning-effects produced by each of them belong to the same basic phenomenon of semantic invention.[15]

Ricoeur is saying that the basic stuff of human discourse is metaphorical imagination and a narrative plot-making imagination.

More, he is insisting that the two modes of discourse must be held together interactively.[16] They construct meaning. No wonder the Bible is not simply narrative, but must break out of narrative again and again. Paul Ricoeur, surely the leading hermeneutic philosopher of our age, offers us a different understanding of narration.

To sense what Ricoeur is after when he insists that narrative and metaphor must be held together, let us turn to the rhetoric of christology, not as an academic discipline, but as the figure of Jesus the Christ as preached. We meet Jesus as a human being in the history of God-with-us. Though Christian scriptures appear to be tacked on to the Hebrew Bible (after the apocryphal books), the life of Jesus from Nazareth falls into place in biblical history. Thus, in sequence, we read of him as a figure in biblical history, a human being under God along with patriarchs and prophets and sages in Israel's story. There are stories of Jesus as there are stories of Elijah, Moses, and others. More, there are collected teachings of Jesus as there are the wisdom sayings of Sirach or recorded words of the Prophets. Further, the stories of Jesus are held within the brackets of myth, the first eleven chapters of Genesis and final eschatalogical visions such as are found in prophetic writings as well as in apocalyptic works such as Daniel and the book of Revelation; thus his life unfolds as all lives do between creation and several visions of God's conclusion.

Notice that Jesus does what every good Jew does: he is dedicated in the temple, he prays, he celebrates Passover. As such he appears in scripture as a child of Israel. More profoundly, he is a human being under God whose life is inter-involved in the purposes of God and subject, as we all are, to unseen improvisations of God's grace. Between creation and eschatological hope, the Bible tells the story of Israel, the full human story—our politics, our sexual adventures, our blundering, and our bravery—but does so as God's story as well. Though Christian writers are striving to indicate Jesus' special chosen role, the pattern of Jesus' life under God is a pattern established throughout the Hebrew Scriptures. Jesus is storied, and his stories are told at the same time as a concurrent story of God-with-us, which, of course, is the way of the whole Hebrew Bible as it tells us of prophets, patriarchs, kings and courtesans, fools and sages. Throughout the Hebrew Scriptures, God is the context of human lives, the conversation partner, the providential improvisor, and shaper of human history. Jesus shows up in the same history under the God of Israel.

But through the centuries, Christian preaching has used the figure of Jesus in other ways. Certainly Jesus is held up, rhetorically placarded if you will, as the image of a true humanity under God. He is the human being we are called to become. So preachers have celebrated Jesus' kindness, his courage, his willingness in all things to bend his will to God's direction, and so forth. Such preaching, *imitatio Christi*, has been criticized, for how can we twenty-first–century types follow in the ways of a first-century rural Nazarene, much less broken sinners bend their lives toward true humanity? Nevertheless, preachers have continued to hold Jesus, the exemplar, high, and likely will continue to do so.

There is another dimension to Jesus' life that preachers preach. We single out Jesus' connections with the structure of every human life. We tell birth stories, temptation stories, eating and drinking stories, suffering stories; for we want to say that Jesus lived our lives, step by step; he shared the passages of our lives from birth until dying. He understands. Such preaching becomes climactic in the Holy Week stations of the cross. He suffered. He was abused, rejected, and humiliated. And see, he died crying for a drink, howling in pain as human beings can. For some of us Jesus' shout, "My God, my God, why have you forsaken me?" is especially significant. In preaching we link Jesus' life with the moving stages of our lives. Thus Jesus is a companion, and perhaps a brave friend in need.

Holding up a person as exemplar and companion is not unknown to the Hebrew tradition. Has not Jewish preaching extolled the lives of the patriarchs, of Moses, of brave prophets and insightful sages? Of course. What is taking place is that, after stories are told, a moral or meaning is added by singling out aspects of character, or by underscoring shared humanity. Certainly some legends of Solomon, told with a nod (or sometimes with a slight wink), celebrate his wisdom and beg imitation. Likewise, the stubborn faithfulness of that impatient sufferer Job is also celebrated. Though Christians may glorify Jesus by holding high his humanity, the rhetorical pattern is nothing new in Scripture.

But there is another way of lifting up the figure of Jesus that is decidedly different. Preachers hold up Jesus as a metaphor for

God. Perhaps the term "Disclosure Symbol" might be better, but the procedure is essentially metaphorical. God is a name that cannot be spoken, because God is transcendent mystery. Yes, God may well be one in whom "we live and move and have our being," but anyone who dares ask childlike questions of life knows existence is essentially mysterious. How on earth can any of us know God?

Traditionally, God has been defined by absolutes. God is omniscient, God is omnipotent, God is perfect in beauty, truth, holiness, and so forth. Think of all those rolling Latinate creeds. Though absolutes are adjectival, stressing the ultimacy of God, as adjectival they must also be denied, for how can human descriptives be used of God? We assume that God is "personal," for God is one God. If we say God is personal, we mean that, though God's hidden personality is mysterious, we can guess God through creation, and retrospectively, we can confess God's providential care as well. No wonder that for centuries synagogue worship has included two great prayers of thanksgiving to God for creation and for providence. An inheritance, such prayers still inaugurate the pattern of Christian eucharistic prayer.

All God-talk is necessarily metaphorical. Metaphor is the only way we can grasp mysteries. Actually, metaphor is the only way we can speak the mystery of self, namely, our own inner world; and metaphor is the only way we can dare approach the mystery of God. Yes, we know that every God metaphor must be countered, corrected, and acknowledged as inadequate: God as warrior, lawgiver, judge, mother, father, you do the naming. The metaphors we use are all necessary and, at the same time, all impossible. Nonetheless, the gift of metaphor-making is all we pokey humans can manage, particularly when we stand before the mysterious holiness of God whose name we cannot name. But if we are trying to get at the personal nature of a living God, Christian preachers have always held up the living symbol of Jesus the Christ. In effect, the person of Jesus is a metaphor for God, giving God a human face and, at the same time, clothing the figure of Jesus with derivative holiness.

In a way, the figure of Jesus held before the mystery of God alters the absolutes. If we claim God is omnipotent, do we really suppose God can do anything? No, God will do what love does, a love we say we see in Jesus the Christ. Love must limit the notion of omnipotence. Likewise, if we suppose that God is omniscient, does God know everything? Is God in on everyone's secrets? No, love respects persons, even the inner privacy of every human self. Precisely the vulnerable figure of Jesus, the Jesus who was beaten up, nailed down, and died in howling pain, tends to redefine the nature of God. Indeed, the Jesus metaphor transforms all our images of ultimacy.

What we are saying is that preaching must always be more than storytelling. Though the Bible may seem to have a narrative structure, notice how, within the structure, again and again, the Bible breaks into different languages—there are the codes of social law, the tirades of the prophets, the hymnbook of Psalms, the stunning poetic ethic of Ecclesiastes, the sensuous lyric Song of Solomon, all in a way metaphorical. No wonder when we preach from Scripture there are many different homiletic styles available. The same diversity occurs in the stories of Jesus. Our gospels are a patchwork of beatitudes, birth narratives, passion stories, hymns, teachings (which, like laws, have been collated), parables, miracles, conflict stories, credos, all within a loosely built frame of narrative. And these excursive forms function more often than not metaphorically.

Christian faith demands more than narration. Maybe Chalcedon's peculiar formula—"truly human, truly Divine"—was fabricated out of the rhetoric of christological preaching. Always there is the story of Jesus a human being before God, a human being among human beings. Yes, but also the lifting of Jesus in metaphor; Jesus Christ as a living symbol held before the high, holy, mystery of God.[17]

On Telling a Story

There are many ways to tell a story. Years ago Eric Auerbach in his book *Mimesis* noted a difference between Hebrew storytelling and the Greek storytelling of Homer.[18] Auerbach noted that Bible stories are told reporting what people do and say without much inner motivation on display. We must fill in the "Why" for what people say and do. Therefore the terseness of biblical storytelling hints something untold, something essentially mysterious. By contrast, Auerbach noticed that Greek stories fill in the "Why" with human emotion or motivation. As a result, please note, there is little room left for the instigations of God. Auerbach's contention speaks to our age bulging with gnostic psychobabble; we fill in all the "Whys" we can.

Earlier I groaned when referring to "I Nicodemus" biographical sermons. Why? Because, though such excursions are packed with biblical background, they are also big on psychological conjecture. Thus Auerbach's concern applies. My problem with biographical preaching may well be *my* problem, but there may be a general concern worth noting. How can we tell stories of the human world, now or in biblical times, so that *theological* meanings emerge? How can we spin stories that, without direct reference, are nonetheless filled with the unseen mystery of presence? The question is not aesthetic, but urgently theological. Why tell stories from a pulpit, even Bible stories, unless our stories have something to do with the knowledge of God?

Many ministers have grooved on narrative preaching because they believe it is "natural" or "easy" to tell stories and enjoy them. However, to tell a story so that theological meanings form in the minds of listeners is much more difficult than preachers realize. The psychological stuff comes readily—we live these days in "the triumph of the therapeutic." But how can we depict in preaching the deep mysterious movings of grace? Narrative preaching is exceedingly difficult. Either it demands the genius of, say, a John Updike, which most of us do not possess, or more hours to design sermons than a minister's schedule will allow. But the demand that storied sermons produce theological understandings in a listener's understanding cannot be dismissed.

Another gambit: How do we tell stories? Do we stand there and simply rattle off a good story—I, storyteller, you, listeners. The story itself can take over. The unfolding world of the story will claim precedence, so there's no room for conversational intrusions between the speaker and a congregation. But good preaching is always conversational in style. A story sermon will have to be told to allow interactional commentary. Probably we should tell a story as if we and the members of the congregation are hearing the story together and can react as the story strikes us episode by episode. If the story is recited as an art form, sermons will become performances and the purposes of preaching will be subverted. No, narrative preaching must be an open form permitting some time and space for pulpit asides, reactive tangents, and so forth. But there are more serious questions, hermeneutic questions. How do we tell God stories? How plot the narration? Should God stories seem to unfold as if from creation, full of novelty and surprise? Or should God stories unfold as if under the grip of a wondrous future? Or should every sermon stop action and celebrate hero Jesus? The task of plotting a narrative sermon is always a matter of theological discernment. The "How" of storytelling is no small matter.

Here's where again we must stop and appreciate Gene Lowry, who has offered us a "loop," which is his helpful rhetorical strategy. In *The Homiletical Plot,* he outlined a strategy:

1. Upsetting the Equilibrium,
2. Analyzing the Discrepancy,
3. Disclosing the Clue to Resolution,
4. Experiencing the Gospel,
5. Anticipating the Consequences.

To express the emotional nuances involved, he abbreviated the sequence amusingly: "Oops, Ugh, Aha, Whee, Yeah." When I first read the schema, I wondered if Gene was offering us a kind of *Ordo Salutis.* Was his system designed to move listeners from disinterest to saving faith? Was he proposing a strategy for conversion? Since then, in his more recent book, *The Sermon,* he has modified the scheme to:

1. Conflict,
2. Compilation,
3. Sudden Shift, and
4. Unfolding.

No one, not even Aristotle, can chart the movement of every narrative. But Gene is offering considerable wisdom about preaching a story. What's more, there is perceptive theological reasoning involved. Maybe biblical thought does run counter to every cultural formulation, thus a sense of conflicted meaning, a questioning. We sense that to live biblically will complicate our lives. Then, according to Gene, there can be a moment of clarity, a being grasped, perhaps. Finally, listeners may begin to see the shape of their changed lives. Gene is not merely suggesting patterned excitement in sermon design, he is chasing down the movement of subjective response to the gospel message.

In his *Homiletical Plot,* he located the arrival of the gospel as a fourth moment in his "loop." But in *The Sermon,* he claims that the gospel message is not always found at a particular point in his scheme. Indeed, he notes sermons in which the gospel message seems to arrive quite differently. Of course. The gospel is, if you will, the horizon of every Christian sermon, and always with us who preach, guiding our rhetoric with theological smarts.

The Shift in Homiletic Thought

Listen to words from Eugene Lowry:

> For at least twenty-five years now, the discipline of North American homiletics has been in the throes of an emerging new homiletical paradigm. Many of us mark its beginning with the publication of Fred Craddock's first book on preaching... I once suggested that Craddock kicked in a door that cannot now be closed. Given the current wrestling with postmodern thought—as well as a reappraisal of the "eclipse of biblical narrative"—I think it fair to say the hinges are no longer on the door.[19]

Lowry's appraisal may seem somewhat strenuous given that preaching is not a subject often featured in human discourse these days. Talk shows are not talking about preaching. Teenybopper superstars do not trill homiletic angst. But, yes, people in the homiletic field quite understand Lowry's images. Fred Craddock's slim volume, *As One Without Authority* (1971), did stir up the discipline, a discipline then groping for renewal. Craddock followed with his Kierkegaardian Beecher lectures, *Overhearing the Gospel* (1978), which were equally challenging.[20] Then, along with Craddock, there were others doing new things: David Randolph, Henry Mitchell, Eugene Lowry, Thomas Long, Ron Allen, Paul Scott Wilson, and even tag-along, David Buttrick.[21] Theorists in the seventies and eighties were doing quite different things, but as a gaggle of scholars they do represent a field rethinking itself. Most of those writers were concerned with biblical preaching, for, in general, they emerged from or were influenced by the biblical theology movement. They were trying to be free from pulpit arrogance ("As One *with* Authority"?), as well as an older rationalist point-making homiletics that had become a somewhat static convention.

But with the crumbling of the biblical theology movement, and the methodological disarray in pulpit practice these days, what now? Here are some of my own reflections: *First,* let us admit the failure of the biblical theology movement. There isn't *A* biblical theology, but within scripture there are different hermeneutic readings of the ways of God-with-us. The symptom of the failure of biblical theology is that people in our churches, even if biblical, seem to be incapable of theological reasoning about what's going on in their world. There is no evident "Public Theology." And in church, there is very little theological thinking about much of anything. A hundred years ago, if you scratched a Presbyterian you discovered an amateur theologian. Nowadays, about all you'll get is a Republican. Ignore the wise crack, for here's the issue: Without theology we are left with partisan orientations drawn from our occupations, our political alignments, our racial preferences, our social locations. The problem is one of education in our churches, yes, but it is surely a problem for preachers who speak to congregations as well. Can we restore the church's theological mind?

Second, with regard to speaking: we are living at a time where there is no ruling rhetorical wisdom; proposals abound. During the rise of the biblical theology movement there was some Barthian rejection of rhetoric. Rhetoric was Greek thinking or secular wisdom intruding on the province of true biblical wisdom.[22] However, this is not the case, ever since Augustine rhetoric has proceeded hand in hand with both scripture study and theology. We need to restore the notion of homiletics as sacred rhetoric so that sermons will once more be well-designed, smart, witty, and compelling. The rhetorical notion of "persuasion" does not mean that sermons will become seamy advertising or political spin, but has much to do with human understanding. Whether we preach narrative sermons, or engage in making points, or set up a moving argument, we will be engaging in a thoughtful discipline—How can people hear, understand, and be enthralled by the gospel message? Once more homiletics must recover its origins in rhetoric. Moreover, homiletics must recover respect for the unique power of a human being speaking to assembled others, a rhetorical conviction, rather than chasing the chimera of other media.[23]

Third, (see, three points without a poem), I am astonished at how fearful fledgling preachers seem to be these days. They will be therapeutic caregivers, but when it comes to the prophetic dimensions of gospel they're in retreat. Who's to blame preachers?

Every week about a thousand clergy are routed from their churches. Nowadays America is contentious, not merely over politics, but over social styles, religious practices, and almost anything else conceivable. The term "culture wars" may be apt. Nevertheless, the prophetic dimension of the gospel has been smothered of late. Clergy are fearful. As a result, when America invades another nation preemptively, local pulpits are silent. When American policy is rewritten to endorse human torture, again local pulpits are largely silent. Maybe story can be preached without a prophetic dimension. But Jesus the Christ cannot; the Jesus who himself was beaten by soldiers, tortured, and brutally killed off. Jesus' gospel includes the Beatitudes, which would seem to describe God's promised social order where the hungry are fed, the oppressed are liberated, the powerless are empowered, peacemakers are approved, and those who weep for the ways of the world will rejoice. Whatever impedes the future of God is of prophetic pulpit concern; Jesus as a living metaphor for God bears witness.

The "New Homiletic" in which many of us were engaged was probably a useful theological movement. Now once more we are called to rethink the task of preaching, but in a very different cultural moment. Now we must be modest. During the height of the biblical theology movement a triumphant christology ruled our discipline. Homiletic types wrote on the finality of Christ, or the ultimacy of Christ, or the singularity of Christ. With Barth, we insisted that faith in Christ was true *faith* in a world where all the other options were mere *religions*. But now, after 9/11, we sense that all our religious identities, including a more modest Christianity, must learn to converse, discovering one another, and indeed rediscovering ourselves before God.

8

Out of the Loop

The Changing Practice of Preaching

THOMAS G. LONG

About ten years ago, I was wandering down a side street in Seoul, Korea, when I stumbled across a tiny theological bookstore jammed in between a noodle shop and a fruit and vegetable stand. Even viewed through the dusty storefront window, this unlikely place looked interesting, books new and used spilling off of shelves and onto stacks piled up on the floor. Curious, I went inside. I don't read Korean, but some titles on the shelves were unmistakable: Barth's *Romans,* Moltmann's *Theology of Hope,* and Tillich's *Systematic Theology* among them. Tucked over in a corner was a section of volumes that was clearly homiletics, mostly Korean authors whom I did not recognize. But at eye level was a whole shelf filled with a single title, a dozen copies or more of Eugene Lowry's *The Homiletical Plot.*

This book was obviously a hot commodity in Korea, and standing there, thousands of miles from home, I was reminded of the widespread and enduring impact of Eugene Lowry's work in preaching, especially the "big idea" Lowry advanced so persuasively in *The Homiletical Plot.* First published in 1980, *The*

115

Homiletical Plot is still in print (now in an expanded edition) over a quarter of a century later, a track record for staying power and popularity in our consumer culture perhaps matched only by the Rolling Stones.

Lowry's "big idea," as is now well known, was to think of the sermon in its essential form as "a premeditated plot which has as its key ingredient a sensed discrepancy, a homiletical bind."[1] In short, Lowry was claiming that sermons, like old time Westerns, don't really get going until trouble comes to town. When listeners smell trouble in the air (the "sensed discrepancy"), they will enter a state of restless ambiguity and will have a powerful desire to see this ambiguity resolved, which can happen only when they call upon the capacity of narrative to repair the gap and to see that the trouble is satisfactorily addressed.

By seeing sermons this way—as processes for addressing ambiguity in hearers—Lowry was, with a single stroke, able to score two homiletical goals. The first was to summon the sermon away from bland abstraction. The first task of the sermon is to evoke (or perhaps to provoke) the kind of trouble that listeners would recognize as urgent and real. Lowry sniffed, for example, at sermons on Joshua 24:15 that dramatically challenge listeners to "choose this day whom you will serve, God or Baal!" God or Baal? This is not the choice, this is not the conflict as people perceive it, as real people live it, argued Lowry.

> People are not caught between a generalized good and a generalized bad. They are caught in the bind of two quite specific goods or two specific bads—or (perhaps more likely) among several options, none of which is good or bad.
> …The homiletical plot must catch people in the depths of the awful discrepancies of their world—social and personal. It is to these very real discrepancies that the gospel of Jesus Christ is addressed.[2]

Lowry's second achievement, and this is the one for which he is justly celebrated, was to realize that ambiguity at the beginning of a sermon is best resolved through a plotted sermon, a sermon with a narrative-like process, a developmental sequence of existentially oriented steps. In doing so, he challenged all static models of sermon design. Sermons don't have structures; they are events unfolding temporally. "Because," he said, "a sermon is an *event in time*—existing in time, not space—a process and not a collection of parts, it is helpful to think of a sequence rather than a structure."[3]

Lowry prescribed a five-fold plot sequence. The sermon (1) begins with a salvo of conflict and tension, which upsets the listeners' equilibrium and pushes the plot downward; (2) analyzes the conflict, which keeps the plot plummeting; (3) draws upon the gospel to disclose the clue that will ultimately resolve the conflict, an epiphany that precipitates a sudden reversal and causes the plot to loop upward; (4) elaborates the clue to resolution in ways that cause the listeners to experience of the gospel and that keep the plot moving upward; and finally 5) builds upon the resolved conflict to anticipate the future, basically ethical, trajectory of the sermon in the lives of the listeners.

Because this master sermon design contains a roller coaster–like reversed circuit in the middle, it garnered the nickname "the Lowry loop," but what we actually have here is a schematic diagram for an Aristotelian tragic-comedy. The sermon is plotlike in the sense that it flows from "itch to scratch," as Lowry liked to put it.[4] The plot action descends steadily until the denouement, at which point it reverses course and is constituted by an unremitting rising action.

Looking in the Rearview Mirror

Lowry has fiddled with the pieces of his model over the years, making adjustments here and there, but the basic idea of the sermon as a tension-resolving, narrative-like plot has been a constant in his work over the decades.[5] To read *The Homiletical Plot*, now nearly three decades after it was first published, is to be thrown back to those heady days a generation ago, when homiletics was frothing with ferment and change. By the early 1970s, it was apparent to many that the sermon as a form of communication was in serious trouble. It had been done in, not to put too fine a point on it, by the firestorm of the sixties' revolution. Dramatic changes in society, church, authority, and communication had converged to make preaching look as remote, hopelessly authoritarian, and outdated as a swallowtail coat.

For those with a long, historical view of such matters, none of this was surprising. Homiletics goes through a nervous breakdown every half century or so, and it was due. But many seminaries, convinced that this was truly the homiletical apocalypse and that preaching no longer deserved its role as the signature practice of ministry, dropped their required courses in preaching (most have now restored them, some not). While the majority of pastors still soldiered on dutifully with the Sunday sermon, the fire in the belly for preaching was cooling, and many ministers began to search for more productive ways to be meaningful, such as pastoral therapy or taking to the streets in political protest. In response, the academic discipline of homiletics entered a period that can be variously described as "a time of creative experimentation" or, less charitably, "a season of unmitigated panic."

The first task for homiletics in the midst of this crisis was to stop the bleeding and to find out what went wrong. In short, homiletics needed a villain, and it quickly found one: the didactic, sermon with "points." No wonder preaching was in disarray, we homileticians announced, slapping our foreheads. Somewhere back down the road it had entered into an unholy alliance with a nasty and demanding partner, namely, linear, propositional logic. Homileticians gleefully declared that this illicit romance was over, that the "three points and a poem" sermon was now dead, and we frolicked like merry widows on its grave. In its place came a host of new proposals for less authoritarian, more communicative sermon forms: inductive sermons, story sermons, metaphorical sermons, nonlinear sermons, dialogue sermons, multimedia sermons (yes, pre-PowerPoint), and a variety of other innovations. Writing about this volatile period in homiletics, Fred Craddock says the following:

> Something needed to be done; the churches insisted and so did the preachers. The burden seemed naturally to fall on those who taught homiletics. Some repeated the old saws, but raised the volume. Others busied themselves in a frantic search for new and lively forms and styles. Experimentation abounded. Anything short of Russian roulette was taken into the pulpit to create a pulse, to make some nerve twitch, to break out of the general state of ennui. Needless to say, mistakes were made. Substance was at times denied access to the pulpit while some new style was being tried. Unhappy marriages between form and content could not last. Many books were written: heavy

volumes calling Israel back to her tents; thin paperback saying by their size and cut, "Maybe this might work, but if not, the price is only \$5.00."[6]

Somewhere in the 1970s, amid this quest for some new approach to preaching, homiletics stumbled across the concepts of story and narrative theory, and it grasped them as if it had suddenly uncovered the Holy Grail at a flea market (actually, theology generally, by now in its own doldrums, had also discovered the tonic of narrative theory.) The problem with preaching, it was now decided, was that preachers were shoving propositions and points down peoples' throats, when that was an alien way of thinking and processing information about deep life concerns. People address life's most profound issues not by applying principles but by fashioning narratives, and preaching needs to assume the story form in response. Moreover, the gospel itself is composed of hundreds of small narratives woven into a grand and overarching biblical story. Typical of the period is the excited "Eureka!" uttered by the authors of *Preaching the Story*, a state-of-the-art textbook published in 1980, the same year as *The Homiletical Plot*, when they unveiled the mother of all homiletical metaphors: the preacher as a storyteller. "We are trying," they said,

> to find that formative image that could both articulate what preaching is and free people to do it. Is there an image adequate to shape the form, content, and style of preaching? If we had to say, in a word or two, or in a picture, what preaching is and how it is done well, what would that phrase or picture be?... Let us consider the storyteller... If we were pressed to say what Christian faith and life are, we could hardly do better than *hearing, telling, and living a story*. And if asked for a short definition of preaching, could we do better than *shared story*?[7]

In one sense, Lowry's *The Homiletical Plot* was simply one more entry in this dizzying sweepstakes to rescue preaching from oblivion, one more narrative innovation in a time of homiletical uncertainty. What set it apart, however, from many other books of this era, and what has no doubt contributed to its longevity, is that it was neither the product of panic nor the result of a wild experiment performed with a chemistry set in the homiletical cellar. Lowry's book is based on solid literary and psychological notions of narrative structure. Beneath that, and here we come to a most important matter, Lowry's ideas about plotted sermons rest ultimately upon clear and widely held assumptions about the narrative shape of experience. Lowry joins many others, before and since, in assuming that human life gains full meaning only when narrated. He quotes Laurens Van Der Post, "[W]ithout a story you have not got a nation, or a culture, or a civilization. Without a story of your own to live you haven't got a life of your own."[8] The claim here is that people don't merely enjoy stories; we *are* stories. Our lives, when they are seen in true light, are not simply "one damned thing after another"; they have beginnings, middles, and ends. They flow from a remembered past toward some denouement, some meaningful future in which the ambiguities and gaps that have puzzled and bedeviled us are finally resolved. In short, we are "plotted."

So Lowry develops his plotted scheme of preaching not simply because this sequence of movements will be more engaging and interesting to listeners. No, Lowry settles on narrative structure because of his conviction, widely held by others, that listeners are intrinsically makers of narrative and dwellers in narrative. Lowry's narrative structure is designed to match a narrative-shaped, ambiguity-resolving, meaning-constructing capacity in human consciousness. He approvingly cites Barbara Hardy:

> For we dream in narrative, daydream in narrative, remember, anticipate, hope, despair, believe, doubt, plan, revise, criticize, construct, gossip, learn, hate and love by narrative. In order really to live, we make up stories about ourselves and others, about the personal as well as the social past and future.[9]

Charles Taylor in *Sources of the Self* agrees with Hardy and Lowry. "[A] basic condition of making sense of ourselves," he says, "is that we grasp our lives in a narrative...as an unfolding story."[10]

But is this true?

Is Narrative the Whole Story?

Recently, significant challenges have been raised to the prevalent idea that narrative is the underlying and defining quality of human life. For example, in a provocative essay making the rounds in university circles these days, "Against Narrativity,"[11] Galen Strawson identifies—in order to attack them—two narrative theses that are currently popular in such fields as philosophy, theology, sociology, and psychology. The first, which he calls the *psychological Narrativity thesis* (he routinely capitalizes Narrativity to make sure we know what a formidable beast it is) involves the widely held claim "that human beings typically see or live or experience their lives as a narrative or story of some sort, or at least as a collection of stories." The second, which he terms the *ethical Narrativity thesis*, "states that experiencing one's life as a narrative is a good thing; a richly Narrative outlook is essential to a well-lived life, to true or full personhood."[12] In short, thesis 1 says that we need narrative to be human, and thesis 2 claims that we need narrative to be good. While conceding that these two theses are not necessarily intertwined—one could be false without implicating the other—Strawson believes that both are false. "There are," he states, "deeply non-Narrative people and there are good ways to live that are deeply non-Narrative."

Strawson's argument is long, convoluted, and philosophically sophisticated, but the most interesting and compelling parts of it are personal and, in the way that Strawson would have us understand the word, autobiographical. He divides human beings into two broad tribes, Diachronics and Episodics. Diachronics are people who see themselves as living out narratives, who see themselves as having continuous "selves," "something that was there in the past and will be there in the future."[13] (*The Homiletical Plot* was written for Diachronics—indeed it assumes that people are, by nature, Diachronics.) But contrary to the prevailing view that *everybody* is a Diachronic, Strawson insists that there are also the Episodics, a somewhat smaller group of people, but Strawson includes himself among them. An Episodic, he says, "does not figure oneself, considered as a self, as something that was there in the (further) past and will be there in the (further) future." In other words, Episodics live completely in the present tense, with little or no regard for the past or the future. They in no way see themselves crafting or living out a narrative, and, Strawson, argues, they can be just as joyful, fulfilled, and ethical as anyone else.

Strawson knows, of course, that he has a past and that he is likely to live into the future, so how can he claim to be an Episodic person, a person whose life has no narrative shape? He addresses this difficulty by making a distinction between two versions of his self. On the one hand, there is the Strawson who was born, had a childhood, grew up, and hopes to live a long and full life (a self he refers to using such terms as "I," "me," and "myself"); then there is the Strawson who is an inner mental presence attending to and living in the present moment (a self he refers to using asterisks as "I*," "me*," and "myself*"). He knows that certain things happened to him in the past. As a boy, he once fell out of a boat, for example, but Strawson insists that, even though past events like this happened to "me," nevertheless "I think I'm strictly, literally correct in thinking that they did not happen to me*."[14] How could it be that something that happened to "me" did not happen to "me*"? Because I* am the self who exists only in this moment, attends only to that which is present to me* now. The little boy who fell out of a boat was, Strawson would say, another me*, different from the me* who now exists. The "I*" is constantly changing and lives episodically, from moment to moment. The I* doesn't have a past (or a future). Past experiences are present to the "I*" only in the sense that last Thursday's piano practice is present for a pianist in today's piano concert. It's there, but not in the form of explicit memory or story. The pianist is not living out a narrative, moving self-consciously from past to future; he's just playing the piano right now with all that he is in the present moment. Strawson states:

> I have a past, like any human being, and I know perfectly well that I have a past. I have a respectable amount of factual knowledge about it, and I also remember some of my past experiences "from the inside" as the philosophers say. And yet I have absolutely no sense of my life as a narrative with form, or indeed as a narrative without form. Absolutely none. Nor do I have any great or special interest in my past. Nor do I have a great deal of concern for any future.[15]

So, some people, the so-called Diachronics, live narratively, and other people, the Episodics, do not. According to Strawson, both can be fully human; both can be stoutly ethical. In the early part of his essay, Strawson seems to argue for a world in which Diachronics and Episodics attempt the hard work of trying to understand each other and try to live in peaceful, if somewhat puzzled, coexistence. But as the essay proceeds to its conclusion, Strawson takes off the velvet gloves and throws a bare-knuckled punch or two at the Diachronics. He suggests that all attempts to narrate one's life inevitably involve a measure of revisionism. We don't really have access to the past, he argues, so we have to reconstruct it, which no one can do with flawless accuracy. He says, "The implication is plain: the more you recall, retell, narrate yourself, the further you risk moving away from accurate self-understanding, from the truth of your being."[16] If that sounds like a charge that Diachronics are inescapably living lies, well... "Some are constantly telling their daily experiences to others in a storying way, and with great gusto," Strawson says. "They are drifting ever further off the truth."[17]

Strawson saves his knockout punch, though, for those seemingly smug Diachronics, especially the religious ones, who claim that narrativity is crucial to ethical living. "I think," he says, "that those who think this way are motivated by a sense of their own importance or significance that is absent in other human beings. Many of them, connectedly, have religious commitments. They are wrapped up in forms of religious belief that are—like almost all religious belief—really all about self."[18] OK, so much for peaceful coexistence.

James Phelan, editor of the journal *Narrative*, found Strawson's "overall effort to debunk the narrative identity thesis to be both effective and salutary," and he cites the following passage from Michael Frayn's award-winning novel *Spies* as an example of the Episodic perspective:

> This is what I see as I look at it [the old neighborhood] now. But is that the way he sees it at his age? I mean the awkward boy who lives in that unkempt house between the Hardiments and the Pinchers—Stephen Wheatley, the one with the stick-out ears and the too-short grey flannel school shirt hanging out of the too-long grey flannel school shorts. I watch him emerge from the warped front door, still cramming food into his mouth from tea. Everything about him is in various shades of grey...because he's entirely monochrome, and he's monochrome because this is how I recognize him now, from the old black-and-white snaps

I have of him at home, that my grandchildren laugh at in disbelief when I tell them it's me. I share their incredulity. I shouldn't have the slightest idea what Stephen Wheatley looks like if it weren't for the snaps, or ever guess that he and I were related if it weren't for the name on the back.[19]

What can we make of Strawson's position? This is not the place for a thoroughgoing analysis of his essay, but my own overall view of it is best articulated by Strawson himself when, near the close of his argument, he gives voice to an imaginary debate partner, who objects, "I'm sorry, but you really have no idea of the force and reach of the psychological Narrativity thesis. You're as Narrative as anyone else, and your narratives about yourself determine how you think of yourself even though they are not conscious."[20] That's exactly what I want to reply to Strawson, and I agree with Oliver Sacks (and presumably with Eugene Lowry) when he says, "We have, each of us, a life-story, an inner narrative—whose continuity, whose sense, is our lives. It might be said that each of us constructs and lives a 'narrative,' and that this narrative is us, our identities."[21]

So, in my opinion, either Strawson is constructing and living a narrative, just like the rest of us, and is denying this truth, or minimizing it in order to be provocative (probably). Or, perhaps Strawson genuinely lacks the ability to construct, or refuses the task of constructing, a life narrative, which means that he is in many ways denied a satisfactorily shaped identity (more unlikely, but possible). Strawson would, of course, find my response both predictable and laughable, the knee-jerk reaction of a veteran Diachronic. "Well, here we have a stand off," he writes to people like me. "I think it's just not so…"[22] Episodics have, he crows, "truly happy-go-lucky, see-what-comes-along lives," which are "among the best there are, vivid, blessed, and profound."[23]

I disagree, then, with the main thrust of his essay, but I do think that Strawson's views raise crucial questions for all narrative approaches to preaching, Lowry's included. To begin, while Strawson has not persuaded me that the Episodic life is a parallel and equally valid way of organizing reality to narrative, he is nonetheless convincing that there are many people who experience life in a profoundly episodic fashion. People are making narrative sense out of their lives, but not everything in life is readily incorporated into this narrative. James L. Battersby, in an essay strongly critical of Strawson in which he challenges the sharp dichotomy Strawson wants to make between Diachronic and Episodic personalities, nevertheless acknowledges the veracity of the episodic impulse. He describes how a more balanced view of human life recognizes that these tendencies—diachronic and episodic—lie side by side in a single self. Even people who would be firmly on the diachronic side of the ledger nevertheless have a sneaking suspicion that the narrative understanding of human identity has its limits, that not everything in life can be digested narratively:

> Ask me about me, my life, about what I'm doing, where I'm going, where I've been, what I've done, what it's like being me, and I'll tell you a story. And I'll do so because I had a beginning, and ever since I can remember I've been on a journey, moving relentlessly forward; furthermore, even though I've undergone many changes in body and mind, it's been me all along, and I'll keep plugging along into the future until nature decides to pull the plug. On the other hand, what has kept the suspicion alive, though dormant, are the unshakeable, but unexpressed convictions that the whole story hasn't been (and can't be) told, that, indeed, the self is like mercury, not easily grasped, that life is fragmented into many stories and many pieces that are not narrative-like at all, that there are an indefinite number of ways of talking about what, for lack of a better term, we have developed the habit of calling the self...[24]

Second, Strawson's argument may, coincidentally, raise an intriguing possibility about the larger cultural situation in which we find ourselves, the social moment into which we are summoned to preach. Now, admittedly, Strawson is writing about the self, about the inner experience of individuals. But could it be that he is also inadvertently describing the episodic character of the media-saturated, fragmented, storyless culture of affluent Westerners at the beginning of the twenty-first century? Strawson claims that he, and many others, are Episodic personalities. Whether or not that is true about individuals as types, it seems true about our society generally. What Strawson is describing may be less a property of selves and more a tendency in the larger society. We are under cultural pressure to live life in random bursts, our attention fleeting from *American Idol* to the troop movements in the Middle East to the desire to purchase a more powerful cell phone, a kind of cultural attention deficit disorder. This is what Neil Postman in *Amusing Ourselves to Death* called the "Now...This" phenomenon, as in television news when an anchor says, "Six children killed in an apartment fire. Now, Biff Sparkle with sports." It is not that people don't seek a unifying narrative of the self; it is rather that people lack the skills to construct one out of the chards and fragments of life.[25]

Another Kansas City Voice

In view of this discussion of the episodic character of experience, Lowry's *The Homiletical Plot* can be seen in a new light. Rather than a formula for sermons with structures that match the intuitive and native communicational capacities of listeners, Lowry's plotted sermons can instead be understood as sermonic homework, as rather difficult and demanding tasks in narrative construction. Hearers of such sermons must be able to manage a high tolerance for ambiguity and then to track an involved five-step sequential process of resolution. They must be able to sustain attention for twenty minutes or so upon a single project from the beginning of the sermon to the end. In short, they must be able to follow, appropriate, and finally create coherent narratives.

But what if fewer and fewer people in our culture can do this? It is probably true that the O. J. Simpson jury, among other crucial factors, simply could not attend to the long and arduous process of constructing a plausible narrative out of the evidence, preferring instead to fasten their attention on arresting episodes like, "If [the gloves] don't fit, you must acquit." Or again, the very popular and certainly hilarious comedy news parody "The Daily Show" does not appeal to our hunger to fashion livable narratives but rather thrives on a postmodernist zinging of slightly irreverent and cynical one-liners at people who do. Oliver Sacks may still be correct "that each of us constructs and lives a 'narrative,' and that this narrative is us, our identities," but we seem to be shifting into a cultural moment when people lack the requisite tools, or maybe the will, to perform this task. Are people who are watching *Oprah* or *CSI* on television, or who are randomly surfing the Internet, engaged in the hard work of constructing socially and personally viable narratives, or are they simply attending to whatever flickers across the screen until something more glittering comes along?

Little wonder, then, that the whole narrative enterprise in homiletics is under assault from the theological right, middle, and left.[26] We are once again at one of those breakpoints when the cultural communicational context has shifted and a new method of preaching may develop before our every eyes. What new style of preaching will emerge? While some homileticians are predicting, and even advocating, a move toward genuinely conversational styles of preaching, approaches to preaching in which preachers freely relinquish the asymmetrical (and allegedly hierarchical) style of presentation in order to serve as facilitators of free-ranging and nonhierarchical congregational discussions, there is little evidence that such an approach is catching on. In fact, if we look at what is happening on the ground among actual practitioners, what seems to be rising up from the mist is exactly the opposite: a highly authoritative and didactic style, aimed right at episodic listeners.

A case in point is Adam Hamilton, the bright, youngish, articulate pastor of the United Methodist Church of the Resurrection in Kansas City. With close to 15,000 members, Church of the Resurrection is a rare example of a mainline "mega-church." Like Eugene Lowry, Hamilton is an ordained United Methodist minister. Like Lowry, he hails from Kansas City, and he is connected (as a trustee) to Saint Paul Theological Seminary, where Lowry taught for over thirty years. Hamilton and Lowry are neighbors in so many ways. Homiletically, though, they are galaxies apart.

In his recent book on preaching, *Unleashing the Word,* Hamilton spends a lot of time on high-tech matters, such as selecting the right images and video clips to accompany the sermon, but when he gets around to method, he says this about sermon structure:

> Preaching professors sometimes speak of two basic types of sermons. The first type begins with the human condition or the problem facing human beings and then draws the hearers toward the teaching of scripture and God's solution to the problem. This first type of sermon starts where we itch, and then brings the scripture to bear offering God's solution...The second type begins with the scriptures,

usually with a scriptural truth, and then seeks to apply that truth to our daily lives.[27]

Although Lowry would probably pick different wording, Hamilton's picture of the first type of sermon structure—from itch to scratch—sounds quite like Lowry's description of the plotted narrative sermon. In practice, however, Hamilton is poles apart from Lowry. Hamilton says, "I use both models in preaching,"[28] but in execution in Hamilton's preaching these two approaches tend to merge into a single method. True, Hamilton's sermons may start with a human "itch" or they may start with some scriptural truth, but, regardless of starting point, they tend to be structured in very similar ways. Hamilton creates sermons with several main points, supported by outlines he shares with the listeners with "fill in the blank" spots to help them pay attention.[29] In contrast to Lowry's five-fold sequence, where no part of the sermon could exist meaningfully apart from the other parts, where the experience of the sermon depends upon following the total flow of the sermon from beginning to end, Hamilton's sermons consist of bursts of insights, often discrete packages of information on a theme. If Lowry draws upon the narrative genre, Hamilton has changed the genre, from narrative to wisdom. Lowry's sermons are sequential plots; Hamilton's tend to be strings of elaborated proverbs. Lowry's sermons are built like short stories, Hamilton's like Web pages.

Ironically, if we take away the fancy computer-fueled technology and the dazzling images appearing on the screen, Hamilton's homiletical approach is straight out of the 1950s. How ironic that after nearly fifty years of our rejoicing over the death of the didactic sermon, "it's ba-a-a-a-ck." Only now, instead of three points and a poem, it's six points and a video clip.

I believe that Hamilton, at least intuitively, knows his listeners well, knows the culture well, and he has recovered the point-oriented, propositional, didactic approach to preaching in response to the communicational needs of an episodic culture. Lowry's approach assumed that the hearer was tacitly saying, "Hey, I have crafted a meaningful narrative for my life, one that gives me a satisfying identity, but there is a slight problem. Some conflict, some tension, some ambiguity, has arisen in my narrative, and I need a gospel-infused process to work this ambiguity through."

Hamilton assumes no such need or ability. Instead, he hears his listeners saying, "I don't have a coherent identity narrative, and I haven't a clue how to construct one. In the meantime, though, I need to manage the day, keep my job, stay married, and raise my children. Can you provide an external set of rules and ideas that will give me what I cannot make for myself: a Christian framework and meaning to my random, episodic life?"

Directions?

If *The Homiletical Plot* assumes a narrative competence that may no longer be fully in place, my fear about the new didactic approach that we see in Adam Hamilton and others is that it may end up reinforcing the worst tendencies of an episodic culture, encouraging people to grasp disconnected principles and rules and insights, provided by an authority figure from the outside, in order to survive in the chaotic whirlwind of life.

If we remind ourselves of our main task as preachers, we are not called to evoke a narrative competence already in place in people, nor are we called to provide wise insights for coping with the stresses of life. We are called to proclaim a narrative that people could not conjure up out of their own resources, the gospel narrative, and then to help people let that narrative become the story that shapes, guides, and clarifies their lives and gives them their primary identity.

If people are going to live into the gospel narrative, then they will need the ability to sustain narrative attention, the very thing that Lowry so provocatively heralded in *The Homiletical Plot.* But in our cultural context, the ability to do this must now be seen as a goal, not an assumed capability. Likewise, as the preaching of Adam Hamilton implies, we may well be in a moment when we need strong and confident teachers of wisdom, but we should not forget that biblical wisdom does not float free from the story of God and God's people but always rests on a narrative substrate. Lose sight of the narrative, and even biblical wisdom forfeits its edge and becomes a banal form of the power of positive thinking.

The next generation of preaching, then, is going to have to be rhetorically nimble. As Battersby says, "There are, then, many truths we can tell, in long and short forms, about selves, and many ways of telling them, but there is no way to get at the whole truth in any way of telling."[30] Because we are proclaimers of God's story, we will always be storytellers. But now, in order to tell this story, we must also stand back from it and become teachers and sages and ethical guides. No single homiletical formula will do; no one way of structuring sermons, however compelling, will accomplish the task; no solitary rhetorical strategy will open all the doors of the faithful imaginations of our hearers. We must help people in a fragmented and episodic culture to repair their ability not only to hear the gospel story but also to know what a powerful story is in the first place, how it works, and what possibilities it affords for identity and ethical living. We must use every gift of language, every responsible strategy of communication, to help people see, in practical and concrete ways, the shape of life that results when one builds a nest in the wide and embracing branches of the gospel story.

9

Jazz Me, Gene

Narrative Preaching as Encore

ROBIN R. MEYERS

How does one prepare to write about the future of narrative preaching, while honoring the life of Eugene Lowry? Well, of course, first you could pull down off the shelf all the Lowry books you own and read them again. Then it will all come back—how much he cares about time, about movement, about plot—because for Gene Lowry, timing is everything.

Then perhaps you could pull out a few scholarly articles from the Academy of Homiletics, to dip your toe once more into that endless debate about the so-called New Homiletic, for which Gene is a credentialed and embodied pied piper. He calls it "evocatively sequenced or eventively-plotted preaching." Critics call it dangerous, as if caring ultimately about the experience of the listener cannot possibly be the same thing as caring ultimately about the text.

But for me the best way to prepare to write this chapter was to dig out Gene Lowry's CD called "Jazz and Christianity," a lecture and concert recorded in 1995 with Milt Abel on bass, and play it in the stillness of a mountain cabin where I had retreated to write. It was the season of Advent, snow was on the ground, and the church was rightly in a minor key. Listening to Gene Lowry do what he does best (playing and preaching as call and response for the hopelessly uptight) made for the perfect musical backdrop to the writing of these words.

They are words of gratitude for his life and work; they are indirectly words of sympathy and sadness over the death of his son; and they are words of hope—a stone of hope, thrown into the lake of tomorrow on behalf of all narrative preachers who must not retreat from what we have learned, and cannot unlearn, about creating an experience of the word of God. We do this with the help of the Holy Spirit, of course. None of us work alone.

My offering will be divided into three parts: (1) a brief word about Gene Lowry's contribution to narrative preaching; (2) a sympathetic defense of the so-called New Homiletic; and (3) a set of musical metaphors, *boogie-woogie* and *encore,* as a means of understanding the future of narrative preaching.

Play It Again Preacher: This Time with Feeling

Eugene Lowery is an accomplished jazz pianist, and as such his homiletic is unmistakably musical. Although a non-musician myself, I recognize his preoccupation with time, with movement, with repetition and refrain, with improvisation, with dissonance and harmony, with cadence and chords, and with the transconscious nature of melody to tap both memory and hope as the basis for deep insights into the "musicality" of preaching. Jazz was born in the church, he rightly reminds us. It was born of great pain and amazing grace. It is, in fact, *antiphonal*—the musical equivalent of call and response.

Gene and I have at least two things in common. We both had the good sense to marry dark-haired women of extraordinary grace, and then managed to fall under the spell of the wisest, albeit the shortest of the homiletical magi: Fred B. Craddock. His 1971 book *As One Without Authority* was called the Copernican revolution in North American preaching for good reason, and solidified a seismic shift in thinking about the purpose of preaching itself. With roots in the hermeneutical work of Gerhard Ebeling and Ernst Fuchs, and accompanied by an increasingly existential view of the nature of language and faith formation, the teachers of preaching shifted their focus from the mouth of the preacher to the ear of the listener. Or, as Gene Lowry put it, our previous concentration was on the transmission of an idea. Our new focus is on mediation—better yet, on preaching as an "act of evocation."[1]

It was certainly not the case that sermon content no longer mattered, but rather that what one said was inseparable from how one said it, since the Word of God is not authoritative as it lies on the page. Rather it becomes the Word of God when encountered and responded to by listeners in a beloved community. In a sense, the New Hermeneutic made a New Homiletic inevitable, because, as Craddock reminds us, not a single word of the Bible is written to a single one of us. We are on our knees as it were, listening through a keyhole to ancient conversations not intended for us. We overhear the gospel.[2]

Thus turned from our historic preoccupation with what a sermon is to what a sermon *does*,[3] preaching could once more be seen (with understandable reservations) as a "performance." Not a dirty word to Charles Rice or Richard Ward, the sermon as performance merely acknowledges that all effective preaching involves "embodiment," and that any experience of the Word of God comes dressed in someone's clothes and rides the breath of someone's mouth. What's more, that "someone" ignores the elements of effective speech, authentic passion, and artful poetics at his or her peril. Narrative preaching is inescapably a performance, where "the selfhood of both preachers and listeners are reconstituted during the preaching event."[4]

If preaching can be understood as a performance without conjuring images of the egomaniac trolling for applause, but rather the preacher as a servant of the word, then paying attention to every aspect of the performance of the sermon is not only legitimate, but essential. Enter Gene Lowry to talk about time and place, task and goal, act and art, shape and strategy, preparation and presentation.

With an abbreviated precision, he summarizes the constellation of new metaphors for a New Homiletic as "Davis's *tree* and

Craddock's *trip*…R.E.C. Browne's *gesture,* Tom Troeger's *music of speech,* David Buttrick's *move,* Henry Mitchell's *celebration,* Lucy Rose's *conversation,* David Schlafer's *play,* and Paul Scott Wilson's *spark of imagination*—as well as [his] *plot* of course!"[5]

Whether Gene is at the piano, or in the pulpit, he is rightly obsessed with *response.* Be it the tapping of toes, or the amazing repertoire of listener responses in the black church, it's good to know that something is actually happening out there. He is convinced that out of an almost infinite variety of possible sermon shapes, one thing remains constant if the goal is evocation: the sermon must have a *sequential* form, because that is how anticipation is achieved.

Hence it is difficult for Lowry to write two pages without making a musical allusion, whether it's Stephen Crites work in the temporality of rhythm and melody line, which create a "unity through time,"[6] or Tom Troeger's "music of speech" that makes the imagination dance.[7] Daunting as it may seem, all of us who are called to preach must aspire to be rhetorical virtuosos (as Martin Luther King Jr. was called), because our voices are instruments, and all of the dynamics of music apply: rhythm, pitch, volume, inflection. So whether we use manuscripts, notes, or nothing but memory and the Holy Spirit to guide the sermon journey, make no mistake—we are singing.

Yet when we sing, or play an instrument, are we not practicing the ultimate form of "sequencing"? Isn't music powerful precisely because it is grounded in memory and hope? Like preaching, does it not depend on the power of *recognition,* and is not every piece of music, from a Woodie Guthrie ballad to a Beethoven symphony, "plotted" by design? It is both framed by time (it begins and ends) and responded to on the basis of timing (it has a beat, it moves, it pauses, creating anticipation—it even ties itself into dissonant knots only to "resolve" itself in the return of "Prodigal Harmony"). In fact, we all take sequencing for granted, even though something as simple as "tick/tock" is undone when we try to imagine "tock/tick."[8]

Music is also inherently inductive, since the crescendo is never heard first, and most arrangements begin slowly and softly, move through various "conflicts" and "complications," experience "sudden shifts," (akin to the good news) and then "unfold" in the experience of the listener in ways that make something hidden clear again, something forgotten remembered again, something lost found again.

For Lowry, sermons that unfold as a "narrative plot" are not just story sermons. They are musical acts of rhetorical evocation. We compose them. We sing them. And the response can be, might be, even sometimes is—an experience of the ineffable.

Is the New Homiletic a "Private Affective Goose Bump"?

This marvelous phrase belongs to Gene Lowry, in response to the charge made by critics of the New Homiletic, that our sermon goals are little more than an attempt to provide a "psychological gestalt."[9] When homiletics shifted its emphasis from the preacher's mouth to the listener's ear, it was assumed by some that we had entered dangerously subjective territory, while abandoning the text as the locus of authority and objectivity. If one is concerned with creating an experience in the heart, mind, and soul of the listener, critics reasoned, then we have opened the door to a shift in authority—from the infallible text, which is located in a particular place (the Bible), to a fallible relationship between the preacher, the text, and the congregation (a not-so-holy trinity located in that therapeutic netherworld where the "self" is superior to all else, and "experience" is the only authority that matters).[10]

The way that we sometimes talk "past" each other about such things reminds me of the media's favorite way of describing a divided America: red state/blue state. To their critics, the New Homiletic folk obviously live near the ocean, and have been seduced by the sounds of the New Hermeneutical waves as they came crashing in on the shore of our failing pulpits. Now what we want most of all is to be "with it," rather than to be obedient, and so we have sold our souls to be "relevant." By putting so many of our homiletical eggs in the basket of the listener's experience, we have turned our backs on propositional preaching meant to transfer eternal truths sufficient for salvation. Now, instead of "telling it like it is," we embrace "feel good" models of the Holy Spirit, and confuse conversion with self-actualization.

Some evangelical critics even complain that the New Homiletic has given too much attention to the parables, which is strange, given that parables were the principle teaching device of Jesus. Could it be that because of their open-endedness, their subversive form, even their strange and sudden reversals, they lack the "certainty" that evangelicals prefer? What if the listener gets it wrong? Can we take that chance? Jesus apparently did, because did he not say, "Let those who have ears hear"?

Taking aim at Fred Craddock, one critic quotes the following out of context: "It is, therefore, pointless to speak of the gospel as Truth in and of itself; the gospel is *Truth for us.*"[11] The point is to argue that the New Homiletic, because it views the sermon as an event in which preacher and listener are co-creators of an experience of the word of God, cannot possibly be "biblical." Authority is to be found in the text, the critics say, even before a word is spoken.

Still others quote David Buttrick's verdict, "The movement came and went with startling dispatch. Probably the fatal flaw was a lurking assumption, namely that the gospel addresses human beings in their existential self-awareness."[12] Or this by John Skoglund: "The real question comes: Is Word-event really happening? What appeared to be a most promising homiletical theory has not produced, in spite of all the scholarly care that has gone into its formulation, a significant new movement in preaching."[13]

Really? So it's either a "Copernican Revolution" or a "movement that came and went with startling dispatch"? But it surely can't be both. Perhaps we are confusing the New Homiletic with some of its less skilled practitioners? For it was never the intention of James David Randolph, Fred Craddock, Charles Rice, Gene Lowry, Ed Steimle, Lucy Rose, Tom Troeger, or Henry Mitchell, et al., to suggest that "narrative preaching" be misconstrued as throwing together a few good stories and hoping that "a meaningful sermonic time will be had by all."

As for the verdict rendered by John Skoglund above, that a new movement in preaching has not materialized, despite "all the scholarly care that has gone into its formulation," that hasty conclusion was reached in 1967, four years *before* the publication of Craddock's *As One Without Authority*. Perhaps some preferred that the New Homiletic might die before it was even born. Change is difficult, as the early Christians discovered.

Critics of the New Homiletic are most unnerved by the changes that the study of language itself has wrought. Because the phenomenon of language itself is symbolic, temporal, and inherently subjective, understanding is necessarily existential, involving a "hermeneutical circle" in which the self and the text come together in daily life.[14] There are enormous interpretive obstacles presented to the modern reader/listener that must be overcome by translation of the text into new forms.

This means that the "original meaning" of the text, which many believe must remain fixed and immutable, is compromised in a process of reinterpretation and translation. Here is the argument:

> Whereas Evangelicals regard the Bible as the revelation from God, the God-inspired book, advocates of the New Homiletic emphasize the preached words as event/experience with the listener encountering God in the spoken word. This understanding raises serious questions about the nature of inspiration and biblical revelation. In addition, this perspective limits sermonic language as primarily a symbolic expression of experience.[15]

This is confusing. I have yet to meet a card-carrying member of the New Homiletic who does not believe that the Bible is a revelation from God, or "God inspired." But how can anyone remain convinced that this means giving equal and uncritical weight to texts in their native form, especially those defending slavery, denigrating women, or assuming that disease is caused by demon possession? Demythologizing, as Rudolf Bultmann put it, is not a sign that one wishes to abandon the authority of the Bible, but to rescue it. Preachers who work in the paradigm of the New Homiletic want the text to have a present and a future, not just a past.

As for the belief that the preached word as an "event/experience with the listener encountering God in the spoken word" raises "serious questions about the nature of inspiration and biblical revelation," this is precisely the biblical *model* for inspiration and revelation. The disciples encountered God in the event/experience of Jesus and the astonishing words that proceeded out of his mouth. "He taught them as one having authority, and not as their scribes" (Mt. 7:29). If indeed we are to fear new ways of interpreting our own tradition, then we ought to abandon the example of Jesus' teaching, and try to forget how often he began, "You have *heard* it said, but *I* say…"

Advocates for the New Homiletic, and its most common (though not exclusive) synonym, "narrative preaching," do not believe, as critics charge, that narrative form is the *only* way to preach, regardless of the text. We are also aware that emphasis upon the listener must not obscure or compromise our primary responsibility to the text, and the inherited truths of the gospel— we're just not sure that anyone has been paying attention to the real experience of the listener. We also know that, despite claims to the contrary, the Holy Spirit plays a vital role in narrative preaching. Like all preachers, we are, in fact, regularly, and mercifully saved by the Holy Spirit.

Finally, as to the claim that the New Homiletic "limits sermonic language as primarily a symbolic expression of experience," one is left to wonder what other kind of language there is, or to what other use the words in a sermon can be put? The answer must be that the sole purpose of the sermon is to convey the doctrinal information necessary for salvation. That might indeed be good enough, if only more people believed that knowledge was redemptive.

A Two-Handed Homiletic: The Future of Narrative Preaching as Encore

We often speak in the Academy of the enormous shift in thinking that has occurred in homiletics in the last thirty-five years as a kind of "break" with conventional understandings of rhetoric. Tom Long is correct when he says that, for a long time, rhetoric and homiletics were a "mixed marriage" of convenience—homiletics being Jewish and rabbinical in background; rhetoric being Greek. But the idea was simple enough: "Homileticians knew what preachers were supposed to say, and rhetoricians knew how they were to say it, so that listeners could hear it and be persuaded by it."[16]

Yet those of us who preach and teach preaching have not always been aware that a considerable shift in rhetorical theory has been occurring simultaneously "across the hall" in many communications departments. We continue to think of rhetorical theory as unrepentantly Greek, wooden, deductive, and propositional—the making of eloquent extended arguments that were thought to work on contact like a hypodermic needle. But while we have been preoccupied with the New Homiletic, professors of rhetoric have been busy teaching their students the New Rhetoric.

Many of the same forces that caused a shift in our thinking about preaching have also shifted rhetorical theory away from so-called "message-centered persuasion," to what is now called "listener-centered persuasion." Not surprisingly, preachers such as Hugh Blair, George Campbell, and Richard Whatley foreshadowed these changes in the eighteenth and nineteenth centuries, because they were already trying to rescue their sermons from the tedium of the sermon as deductive monologue. When the social sciences, especially psychology, began to teach us all more about what went on inside the listener's head, and language studies gave us new insights into how human beings "make meaning" through words, rhetoric did not stand still. It moved also—from the mouth to the ear.

Rhetoricians began saying many of the same things that homileticians were saying, but in different ways. Under the rubric of "self-persuasion," which became an area of special interest to me, persuasion shifted on its axis, from what a message does *to* a listener, to what a listener does *with* a message. One theorist went so far as to say, "In a real sense, we do not persuade others at all; we only provide the stimulus with which they persuade themselves."[17]

This caused me to wonder if preaching might be thought of with benefit as an intentional act of "self-persuasion"? The preacher, in this case, might also fall under the spell that he or she is trying to cast for the listener. What's more, if more preachers wrote sermons for their own ears, might they not better understand what kind of language, and what kind of movement, will create the most effective response in the listener? After all, the first person to be bored by a boring sermon should be the preacher. Likewise, if the preacher can't be seen and heard as fitfully, compulsively, joyfully "embodying" the many moods of the sermon, then what is there for the listener to emulate? Like it or not, all preachers end up with the kind of listeners they deserve.

What's more, if preachers modeled a *dialogical* method in the pulpit, as both speakers and listeners, then wouldn't they help to *create* dialogical listeners? It seems to me that the most ignored concept in homiletical theory today is the notion of *vicariousness*. One has only to sit before great preachers to know that they often seem "possessed" by the need to exorcize the "demon" of meaning from the text. They do not "work a sermon up" so much as "work it *out*"—like Jacob, wrestling with an angel named "germinal idea" in front of, and on behalf of, everyone in the room. The "point" of the sermon is like an irresistible intruder, and they engage it not just to be polite but because it won't go away.

That engagement is both contagious and instructive. What preachers have heard "whispered" in the study must now be "shouted from the housetops" of the sanctuary. If that shout is not to sound shrill, it must be musical. What's more, when that shout is harmonic, the listener picks up the beat and we all get lost in the music. That's when preachers discover that they are no longer working alone. We've heard about the "cloud of witnesses." What about the "chorus of listeners"? That brings us back to Gene Lowry.

If you don't understand him as a musician, you won't understand him as a preacher. Whether it's the jazz he loves to play, or the text that he has plotted into a sermon, music, like preaching, is all about *call* and *response*. The quality of that call will be matched by the quality of the response, which may explain why so many of our sanctuaries are so quiet. Emotionally speaking, the call itself is barely audible.

Europeans have trouble understanding jazz, Lowry teaches us, because it is so much more complicated, and improvisational than any other form of music. For Europeans, music is "the frosting on top of a middle class cake."[18] It is like Muzak in the dentist's office, something that distracts us rather than defining us—soothes our terror, or muffles the hard edges of our lives—but not something that *expresses* life itself.

It was the black preaching tradition that awakened Lowry to preaching as a community act. It was his knowledge of jazz, and his gift for playing it, that opened up his understanding of call and response—because jazz is born of suffering, and its beat comes from the cadences of the sermon. It's no wonder that some of those cadences were originally set to the rhythm of the sledgehammer. Jazz is the musical incarnation of unbearable pain answered by amazing grace.

Of all the wise things that Gene Lowry has said about the relationship between jazz and the gospel, one struck me with peculiar force, and gave birth to a metaphor that might explain why narrative preaching and the New Homiletic are not really new at all. In trying to explain the jazz musical form known as "boogie-woogie," Lowry quotes a jazz great, T-Bone Walker as saying, "The first time I heard boogie-woogie was the first time I went to church."[19]

Lowry goes on to explain that in this particular jazz form, the left hand "walks" up the chord, staccato-like, makes a U-turn and walks back down it, while the right hand "does whatever it wants."[20] If you've ever heard boogie-woogie you know exactly what this sounds like, but Gene goes on to make an astute theological analogy. It's as if the left hand is the daily grind, the trudging, measured, one-foot-in-front-of-the-other world of everyday life with all its chores, its obligations, its plodding predictability—even its pain; while the right hand runs away to play, flies off toward joy, and sings a song of hope and freedom. It is the musical equivalent of the tension between pain and grace, between putting one foot in front of the other "on the one hand," and wanting to fly away "on the other."

Let's extend this marvelous metaphor even further. In narrative preaching, we might think of the left hand as the *text*, not because it is plodding or even necessarily painful, but because it is familiar, foundational, part of the "walk" through the canon that that is "normative for our faith and life." The preacher walks up and down that text with his linguistic left hand—back and forth, like the left hand in boogie-woogie—as if such a measured stride is the preacher's obligation, because it is. But there is more to preaching than one-fingered, single-note renditions of those ancient scriptural songs.

At the same time, the preacher's rhetorical right hand *improvises*, taking off in flights of fancy, but always exegetically tethered to the left hand's solid, scriptural beat. The right hand, with its right-brain proclivities, tells new stories, creates new melodies, turns what might otherwise seem like a plodding, unfamiliar, heavy-footed ancient walk into something that feels more like skipping, even running with joy. Narrative preachers "walk the exegetical walk" on one hand, because we don't get to make up the gospel as we go. But we *sing a new song* to accompany that old walk on the other hand—precisely so that our preaching doesn't sound like "Chopsticks."

What's more, the inherited wisdom of the textual left hand is not self-authenticating, self-evident, or even necessarily the Word of God in its plodding, lectionary familiarity until the right hand performs the essential task of *interpretation*—singing a new song that brings recognition and relevance to the listener. The left hand of the preacher walks around the text, over it, under it, ahead of it, behind it. But the right hand has improvisation on its mind. It is after *evocation*, not just edification. So it begins to make new melodies using the same textual "chords," and creates, in the same "key," a series of new refrains: examples, analogies, anecdotes, metaphors, illustrations, stories—not to replace the text, but to *reconstitute* it. These improvisations are not just for entertainment, but also to lift what might otherwise be a lifeless walk and turn it into an encounter, a present-day Emmaus experience.

Narrative preachers don't sing new songs to be "with it," or to ground the total activity of God in the subjective world of the listener's experience. We do this because it's biblical. We do it because the New Homiletic is really the First Homiletic.

Was it not the exiled children of Israel who first called for the singing of a new (old) song? Their left hand wept, but their right hand remembered the songs of Zion and thus the hope that their identity and faith could be reconstituted. Did the prophets not come before the kings again and again to say that while the beat of the law may be in your "talk," on one hand, the melody of compassion is missing from your "walk" on the other?

Then there's Jesus. While the left hand of Israel's measured hope for a messiah that would lead them to greatness played on, the Son of God was in their midst playing a new song from God's right hand—coming not to abolish that law, but to complete it. The new sound was grace in the flesh, and while it sounded fetching and harmonic to some, others found it breezy and unsettling, even dangerous and frightening. Radical freedom still frightens us. That's why so many of us are afraid to dance.

When the gospel writers sat down to create persuasive portraits of Jesus, they started with the great themes of Judaism as a baseline with their left hand, and then with their right, they reinterpreted those very stories in light of the coming of Christ. The left hand played Adam, the right played the New Adam. The left hand played the old tune of the house of David, while the right improvised Bethlehem, angels, shepherds, and flights into Egypt.

The left hand played Moses, and Elijah as the great lawgiver and prophet. The right hand played "transfiguration," where on the mountain of a new melody both come to pay honor to the one Christians laud as the greater Lawgiver and the greater Prophet. The left hand knows the tune of the confusion of tongues at Babel, but the right hand wants to play something new and miraculous: the translinguistic miracle of Pentecost. The left hand preserves *tradition*. The right hand *interprets* it in light of new situations, new challenges, and new revelations. God is still speaking, and this is how we should preach—with both hands.

In narrative preaching we have not invented something new, but have carried forward the form of the gospel itself, which is a story that is constantly being improvised by God. The gospels are faithful improvisations in narrative form. The epistles show how fluid and adaptive the pastoral care of the church must be. How then can preachers be other than faithful narrative improvisers when they are called not just to *tell*, but also to *retell* the old, old story?

Our left hand studies, remembers, and acknowledges the inherited wisdom of the faith, but it's not enough to play with only one hand. Knowledge is *not* redemptive. Hearing the Word of God and being changed by it is. So we start out walking, then we skip, and finally we run, because joy comes with the morning.

One of the universal experiences of listening to great music holds a lesson for preaching. When we are moved by what we have heard, we know how to ask for more. In concert halls, great and small, the word we use is *encore*. That's what the audience shouts out because it is not yet ready to return to the silence that came before the experience of having it so artfully, soulfully broken. The music has carried us off to a place "beyond," a place that we are not eager to leave—not just yet.

When we shout "encore!" we are not asking for musicians to abandon all that is familiar to us, because in music, as in preaching, the power of recognition is the spiritual baseline. But we love to hear what we think we have already heard played in a new way. It will be like hearing it again for the first time.

If the musicians truly care for us, they will play with both hands. If the preacher cares for us, he or she will do likewise. The gospel of Jesus Christ is a two-handed invitation to trust that God was, and is, and will be the definitive word of unconditional love, grace, and forgiveness in a suffering and broken world—but only if the left hand knows what the right hand has to offer, and the right hand never forgets where it came from, where it's going, and to Whom it belongs.

As narrative preachers we sing a new song because every preaching moment requires a fresh improvisation, and the church's version of "encore" is when people come back, Sunday after Sunday, to hear it again, as if for the first time. Thank goodness we don't have to start from scratch just to be "with it." We still have the beat in our left hand, and the improvisational gift of imagination in our right hand.

That's when we "dance the edge of mystery," as Gene would say. That's when we gesture toward the ineffable, and draw the curtain back. For all the times we fail, and seem to preach "one-handed," there is something that surely frightens us more than failure—and that's how often we succeed, by God's grace, and people want more.

The New Homiletic is really the First Homiletic, and narrative preaching is not a recent discovery; it's the latest version of an old, old song that people keep asking us to play so they can hear it again, as if for the very first time. Thanks to Gene Lowry, and his lifelong commitment to a two-handed homiletic, the listeners have spoken.

Encore!

PART III

Prospects

*What Fresh Shapes Might
Narrative Preaching Take?*

10

Making Music with What You Have Left

The Paradigm of Hope in African American Preaching

FRANK A. THOMAS

Through the generative seed of a book, *The Homiletical Plot: The Sermon as Narrative Art Form,* Eugene Lowry explained to a young novice preacher from a methodological perspective what real preaching looked like. As part of the oral African American preaching tradition, I had known narrative. I had seen it, felt it, and experienced it all of my life, but no one could explain to a rational type like me how it was done. Lowry gave methodological explanation to what I came to know as the genius of the African American preaching tradition, what I call a "paradigm of hope." Gene Lowry provided the methodological explanation for what had been buried down in my soul as part of the African American preaching tradition. After seventeen years of teaching preaching, *The Homiletical Plot: The Sermon as Narrative Art Form,* albeit now the expanded edition, is still required reading in every class as a way of helping my students understand how they can undertake preaching in a paradigm of hope.

I have recently begun to study hope. I am always on the lookout for it, particularly when there does not appear to be any obvious and rational reason to hope, and yet, somehow, someone in the grip of tragedy and disappointment manifests the courage and resolve to summon it. I come from an African American preaching tradition that, at its best, has as its genius delivering and imparting hope. If asked, "What has sustained and liberated African American people amidst more than four hundred years of systemic slavery, racism, hatred, violence, and second-class citizenship?", I would respond unequivocally: "The reality of hope offered within the African American sermon." The African American preacher has operated within the paradigm of hope to liberate and sustain African American people. In this chapter, I will define the African American preaching tradition's understanding of that paradigm, utilize the work of Jerome Groopman and Martin Luther King Jr. to clarify that understanding, then conclude with an exhortation for preachers to make hope an essential characteristic in their preaching.

The African American Preaching Paradigm of Hope

Valentino Lassiter, in his book *Martin Luther King in the African American Preaching Tradition*,[1] helps us understand that such tradition operates within the "paradigm of hope." He lists four central tenets in African American preaching: (1) God is the unquestionable sustainer of the world; (2) the world maintains a physical and permanent moral order; (3) the Sustainer and Gracious God is loving, caring, yet remains in full control; and (4) the unquestionable divine ability (God is "able") extends grace and mercy (God is "good"). These four premises are theological core beliefs in which African American preaching is historically and spiritually grounded. Whenever African American preaching has had to face alienation, oppression, slavery, segregation, hatred, death, sickness, hardship, and the like, these core beliefs have been utilized to construct a "paradigm of hope."

Hope, then, is the ability to look at the brutal reality of a fundamentally flawed world and still believe in the power and goodness of God, who offers freedom, deliverance, and healing. The African American preacher, recognizing a fundamentally flawed America, does not drop out, give up, or become cynical, but continues to portray positive solutions, even if those solutions are left to God. One of our most illustrious native sons, Martin Luther King Jr., given the reality of alienation in African American experience, did what generations of African American preachers have done: function in a paradigm of hope, and deliver it to people. Few African American preachers have done it as well as King in the totality of preaching and protest, but the unquestionable fact remains that King operated from squarely within this African American preaching paradigm.

King expressed a rhetoric of hope across the entire career of his public discourse; but in the last year of his life, it became more clearly and sharply defined, and ultimately more radical. Hope is hammered out in the midst of adversity; and the greater the adversity, the greater potential for hope. King, in his last year of life, faced his most determined opposition to nonviolence; suffered the most vicious personal attacks on his motives, integrity, and leadership; endured unparalleled harassment, hounding, and investigation; encountered more personal death threats; and all in times of his most intense personal depression. Despite this daunting matrix, King proclaimed the reality of hope, and utilized it to move forward with his mission to save the soul of America.

The Anatomy of Hope

One of the best contributions to this discussion of hope is the recent work of Jerome Groopman in *The Anatomy of Hope: How People Prevail in the Face of Illness.*[2] Groopman represents a new attempt to integrate the perspective of hope into the discourse of medicine, seeking to discover how hope factors into the equation of healing. Groopman holds the Dina and Raphael Recanati Chair of Medicine at Harvard Medical School, and is chief of experimental medicine at Beth Israel Deaconess Medical Center in Boston. He is staff writer in medicine and biology for *The New Yorker*, and has authored several popular books. Groopman concludes the following:

1. Hope can change the course of a malady, and help patients overcome it.
2. Hope has proved as important as any medication he has prescribed and any medical procedure that he has performed.
3. His own personal experience of a failed spine surgery, constant relapses into pain and debility, and subsequent freedom through hope confirms the healing properties of hope.

4. The medical community must integrate hope as a major component of its therapeutic processes (which he calls a "biology of hope").

The medical community is moving toward what the religious community has always understood: the healing properties of hope.

On the way to persuading the medical establishment, Groopman defines hope in a manner that allows us to give clarity to King's rhetoric and the African American preaching tradition. Following experimental psychologist Richard Davidson, one of the world's experts on the biology of positive emotions (joy, resilience, and motivation), Groopman argues that the *anatomy of hope* has two distinctive components, which can be described as (1) cognitive and (2) affective.[3]

The Cognitive Component of Hope

According to Davidson, the cognitive component of hope involves "employ[ing] to some degree our cognition, marshaling information and data relevant to a desired future event."[4] In effect, through our cognitive belief systems, we generate a different mental vision of our condition. A person suffering with a serious illness paints a different picture of improvement, or even a cure, "by assimilating information about the disease and its potential treatments"[5] by means of the cognitive, rational dimension of human personality.

My argument is that from the cognitive side, King's rhetoric of hope develops a radically different vision of the human condition. King paints a picture of improvement, even a cure, for the societal illness of America and the world. A close reading of *A Time to Break Silence*[6] has identified several cognitive themes (principles or belief systems) contained in King's rhetoric of hope: nonviolence, the oneness of the entire human family, and a revolution of values. These themes can be traced through the discourse of King's entire public ministry, but they are most pronounced in the last year of his life.

1. *Nonviolence is a strategy that overcomes the social dialectics of race and class.* King refused to respond to human beings from the perspective of violence because violence hardened and intensified the tensions of race and class (and, I would add, gender and

sexuality). Violence heightens tensions and hardens divisions. In *A Time to Break Silence,* King sought to move both "angry young [black] men" and the "U.S. government" from the belief that violence could solve problems. King says:

> As I have walked among the desperate, rejected, and angry young men, I have told them that Molotov cocktails and rifles would not solve their problems. I have tried to offer them my deepest compassion while maintaining my conviction that social change comes most meaningfully through nonviolent action. But they asked, and rightly so, "What about Vietnam?" They asked if our own nation wasn't using massive doses of violence to solve its problems, to bring about the changes it wanted. Their questions hit home, and I knew that I could never again raise my voice against the violence of the oppressed in the ghettoes without having first spoken clearly to the great purveyor of violence in the world today: my own government.[7]

King equally critiqued "the violence of the oppressed" and the role of the U.S. government as "the greatest purveyor of violence in the world today." If America, or any nation, was going to heal the tensions of race and class, then nonviolence was the only option.

2. *Nationhood (nationality) and religious distinctions are overcome by an underlying oneness in being of the entire human race.* King places Buddhist, Hindu, Jew, and Christian all one under one banner in a vision of global community of citizens who seek to resolve conflict through nonviolence, and live in a climate of peace and love. King advocates a worldwide fellowship beyond race, class, nation, and religion, which he calls, "the sons [and daughters] of the living God." He says: "Beyond the calling of race or nation or creed is this vocation of sonship and brotherhood… This I believe to be the privilege and the burden of all of us who deem ourselves bound by allegiances and loyalties which are broader and deeper than nationalism, which go beyond our nation's self-defined goals and positions."[8]

Many would argue this ethic is impractical, naïve, and unattainable in the real world, especially at the level of international politics, but the undaunted King marches boldly into rhetorical and symbolic space. King, in one stroke, through the ethic of love in the Christian Bible, unifies the Hindu-Muslim-Christian-Jew-Buddhist into a worldwide fellowship:

> This Hindu-Muslim-Christian-Jewish-Buddhist belief about ultimate reality is beautifully summed up in the first epistle of Saint John: Let us love one another, for love is God. And everyone that loveth is born of God and knoweth God. He that loveth not knoweth not God, for God is love… If we love one another, God dwelleth in us and his love is perfected in us. Let us hope that this spirit will become the order of the day.[9]

King calls for a worldwide fellowship that lifts neighborly concern beyond one's tribe, race, class, and nation.

3. *A revolution of values is necessary if we are to continue as a human race.* In *A Time to Break Silence,* King moved to identify American evil specifically. He believed that the war in Vietnam was but "a symptom of a far deep malady within the American spirit."[10] America, he thought, "was on the wrong side of a world revolution."[11] American values gave rise to racism, militarism, and extreme materialism. King said:

> I am convinced that if we are to get on the right side of the world revolution, we as a nation must undergo a radical revolution of values. We must rapidly begin [applause], we must rapidly begin the shift from a thing-oriented society to a person-oriented society. When machines and computers, profit motives and property rights, are considered more important than people, the giant triplets of racism, extreme materialism, and militarism are incapable of being conquered.[12]

For King, the positive values of human life, freedom, peace, justice, and love replace extreme materialism, racism, and militarism. Greedy capitalism is overcome by a "person-oriented society." These three cognitive themes combine to function as a cure for societal illness and disease and supply the rational basis for King's rhetoric of hope. King, through cognitive belief systems, marshals information and data relevant to a desired future event—the freedom and liberation of America from racism, materialism, and militarism.

The Affective Component of Hope

Hope has a cognitive element, but also has an affective element, or what Groopman/Davidson call "affective forecasting."[13] Hope is the comforting, energizing, and elevating *feeling* that comes from projecting a positive future. From Groopman's perspective, when we project a positive future, the brain generates a different feeling state that is intensely visceral, sensed as a sharp upward shift in mood. We are "lifted by" hope, and "hope has wings," Groopman says.[14] Hope facilitates this upward shift in mood through the following characteristics: belief, expectation, memory, and resilience.

1. *What people believe, as located in the intuitive aspects of human personality.* Human awareness involves three aspects of self: the cognitive, the emotive, and the intuitive. The cognitive is the faculty for reason and rational thought. The emotive is the base for the arousal of feelings and affections. The intuitive is the capacity for direct knowing or learning without the conscious use of reasoning. Within the intuitive is the collection of core beliefs, which are broad principles for living shaped by the intuitive evaluation of life and experience.

Faith, for example, does not reside in the cognitive, or the emotive, but in the intuitive aspects of human personality, or what could be called the "gut." Faith is born in a "reasonable encounter,"[15] within an emotive context, and then moves to reside as a principle in the intuitive that shapes the opinion and behavior of the people. Henry H. Mitchell writes:

> Our intuitive responses to various experiences are like tapes placed deep down in consciousness. If in early life we forged a habit of believing that the planet was safe, and God was caring for us, that amounts to a tape. In a crisis, we tend to "play" it again and live by the same habit of trust. If a child was mistreated or poorly cared for, that child will have emotional habits or tapes of fear and distrust.[16]

Our ability to hope is connected to our belief in core belief, which amounts symbolically to a "tape" of our habits of trust or distrust shaped by intuitive evaluation of life and experience.

2. *Expectation.* Expectation is looking forward to something in the future. In the case of hope, it is to look forward to something based upon our habit of trust located in core belief. To hope is

to wait with positive confidence for that which is desired. The apostle Paul, who spends a tremendous amount of time and energy defining and living in hope, says: "Hope that is seen is no hope at all. Who hopes for what he already has? But if we hope for what we do not yet have, we wait for it patiently" (Rom. 8:24—25, NIV).

The author of Hebrews links faith and hope: "Faith is being sure of what we hope for and certain of what we do not see" (Heb. 11:1, NIV). Hope is to expect in confidence, which gives one the courage to wait patiently for that which one hopes.

In King, hope expresses itself in the expectation and confidence of a liberated future. In his last public address, the last full night of his life, he uttered this phrase that after his death was played as a clip many times a day on WVON (a black-owned radio station in Chicago) for many years of my youth, "But I want you to know tonight that we as a people will get to the promised land." King offers hope, the expectation and confidence in a positive and liberated future—the promised land.

3. *Memory.* Memory draws on experiences of the past, "seeking models and directions from other individuals who endured and overcame long odds."[17] Memory brings to consciousness a redemptive past, a former time when we or others were in trouble, but were successful or victorious. It does not have to be a personal experience of redemption; it could be a story found in religious faith such as the Bible, Koran, or other holy book. It can be a hero or heroine from family, literature, history, poetry, or philosophy, but is usually based in an authoritative text or tradition. The key is identification, the ability to relate one's life or condition to the condition or life of another. One sees the struggle and life of another, and vicariously connects to it. When that other is victorious, vicariously we are victorious. The sports fan, for example, identifies with his or her favorite team, and when the team wins the fan wins. And it is from this vicarious identification with individuals who endured and overcame long odds, residing in memory, that one garners faith or confidence in the future.

4. *Resilience.* Groopman/Davidson define resilience as the maintenance of high levels of positive feelings and well-being in the face of significant adversity.[18] Resilient people have negative feelings, but Groopman insists that the negative feelings do not persist. Davidson quotes a 1957 study that followed ten thousand men and women from high school graduation to their advancing

years in the attempt to develop a profile with respect to their affective style. Out of the group of ten thousand, Davidson selected a representative sample of five hundred elderly women whose mean age is now seventy-five. Davidson argues that the results suggest that in response to a negative experience, "resilient" women "did not show a sharp rise in cortisol [stress hormone]; this indicated that they would psychologically modulate their response to severe stress."[19] In contrast, Davidson labeled the group that was less resilient as "vulnerable." While recalling difficult experiences, they had a markedly different cortisol profile. The amount of cortisol released was significantly higher in the nonresilient, vulnerable women compared to the resilient ones. Davidson concludes that this indicates that "women can dampen the fear response."[20] While Davidson's goal is to map the ways in which bodily health can be modulated by each person's affective style, a key component of the modulation is resilience. Resilient people modulate the stress hormone cortisol and maintain high levels of positive feelings and well-being in the face of significant adversity.

Groopman's work is important. If a scientist can come to believe that hope can change the course of a malady, and help patients overcome—what about preachers? If a medical doctor can come to the conclusion that hope has proved as important as any medication he has prescribed and any medical procedure that he has performed—what about biblical scholars and professors? If the chief of experimental medicine, based upon his personal experience of a failed spine surgery and constant relapses into pain and debility and subsequent freedom through hope, can authoritatively and passionately testify to the healing properties of hope, what about homileticians? Finally, if a writer in biology for *The New Yorker* can call the medical community to integrate hope as a major component of its therapeutic processes, and call it a "biology of hope"—what about pulpiteers: bishops, apostles, evangelists, priests, prophets, gospel pushers, heralds, holy mothers, divine fathers, sermonizers, and those who proclaim the gospel story? What about those whose job it is to look at the brutal reality of a fundamentally flawed world, including racism, segregation, oppression, death, sickness, and still believe and proclaim the power and goodness of God who offers freedom, deliverance, and healing? Let me say it the way that we say it in the African American church: the preacher should be able to stand and proclaim that God is "able" and God is "good."

Always on the lookout for hope, I found it in an article written by Jack Riemer that appeared in the *Houston Chronicle*:

> On November 18, 1995, Itzhak Perlman, the violinist, came on stage to give a concert…If you have ever been to a Perlman concert, you know that getting on stage is no small achievement for him. He was stricken with polio as a child, and so he has braces on both legs and walks with the aid of two crutches.
>
> To see him walk across the stage one step at a time, painfully and slowly, is an unforgettable sight. He walks painfully yet majestically until he reaches his chair. Then he sits down, slowly, puts his crutches on the floor, undoes the clasps on his legs, tucks one foot back and extends the other foot forward. Then he bends down and picks up the violin, puts it under his chin, nods to the conductor and proceeds to play.
>
> But this time, something went wrong. Just as he finished the first few bars, one of the strings on his violin broke. You could hear it snap—it went off like gunfire across the room. There was no mistaking what that sound meant. There was no mistaking what he had to do.
>
> People who were there that night thought to themselves: "We figured that he would have to get up, put on the clasps again, pick up the crutches and limp his way off stage—to either find another violin or else find another string for this one."
>
> But he didn't. Instead, he waited a moment, closed his eyes and then signaled the conductor to begin again. The orchestra began, and he played from where he had left off. And he played with such a passion and such power and such purity as they had never heard before. Of course, anyone knows that it is impossible to play a symphonic work with just three strings. I know that, and you know that, but that night Itzhak Perlman refused to know that.
>
> You could see him modulating, changing, recomposing the piece in his head. At one point, it sounded like he was de-tuning the strings to get new sounds from them that they had never made before.

When he finished, there was an awesome silence in the room. And then people rose and cheered. There was an extraordinary outburst of applause from every corner of the auditorium. We were all on our feet, screaming and cheering, doing everything we could to show how much we appreciate what he had done.

He smiled, wiped the sweat from his brow, raised his bow to quiet us, and then he said, not boastfully, but in a quiet, pensive, reverent tone, "You know sometimes it is the artist's task to find out how much music you can still make with what you have left."[21]

The preacher's task is to convince people that they can still make it with what they have left. The preacher's task is to show and convince people that they can modulate, change, and recompose their lives. The preacher's task is to convince people that life is not over just because a string is broken, even if they have braces and must walk with crutches. The preacher's task is to call forth the creative genius that is buried within us all, and when that creative genius is summoned and expressed, it looks like hope. Scientists and musicians are telling preachers and professors of homiletics that our task is hope: to proclaim to people that they can make music with what they have left through the God revealed in the life and ministry of Jesus Christ. In the African American church, we would quote a hymn right about now: "My hope is built on nothing less, / than Jesus' blood and righteousness."[22]

11

Gasping for Breath

Women Listening,
Women Telling Stories

BARBARA K. LUNDBLAD

Consideration of narrative preaching is not only a matter of how the narrative moves, but which narratives are worth hearing and preaching. This is true whether the narrative is in the Bible, in contemporary literature, film, public media, or in people's lives. When Eugene Lowry wrote *The Homiletical Plot* in 1980, most of the books now considered classics of feminist biblical interpretation had not yet been written. Seminarians were beginning to read the early work of Rosemary Radford Ruether and Letty Russell in the late seventies, but few texts by feminist biblical scholars were available until later. *God and the Rhetoric of Sexuality* by Phyllis Trible was published in 1978, but her earth-shaking book *Texts of Terror* didn't come until 1984. *In Memory of Her: A Feminist Theological Reconstruction of Christian Origins*, Elisabeth Schüssler Fiorenza's book on women's leadership in the New Testament, was published in 1983, followed the next year by *Bread Not Stone: The Challenge of Feminist Biblical Interpretation*. The feminist insights of Adela Berlin, Adele Yarbro Collins, J. Cheryl Exum, Johanna W.H. Bos, Carol Newsom, Sharon Ringe, and many others have all been published in the last twenty-five years.[1] The categories of biblical studies, theology, Church history, and ethics haven't remained neatly separated in women's writings. Theologian Delores Williams was drawn to the biblical story of Hagar as she listened to African American women tell the narratives of their own lives:

> Hagar has "spoken" to generation after generation of black women because her story has been validated as true by suffering black people. She and Ishmael together, as family, model many black American families in which a lone woman/mother struggles to hold the family together in spite of the poverty to which ruling class economics consign it. Hagar, like many black women, goes into the wide world to make a living for herself and her child, with only God by her side.[2]

Williams's engagement with Hagar not only led her to criticize white feminists who tended to speak for all women, but to challenge the liberation theology of the African American brothers who often neglected women's survival and well-being in their emphasis on exodus and freedom.

Hagar and Ishmael are left behind as the primary narrative of Abraham's other descendants moves on. Which narratives are told and retold in the formation of a community of faith? Which biblical narratives count as theologically significant? Even though all four gospel narratives feature faithful women as the first witnesses at the empty tomb, the Church has paid far more attention to the narratives of Jesus and the male disciples—even insisting that only men could be ordained since all the disciples were men. In John 11, Martha made a bold confession of faith, saying, "Yes, Lord, I believe that you are the Messiah" (Jn. 11:27). Yet, the Church was founded on Peter whose confession was almost identical to Martha's. When Elisabeth Schussler-Fiorenza's book *In Memory of Her* was published, a celebrative party was held at Harvard Divinity School. Krister Stendahl, the dean, and an ardent supporter of women's ministries, praised the book. Then he added a note of cautious realism: "You know, Elisabeth, it's all wonderful, but it's still like looking at a bird beside an elephant."

This wasn't a criticism, but rather a reminder that the stack of biblical stories about women will always be tiny alongside the tall stack of stories about men. If the Church is a people shaped by the narrative of the biblical canon, how is that narrative remembered, and how is it preached when women are often in the margins?

Listening to the Gasps

When I was a pastor of a Lutheran congregation in upper Manhattan, we shared worship space with Beth Am, a Reform Jewish congregation. Over the course of ten years, Rabbi Margaret Moers Wenig became not only my friend, but my rabbi. One day she told me about a time when she was leading a text study with a group of women from Beth Am on Genesis 22 — the *akedah,* the near sacrifice of Isaac by his father Abraham. This circle of women knew the story well. They heard it every year on Rosh Hashanah. Most of the women were well over sixty. Each could have told it from memory. When the rabbi came to the place where Abraham raises his knife to slay his son, the women gasped. Even though they knew what was coming, they couldn't bear to hear it. Their bodies and their breath protested involuntarily. They could only gasp at the violence of a parent about to kill his own child. No matter that the story was evidence of Abraham's absolute faith in God. No matter that they had heard many explanations, including the one about an end to child sacrifice. No matter all the *midrashim* that had been written by rabbis over the centuries. When Abraham raised his knife to slay his son, the women gasped.

What does it mean to gasp at a narrative so central in shaping the people of faith? Is gasping an act of heresy, of refusal to let God be God? Must women trust the God of the narrative even when everything in their bodies screams against the story? In recent years, many Christian women have gasped at the classical doctrine of sacrificial atonement. One of the earliest verses children memorize in Sunday school is John 3:16: "For God so loved the world that he gave his only Son, so that everyone who believes in him may not perish but may have eternal life." Though this verse says nothing about Jesus' death, most Christians have heard death there, as in the words of this gospel chorus:

For God so loved the world, He gave His only Son
To die on Calvary's tree, from sin to set me free;

Some day He's coming back—what glory that will be!
Wonderful His love to me.[3]

Like Abraham, God was willing to sacrifice his only Son, and
no angel was there to stay the knife. For centuries, the narrative
of Jesus' willing and necessary suffering and death has shaped
Christian believers. This narrative has provided the libretto for
hundreds of hymns and much of the liturgy. Susan Bond points
to this problem in her book *Trouble with Jesus*. She imagines
"Reverend Ms. Jones" preaching a sermon on the woman at
Bethany who anoints Jesus. Preaching boldly, she says this woman
is "a boundary violator, a courageous and uppity woman who
wouldn't let anything come between her and an act of devotion."
Ms. Jones hears liberation in the text and she hears Jesus affirm
the woman's daring liberation. But there is another narrative that
takes over as the service continues:

> Now Reverend Ms. Jones takes her place behind the
> eucharist table and begins the liturgy of the sacrament. As
> we eavesdrop on the service we realize that everything she
> has just woven together in her sermon is about to come
> unraveled…She will liturgically reinscribe the virtues of
> willing sacrifice, obedience unto death, and the merits
> of vicarious suffering. In the eucharistic liturgy, Christ
> becomes a victim on our behalf. The Jesus who approved
> resisting victimization in the sermon is displaced by the
> Jesus who embraces victimization in the liturgy.[4]

Reverend Jones probably didn't gasp at the table. Yet, many
women have gasped in the midst of a hymn or a eucharistic prayer.
Gasping has often been the beginning of revelation for women.
But gasping can take your breath away, and most women, as well
as men, want to keep breathing.

Narrative Conversations

Women's gasping has led to a hermeneutics of suspicion that
dares to question narratives proclaiming the righteousness of a
father requiring the death of his son—whether the son was Isaac
or Jesus. This hermeneutic has led feminist scholars to name the
patriarchal bias of the narratives, including narratives that have
become "seminal"—an apt description of texts written almost
exclusively by men. Yet, the biblical narrative is also in women's

bones and in their memories. This narrative shaped their ancestors' faith as well as their own. Years ago at a conference, I sat in a circle of women and listened as a Roman Catholic sister spoke of opening her prayer book every morning. She had begun to cross out patriarchal words that she could no longer pray. "Sometimes," she said, "I fear that I will open the book and it will be completely blank." Deconstruction and suspicion were not sufficient for the women who gasped when the knife was raised. Patricinio Schweickart poses a perplexing question: "Why," she asks, "do some (not all) demonstrably sexist texts remain appealing even after they have been subjected to thorough feminist critique?"[5]

Are there narrative conversations that open a space for new understandings of texts, including texts that have been "subjected to thorough feminist critique"? Are there forgotten narratives that might be brought into lively conversation with narratives that have been passed down as theologically essential? Some years ago, Rabbi Wenig opened the ancient scrolls and took me to a story I had forgotten in 2 Kings 4. There are four stories in this chapter, but the story about Elisha and the Shunammite woman is by far the longest (2 Kings 4: 8–37). This detailed narrative tells of a woman who insists on restoring the life of her son who has died. This text is one of the longest narratives about women in the Bible.

"Do you read this story in worship?" I asked the rabbi. "We read it every year," she said. This story is appointed as the *haftarah* reading alongside Genesis 18—22." Those stories I knew: the visitors to Abraham's tent, Sarah laughing inside the tent at the news that she will bear a son, the destruction of Sodom and Gomorrah, the birth of Isaac, the banishment of Hagar and Ishmael into the wilderness, and the near-death of the promised son. (How they could read so many powerful stories at one service, I could not fathom.) Why were Genesis 18—22 and 2 Kings 4 placed together? What sort of conversation might take place between them? Could the story of this persistent mother fill in for Sarah's absence in Genesis 22? Could such a conversation take us beyond gasping for breath?

The narratives in Genesis 18—22 and 2 Kings 4:8–37 both begin with hospitality to holiness. Three strangers visit Abraham and Sarah's tent. They are not just any strangers, for the text is clear: "The LORD appeared to Abraham by the oaks of Mamre" (Gen. 18:1). Abraham invites them to come and eat—and gives Sarah the recipe to bake the cakes. This meeting place by the oaks of Mamre has become a holy place. The Shunammite woman also knows holiness when she sees it. She knows that Elisha is a holy man of God and she wants to be near holiness. So she builds a roof chamber where he can stay whenever he comes her way. In the room she places a bed, a table, a chair, and a lamp—a holy place marked with great detail. Even as Abraham invites the three strangers to come and eat, the Shunammite woman invites Elisha to eat and stay.

For generations, the story of the Shunammite woman has been gathered up with other stories in chapter 4 under such titles as "Elisha's Wondrous Deeds." Sometimes, this chapter is placed in the larger context of 1 and 2 Kings as part of "The Elijah-Elisha Cycle." Second Kings 4 echoes 1 Kings 17: both include stories of poor women and overflowing jars of oil. Both move on with stories of an only son raised from death, with Elisha echoing the actions of his mentor Elijah. When we listen carefully to the narrative, we begin to wonder why all the attention is focused on Elisha, who seems to forget what it means to be a holy man of God.

Both Sarah and the Shunammite woman receive the promise of a son. From inside the tent, Sarah hears the words of the holy visitors: "I will surely return to you in due season, and your wife Sarah shall have a son"(Gen. 18:10). The Shunammite woman hears almost the same words from Elisha: "At this season, in due time, you shall embrace a son"(2 Kings 4:16a). Indeed, the Hebrew *ka'et hayya* ("at this time of spring") is found only in these two places.[6] Sarah and the Shunammite woman are connected over centuries of time and many pages of text. What might these two women talk about? Would Sarah say she was so desperate to bear a son for Abraham that she gave her him her maid Hagar to be surrogate mother? Would the woman of Shunem ask what right Sarah had to give her maid away like a piece of property? Would Sarah wonder why the woman of Shunem never asked for a child? What sort of woman doesn't long for a child? Elisha's servant simply assumes that's what she needs. "She has no son," he tells Elisha, and the holy man decides that's exactly what she must want: "At this season, in due time, you shall embrace a son." But she does not laugh as Sarah laughs. She protests: "No, my lord, O man of God; do not deceive your servant" (2 Kings 4:16b). Does she fear being set up for disappointment? Does she not want to be a mother? Elisha never responds. Her protest hangs in the air and the story moves on as though she hasn't said a thing: "The woman conceived and bore a son at that season, in due time, as Elisha had declared to her"(4:17). There is no indication that she laughs as Sarah laughed when Isaac was born. But if she does, her laughter is short-lived, for the narrative moves quickly toward sadness. Her little son becomes ill out in the field. The details of his death are poignant: "Oh, my head, my head!" he cries. The boy's father calls for his servant: "Carry him to his mother" (4:19). Surely she will know what to do, but all she can do is embrace him on her lap. She holds him until noon and then he dies.

Sarah's son doesn't die as a little boy. When he is old enough to be weaned Sarah seems very protective of Isaac, her only son. But Isaac is not Abraham's only son. Is that what troubles Sarah, the notion that Abraham's oldest son, the son of her maid Hagar, is still the favorite? Does she worry that Ishmael will inherit everything? Sarah becomes the bad woman in the narrative, saying to Abraham: "Cast out this slave woman with her son; for the son of this slave woman shall not inherit along with my son Isaac" (Gen. 21:10). Abraham goes along with Sarah's request. Then Sarah disappears. The narrative says nothing more about her until she dies at the age of one hundred twenty-seven years (Gen. 23:1). Where is she when Abraham takes her only son up the mountain?

The Shunammite woman lays her only son on Elisha's bed in the rooftop chamber. She insists on a connection between the holy man and her son—she will not let Elisha forget who he is and what he promised. She will not accept her son's death even though she never asked for his birth. She takes charge, giving orders to her husband. Get the servants. Saddle the donkeys. The text speeds up, but her husband stops the action with his pragmatic question: "Why go to [the holy man] today? It is neither new moon nor Sabbath" (2 Kings 4:23). Does he even ask about his son? Does he wonder if there was any connection between her untimely trip and the boy? We hear only his concern about the time being wrong. A footnote in the Bible explains: "It was considered more propitious to visit a prophet on holy days."[7]

"It will be all right," is all she says. *Shalom* is the word in Hebrew. *Shalom*, the expansive and elusive word. *Shalom*: it is well. *Shalom*: peace to you. *Shalom*: goodbye, I'm leaving. She heeds neither her husband nor the footnote. For her, this *is* a propitious time. "It will be all right," she says. And she heads off to find Elisha on the mountain.

But Sarah doesn't go to the mountain. Where is she on that day when God calls out to Abraham? "Take your son, your only son Isaac, whom you love, and go to the land of Moriah, and offer him there as a burnt offering on one of the mountains that I shall show you" (Gen. 22:2). Is she inside the tent listening? If she hears those terrible words, does she argue with God? "This is not his only son. You know that he has another son. But Isaac is *my* only son and I will not let him be sacrificed to satisfy you." Does she see the servants load the wood on the donkey's back? Does she see the knife in Abraham's belt? Does she kiss Isaac goodbye? On such matters, the narrative is silent. Sarah is nowhere to be seen or heard as Abraham and her only son head for Moriah.

The Shunammite woman does go to the mountain. When she comes near Mt. Carmel, Elisha sees her coming, but he doesn't go to meet her. He dictates a message for his servant Gehazi to deliver: "Are you all right? Is your husband all right?" We gasp, hoping Elisha won't ask the next question. But he doesn't hear us and he doesn't stop: "Is the child all right?" (2 Kings 4:26).

"It is all right," she said. *Shalom*—though there is none.

With that word she rushes past Gehazi as quickly as she had left her husband. Gehazi tries to push her away, for this is not a propitious time, neither new moon nor Sabbath. "Let her alone," Elisha says, "for she is in bitter distress; the LORD has hidden it from me and has not told me" (4:27). Elisha sees her embracing the empty place where her son had been. The truth once hidden is revealed in her body. "Did I ask my lord for a son? Did I not say, Do not mislead me?" (4:28). What can the holy man say? There is no way to escape her question. Yet he hadn't deceived her. She had given birth in due season. That was the end of it for him, but not for her. Her son is lying on the holy man's bed. She will not let him forget his connection to the child. Nor will she let him forget who he is: he is the holy man of God. Surely, now, he will act.

He sends his servant. Is that all Elisha can manage? Of course, he does give Gehazi his own staff—no ordinary stick. The narrative remembers: the staff turned squirming snake in Pharaoh's court, the staff parting the waters of the sea, Elijah's mantle rolled up like a staff making a path through the Jordan and Elisha repeating the action to make sure he could do it, too. "[Go,] lay my staff upon the face of the child"(4:29). But this will not do, not for the Shunammite woman. "As the LORD lives, and as you yourself live, I will not leave without you" (4:30). Like the persistent widow in Jesus' parable, this woman cannot be dismissed. She is the one who makes things happen. She has spoken: "It will be all right." At her insistence Elisha finally leaves his mountain. Soon it becomes clear that it is not all right. Gehazi bears the bad news: "The child has not awakened"(4:31). Yet, Elisha doesn't turn around on the road.

The holy man seems utterly alone as this last scene begins. He goes into the house, up the stairs to the familiar room—the table, the chair, the lamp, the bed—and the little boy lying still. Is Isaac lying still, tied down on the wooden pyre? Elisha's staff is useless. He closes the door. Now it is just the two of them. Abraham tells the servants to stay with the donkey. Now it is just the two of them, Abraham and Isaac alone on the mountain.

Elisha prays. What else can he do? Does Abraham pray as he touches the knife in his belt? Does he think of untying his son and climbing onto the stack of wood? Elisha climbs up on the bed. Gone is every notion of propriety. He puts his own body where his staff had been. His mouth on the child's mouth, eyes upon his eyes, hands upon his hands. The boy's flesh grows warm, but it is not yet *shalom*. Elisha walks around the room, touching the lamp, the chair, the table, then gets up on the bed again. One more time he bends over the boy. The little boy sneezes seven times and opens his eyes. "Call the Shunammite woman," Elisha says to Gehazi. She comes without a word and bows to the ground. "Take your son" (4:36), he says. Then she takes her son and leaves.

There is no way to know if Sarah embraces her only son when Abraham and Isaac come back from the mountain. Does the boy tell his mother all that had happened? Does he still feel the ropes tight around his body even though they are now gone? Is he scarred forever by the sight of his father raising the knife? The narrative doesn't answer such questions, nor does Sarah appear again. Only men come down from the mountain: "So Abraham returned to his young men, and they arose and went together to Beer-sheba; and Abraham lived at Beer-sheba" (Gen. 22:19). There is no mention of Sarah or of Isaac. Does the boy come down the mountain with his father? The narrative is so evasive that over the centuries rabbis have suggested that Isaac is indeed killed and later brought back to life. Perhaps Sarah dies at the shock of it all.

The central narrative of Abraham's willingness to sacrifice his son is now heard in conversation with a marginal narrative about an unnamed woman from Shunem. In both the sons survive—one through the intervention of an angel, the other through the stubborn intervention of his mother. Abraham's obedience to God in offering up his son is reckoned as righteousness. Is the Shunammite woman's insistence on life and *shalom* for her son also reckoned as righteousness?

If we have put the near-sacrifice of Isaac behind us, the narrative won't let us forget. Second Kings 3 ends with the king of Moab surrounded by the troops of Israel and Judah in holy war. In desperation, the Moabite king "took his firstborn son who was to succeed him, and offered him as a burnt offering on the wall" (2 Kings 3:27). The great woman of Shunem interrupts the holy wars of kings and protests the necessary death of sons. *Shalom* will not be martyred. Perhaps, "in due season," God will be worshiped more fully as the God of shalom rather than sacrifice.

Narrative Interruptions

The narrative of the Shunammite woman has not taken center stage in shaping the people of God. Yet, that often-forgotten story has received a hearing alongside the central story of Abraham and Isaac in the Reform Jewish tradition. That placement invites us into a conversation between the two narratives, seeking for a response other than gasping as the knife is raised. Paying attention to where the story of the unnamed woman comes within the canon alerts us to another clue for narrative preaching: the significance of interruptions. As noted above, 2 Kings 3 is a chapter filled with holy war and the Moabite king's sacrifice of his only son on the wall. Without any logical connection, 2 Kings 4 follows with four stories of wholeness and shalom: debts repaid through overflowing pots of oil, a son restored to life through the persistence of his mother, poisoned stew made edible, and barley loaves sufficient to feed a hundred—with some left over.

Interruptions are important in the biblical narrative. The woman of Shunem interrupts the cycle of violence. She stands between a story of warfare in chapter 3 and the warrior Naaman in chapter 5. There are few more pressing needs in our own time than for hearing stories that interrupt holy wars and vicious circles of vengeance. Rahab enters the narrative in Joshua 2 as one brief interruption in a bloody story of conquest. Can her voice be heard now even in our own violent time?

The book of Joshua begins with the people gathering on the far side of the Jordan, preparing to enter the land. Joshua has been called to lead the Hebrew people where Moses was not permitted to go. But it isn't as simple as crossing the river. There is a problem: "the promised land" is not deserted. Canaanites, Jebusites, Edomites, and Hittites live on the far side of the river. They tend flocks, grow grain, and build cities.

The Lord speaks to Joshua: "No one shall be able to stand against you all the days of your life" (Josh. 1:5a), God promises. "Be strong and courageous" (1:6a). "Then Joshua commanded the officers of the people, 'Pass through the camp, and command the people: "Prepare your provisions; for in three days you are to cross over the Jordan, to go in to take possession of the land that the LORD your God gives you to possess."' (1:10–11).

Of course, it's a problem when you get to the promised land and somebody else is already there. There is great anticipation in the camp, for the people have waited forty years for this moment. But there is also tension, because the land beyond the river is not empty. So before crossing the river, Joshua sends out spies: "Go, view the land, especially Jericho" (2:1), he tells them. Find the weak points. Count the troops. See if there is any way to penetrate the city walls. The spies go off. The narrative tells us very little about what they see, but they do see Rahab. The two men slip inside the city and enter the house of Rahab the prostitute. That seems to be her whole name: Rahab-the-Prostitute. She lives on the very edge of the city—her house built into the city wall. She lives in the wall between her people and their people, in a space that divides insiders from outsiders. Which is which? Who is who?

Why do the spies enter that particular house—the house of Rahab the prostitute? Is it God's planning—or their own longing? Perhaps they come to her house first, just inside the gates. Perhaps they know they will hear soldiers' stories at the house of a prostitute. They spend the night. Actually, the Hebrew text says they "lay there"—perhaps mixing business with pleasure.

But the next day the king sends orders to Rahab. (Perhaps he, too, has spent the night in her house.) "Bring out the men who have come to you" (2:3), the king orders. What is she supposed to do? Who is Rahab to defy the king? What is the value of a prostitute who lives in the city wall? In spite of obvious dangers, Rahab takes the two men and hides them on her roof. Then she says: "True, the men came to me, but I did not know where they came from. And when it was time to close the gate at dark, the men went out. Where the men went I do not know. Pursue them quickly, for you can overtake them." (2:4–5).

Even as she speaks, she thinks of the two men up on her roof, hidden among the stalks of flax bundled for drying. What if the king's men insist on searching her house? They take her at her word. Perhaps they know her well. She hears the gate closing as the king's men go out to into the night.

Why does Rahab lie in order to save the lives of two Hebrews? Why did some people lie to hide runaway slaves in the Underground Railroad? Why did some people lie when the Gestapo came knocking at their doors looking for Jews hidden in the attic or under the floorboards? There are times when bearing false witness is the only way to save your neighbor.

But these men on the roof are not Rahab's neighbors: they are outsiders to her, as she to them. Yet on the rooftop of her house the distinctions blur. Rahab has not stood at the foot of Sinai, nor has she been numbered among the tribes of Israel. But her testimony is bold: "The LORD your God is indeed God in heaven above and on earth below" (2:11b). She tells them she has heard what happened at the Red Sea. How could she have heard? Who brought that message to Jericho? Has the God of Abraham and Sarah spoken also to her?

Rahab is a feisty woman—nobody's fool. "Swear to me by the LORD that you will deal kindly with my family," she says. "Give me a sign of good faith that you will spare my father and mother, my brothers and sisters, and all who belong to them" (2:13). Who knows how many that might be? Perhaps she wants to say, "Spare this great city which is my home. Have mercy on all who dwell within the city gates." That must seem more than she can expect, so she asks for what seems possible. Rahab does what she can to gain some kind of assurance that her request will be granted. Before letting them down by a rope from her window, she asks them for a sign. (She learned long ago not to trust the men who came to her house.)

"Tie this crimson cord in the window" (2:18a), they tell her. "Gather all your family in your house in the wall. And you will all be spared" (2:18b, paraphrase). Can she trust them? Will they bother to tell anyone to save the life of a prostitute? She sends them away, then ties the crimson cord in the window—God's own sign of Passover, the blood-red sign on the doorpost. Now the blood-red sign hangs from her window in the wall. Will anyone look for the red cord at the window? We wait, as Joshua's army surrounds the city. Joshua commands the two spies to bring Rahab and her family out of the city. Then they burn the city to the ground, "But Rahab the prostitute, with her family and all who belonged to her, Joshua spared. Her family has lived in Israel ever since" (Josh. 6:25). Like the Hebrews saved by the sign of blood on the doorposts, Rahab is saved by the blood-red cord. The forces of death pass over her house, and the walls between insider and outsider crumble in her presence.

Is that why Rahab is here—to remind us to beware of making distinctions between "insiders" and "outsiders"? She is the first person encountered in the land of promise—a foreigner to the spies, but at home in her own land. Old Testament scholar Danna Nolan Fewell writes: "Rahab's faith and kindness raise serious questions about the obsession with holy war in the book of Joshua. How many Rahabs are killed in the attempt to conquer the land? How many people with vision and loyalty…are destroyed in the attempt to establish a pure and unadulterated nation?"[8]

Joshua 2 belongs to Rahab. Her narrative interrupts the murmuring of warriors preparing for battle. "Be strong and courageous," God tells the people as they prepare to cross the Jordan. A Canaanite woman who shows both strength and courage interrupts the battle plans briefly There's hardly any mention of what the spies discover on their reconnaissance mission: nothing about the number of troops they might encounter, nothing about vulnerable places in the fortress, nothing about the population of Jericho. They give only a brief report; then, Joshua amasses his troops at the edge of the river.

Under the many narratives of battle, of walls that came a-tumbling down and whole cities burned to the ground, Rahab stands watch at her window in the wall. She is remembered for centuries. The New Testament narrative begins with a long genealogy of Jesus' ancestors. The oddest thing about Matthew's list is the four women who appear: Tamar, Rahab, Ruth and Bathsheba. All are suspect for one reason or another. Rahab and Ruth are both foreigners, and the other two are unfairly remembered for sexual relations. The narrative has remembered Rahab and given her a place in Jesus' family tree.

The red thread of Rahab's story is woven throughout the narrative that has shaped the people of God. Without it, we might see only a story of conquest and holy war moving toward the final Armageddon in the book of Revelation. These early days of the twenty-first century have been filled with the sounds of vengeance and violence, often in the name of religion. Reverend Ted Haggard, the now-discredited former pastor of New Life Church in Colorado Springs, is but one of many Christian preachers supporting violent warfare: "'I teach a strong ideology of the use of power,' he says, 'of military might as a public service.' He is for preemptive war, because he believes that the Bible's exhortations against sin set for us a preemptive paradigm, and he is for ferocious war, because 'the Bible's bloody. There's a lot about blood.'"[9]

There is a lot about blood in the Bible, but the blood-red thread draws us to the window where we must see Rahab's face. She bids us be attentive to those who live in the walls of the city, in apartment buildings being bombed into dust. She pleads with those who would conquer in the name of God—for she knows that the Lord is God of heaven and earth and will not be held captive by any nation.

Whenever anyone speaks of "collateral damage," Rahab begs us to see human beings. Still she sits at the window in the Middle East. Can anyone see the red thread at the window, the window dividing insiders and outsiders? Between those who have been promised the land and those who already live in the land?

The red thread must not be forgotten. It is a sign of life saved in the midst of holy war, a blood-red sign tying Hebrew to Canaanite, binding insider and outsider. The voices of hatred are so loud, the cries of mourning never silenced. But there she is at the window calling us to remember, begging us to see. She comes to us now, even after September 11, 2001, inviting faithful people—insiders and outsiders—to sing a new song.

Gasping Is Not the End of the Story

The Shunammite woman and Rahab have not been central to the biblical narrative nor to shaping the community of believers over the centuries. To honor the narratives of these two women is to see a bird beside an elephant. This elephant has loomed large in the formation of Christians and Jews: God calling Abraham to sacrifice his son and God promising victory in battle over enemies. If theological significance is measured by whether men or women are given the most space in the biblical narrative—well, the winner is surely clear. Yet what a wondrous thing it is that the narratives of these women remain in the canon. Not only have these "birds" found a nest in the branches of the biblical tree, but these narratives are remembered in detail. We come to know these women, their persistence and cleverness, their boldness in saving their families, their willingness to push the boundaries. Listening to a conversation between the Shunammite woman and Sarah "in due season" invites a conversation with women who have gasped when the knife was raised and when God's love was defined primarily by the necessary sacrifice of his only Son. Rahab's interruption of battle plans lasts only one chapter, yet she is remembered for centuries and appears in the genealogy of Jesus, who interrupted the murmuring of warriors in his own life. Perhaps this descendent of Rahab remembered the red thread in her window. Perhaps he heard her pleading for the life of her whole extended family—which would eventually include him. Of course, we'll never know such things, but Jesus surely surprised many when he preached his first sermon in Matthew: "You have heard that is was said, 'You shall love your neighbor and hate your enemy.' But I say to you, Love your enemies and pray for those who persecute you" (Mt. 5:43–44).

Gasping must not be the end of the story, because people's lives are at stake. Who knows how many women heard echoes of their own lives when Phyllis Trible directed our attention to stories we didn't want to hear? In her book *Texts of Terror* she spins out in intricate detail the terrifying stories of women who were cast out, raped, mutilated, and offered as sacrifice for victory in battle. There are no happy endings to these stories unless the readers choose to write them. We, the readers, must move beyond gasping at the terror to create life-giving responses. Trible's chapter on the unnamed woman raped and mutilated in Judges 19 is woven throughout with a poignant plea rising within the text itself: "Direct your heart to her, take counsel, and speak." Yet no one ever speaks to her heart, not in the whole biblical narrative nor in the many centuries that have passed since she was brutalized. The narrative remains unfinished:

> Truly, to speak for this woman is to interpret against the narrator, plot, other characters, and the biblical tradition because they have shown her neither compassion nor attention. When we direct our hearts to her, what counsel can we take? What word can we speak? What can we, the heirs of Israel, say in the presence of such unrelenting and unredeemed terror?[10]

This is an urgent call to those who preach—both women and men—to move beyond gasping. "The story is alive," Trible continues, "And all is not well. Beyond confession we must take counsel to say, 'Never again.'"[11] Never again the knife poised to kill a child as the ultimate sign of faithfulness to God. Never again Jesus' life framed only as God's necessary (but loving) sacrifice. Never again the faces of our enemies erased from our minds and hearts. Never again their lives reduced to collateral damage.

"Why go to him today?" her husband asked, "It is neither new moon nor Sabbath." There is a time for such travel, a more propitious time to ask for blessings from the holy man of God. You must follow the rules. You must heed the traditions of the elders. You must know when to speak and when to keep silence. It is neither new moon nor Sabbath, don't you see?

"It will be all right," is all she says.

12

Except in Parables

Preaching the Riddles of Jesus

Mike Graves

NOTICE: Persons attempting to find a "text" in this book will be prosecuted; persons attempting to find a "subtext" in it will be banished; persons attempting to explain, interpret, explicate, analyze, deconstruct, or otherwise "understand" it will be exiled to a desert island in the company only of other explainers.

BY ORDER OF THE AUTHOR

–Wendell Berry, *Jayber Crow*

When the World's Fair came to New York City in 1964, the Protestant Council, a precursor to the World Council of Churches, knew they had their work cut out for them. How, in the shadow of Madison Avenue, could they compete with the other exhibitors? As it turned out, no one could have imagined the attention one of their exhibits would attract, a 22-minute film called *Parable*. Not all of the attention, however, was positive.

The negative public relations came from the film's content, a parable comparing Jesus to a circus clown. Even some ministers and judicatories on the council's board were outraged. Several persons resigned in protest. However, as is often the case with controversy, the protests only served to make the film more popular. Coverage in *Newsweek* and *Time* drew huge crowds to the council's pavilion. The executive director of the council, Rev. Dan Potter, perhaps with tongue in cheek, noted that the film never says a word about Jesus, and he was right, since there is no dialogue. In an interview for *Time,* Potter stated, "Everyone must make up his own mind about it after he has seen it."[1] Years later, *Parable* is still regarded as something of a classic, a rare gem in the history of Christian film-making in which viewers are truly allowed to decide what it means for themselves. As the film's title says, it's a parable.

Most ministers will recall that the Greek word *parabole* covers a wide range of meanings, including riddle.[2] Like the film, the parables of Jesus are open-ended and riddle-like. Everyone must decide for himself or herself. Contrary to popular opinion and many a Sunday school lesson, not all of Jesus' parables are simple stories told so everyone could understand, even the little kids in vacation Bible school. With many, if not most of the parables, the opposite is the case. They are stories from everyday life, but with a twist designed to blow the minds of thinking adults. They could easily be rated R for radical, even revolutionary; but only for those with ears to hear, since they are riddles. According to C.H. Dodd, Jesus' parables are brainteasers. From a rhetorical standpoint, Dodd's definition still functions quite nicely for preachers: "At its simplest the parable is a metaphor or simile drawn from nature or common life, arresting the hearer by its vividness or strangeness, and leaving the mind in sufficient doubt about its precise application to tease it into active thought."[3] While Dodd's descriptors hardly apply to most sermons preached these days ("arresting," "strangeness," "sufficient doubt," "to tease"), these terms do describe some of the parables upon which these sermons are based. Some of the parables are riddles.

By their very nature, riddles change the communication dynamics between parties. Someone offers a riddle, and suddenly the burden for what comes next shifts from the speaker to the listener. Here's a classic riddle: A road in the forest comes to a fork, with one path leading to death and the other to life. Twin boys guard the paths. One always tells the truth and the other always lies. You don't know who is who, and you don't know which boy is guarding which path. You can only ask one question. What question do you ask; and, based on the boy's answer, which road do you then take?

In Dodd's terms, "active thought" is now required. What question *would* you ask? What road would you take? Do you have any guesses? Would you like to know the solution?[4] The communication dynamics change—as Jesus is quoted as saying after many of his parables: "Let anyone with ears to hear listen!" (Mk. 4:9). The riddle-like parables cry out to be solved.

A Tale of Two Ways

There have always been two ways to communicate, what writer Doris Betts calls "shouts and whispers," although clearly the latter path is a road less traveled. Betts maintains that shouted forms of literature are obvious. Their content may be unsettling, but their message is unmistakable. The approach may be simplistic or sophisticated, but shouts are always forthright. Whispered literature is different; whispers are subtle—you have to lean in closer if you want to hear.

Homiletical theory suggests two ways of preaching as well, and the same terms can be applied. Shouts are the more traditional way of sermons, although the designation has nothing to do with the preacher's volume. Shouts are direct forms of preaching in which little, if anything, is left to chance. Not hints, but pronouncements are clearly sounded. The message is clear. Betts quotes Flannery O'Connor, who claimed, "To the hard of hearing you shout, and for the almost-blind you draw large and startling figures."[5] O'Connor fans know exactly what she means, since the encounter with the holy in her stories is never in doubt. There may be twists and turns along the way, but by the end of the story the message often hits you smack upside the head. Same goes for the shouted sermon. Think of the Reformers whose messages never hinted at anything. The message is clear. Period.

But the direct form of communication is only one option. Recall the Lyman Beecher lectures of Fred Craddock, published under the title *Overhearing the Gospel*, in which he takes as something of a text a line from Søren Kierkegaard, "There is no lack of information in a Christian land; something else is lacking, and this is a something which the one man cannot *directly* communicate to the other."[6] If not directly, then indirectly; and, thus, inductive preaching. Whispered sermons are a form of indirect communication, just what we find in many, if not most, of Jesus' parables. Whispered sermons do not so much make pronouncements as suggest possibilities.

While both options seem valid when it comes to literature, choosing between the two would seem obvious when it comes to preaching. Isn't the goal of preaching clarity? Don't even inductive sermons move toward conclusion? In his survey of homiletical literature, Paul Scott Wilson summarizes the matter succinctly, "Preachers use thesis statements to witness to God as clearly as possible in order to equip the saints for ministry."[7] Is there an alternative? Who would dream of offering gospel hints when the possibility exists that listeners may miss our intent altogether? Miscommunication happens often enough in sermons without our promoting it.

True, but as most of us recognize, the synoptic gospels are full of examples in which Jesus (or the evangelist) runs the risk of being misunderstood via parabolic riddles. How, for instance, does a dishonest steward say something about God's reign among us (Lk. 16:1–8)? How does finding buried treasure on someone else's land bear witness to the God movement (Mt. 13:44)? A whole school of thought in homiletics is based in large measure on those parables, namely the New Homiletic.

The Parables as Paradigm

Although the term New Homiletic originated in the late 1960s with David James Randolph's *The Renewal of Preaching,* the movement is typically dated from Fred Craddock's 1971 volume, *As One Without Authority.* Craddock asked, among other things, why should the diversity of literary forms in the biblical witness be ignored and all our sermons look and sound the same?[8] One answer came in 1980, when the modern narrative movement in preaching was launched with the publication of a slew of books, most notably Eugene Lowry's *The Homiletical Plot.*[9] This movement looked to a wide range of narratives–in culture, the preacher's personal experiences as well as the congregation's–but primarily to narratives found in the biblical witness. While Lowry and other proponents of narrative preaching could have looked to the stories sprinkled throughout the Hebrew Scriptures and/or the stories about Jesus that all four evangelists tell, Lowry in particular looked primarily, although not exclusively, to the stories Jesus told, namely the parables.[10] In a sense, the parables of Jesus became and remain the poster child for narrative preaching.

For Lowry, the essential nature of Jesus' parables and, by extension, the essential nature of narrative preaching is ambiguity. In *The Homiletical Plot* he writes, "I was taught to 'tell them what you're going to tell them, tell them, and then tell them what you told them.' Nothing could be more fatal for a sermon!" Or later, "There is one essential in form which I believe indispensable to the sermon event, and that one essential is ambiguity."[11]

Nowhere is this ambiguity more apparent than in Lowry's famous loop, his original five stages of the homiletical plot: upsetting the equilibrium, analyzing the discrepancy, disclosing the clue to resolution, experiencing the gospel, and anticipating the consequences.[12] Ambiguity is writ large over the loop. Consider the popular abbreviations his students developed for these stages: Oops, Ugh, Aha, Whee, and Yeah. For many preachers Lowry's loop breathed fresh air into their predictable preaching styles. The key? Ambiguity.

But while "Oops" and "Ugh" are the language of ambiguity, "Aha" is the language of ambiguity resolved. In a sense, then, *ambiguity* and *resolution* are the two essentials of narrative preaching according to Lowry. As any minister who has heard him speak about narrative preaching can testify, the sermon must move from "itch to scratch."[13] Scratch is not enough; itch is not enough either, since the sermon moves toward resolution as it approaches its conclusion.

There is a big difference, notes Lowry, between a movie plot and that of a typical television series. Movies start with ambiguity and move toward an unknown resolution. When people see the Academy Award–winning *Crash* for the first time, there's no way they can know how it will end. But with a television series like *Law and Order* or *Cold Case*, though the episode begins with ambiguity, viewers can be fairly certain the bad guys will be caught and justice served. Sermons have more in common with the television kind of plot, Lowry says. Viewers know there will be initial ambiguity or else they wouldn't watch. They also know there will be resolution or else the stars would be killed off and the series canceled. Similarly, the plot in narrative sermons involves what Lowry calls an "unknown middle process."[14]

A Newer Homiletic?

But while the New Homiletic has played with indirect forms of communication for decades now, and while Lowry has championed the essential role of ambiguity (and resolution), the riddle-like parables of Jesus rarely conform to so neat a pattern. Granted, the parables typically begin in ambiguity, but they frequently end there too, with what we might call an "unknown ending." This untidiness leads to some interesting homiletical questions: What if some of Jesus' parables suggest a loop more radical than Lowry's own? If ambiguity is the essential nature of narrative preaching, why must the conclusions of our sermons move toward resolution? What about the power of movies with unresolved plots? What about an itch that encourages listeners to do more of the scratching—even of their heads in bewilderment?

As ministers know, many of Jesus' parables do not bring closure. Their open-ended nature can be mind numbing when we ponder them in our studies, hoping a sermon idea will soon germinate. Consider a few examples. In the final movement of the so-called prodigal son story, when the father converses with the older brother, pleading with him to join the party, there is not the slightest hint as to the response of the son. The parable ends on the porch, so to speak (Lk. 15:11–32). Does he go in? Does he stay outside? If so, what happens next?

In Matthew we encounter one of Jesus' many shorter riddle-like parables: "The kingdom of heaven is like yeast that a woman took and mixed in with three measures of flour until all of it was leavened" (Mt. 13:33). End of story, if you call that a story. The reign (*basileia*) of God is like a woman baking an exorbitant amount of bread who mixes leaven into the dough. How so? No commentary is provided, not by Jesus or by the evangelist. No answers in the back of the book like there were in high school algebra. Ambiguity, to be sure, but not much resolution. Upsetting the equilibrium, yes, but what about experiencing the gospel?

Granted, sometimes Luke gives away the parables of Jesus even before we hear them (something Lowry and the New Homiletic never would condone): "Then Jesus told them a parable about their need to pray always and not to lose heart" (Lk. 18:1). But this is how Luke introduces the story some fifty years later, when writing to his community. Did Jesus amend such sayings to his parables? Not likely. Granted, there are parables in which interpretations follow the story, e.g., the allegorical sower and soils (Mk. 4; Mt. 13), but are these explanations the words of Jesus or the work of the gospel writers? Who knows? Even members of the Jesus Seminar might vote differently: Pink? Gray? Red? Black?[15] One thing is certain: there are plenty of parables in which no words of explanation are provided. What would it mean to preach like that? Not always, but on occasion—to tease listeners as parables do, and not just at the beginning of the sermon.

According to the earliest gospel account, Mark concludes the first parables of Jesus with something of a summary: "With many such parables he spoke the word to them, as they were able to hear it; he did not speak to them except in parables, but he explained everything in private to his disciples" (Mk. 4:33–34). Three aspects of this Markan summary are worth noting: (1) Jesus spoke as his listeners were "able to hear" these parables/riddles; (2) he spoke only in parables/riddles; and (3) he interpreted these parables/riddles to his disciples when they were alone. Each merits examination.

The second observation, that Jesus spoke only in parables, is clearly hyperbole, since, as scholars have calculated, the parables of Jesus constitute only about 35 percent of his teachings.[16] What, then, about the other two characteristics? Are modern-day preachers obligated to ensure that people have the ability to hear the parables, or does that depend on the listeners? Are we obligated to explain these ancient riddles? If so, in private only? What difference does it make that we preach to a wide-ranging group of people, many biblically illiterate? What would it mean for ministers to experiment with parabolic sermons that remain parabolic to the final amen? Could a conversation be generated that extends beyond Sunday morning? Why do we preachers think that our sermons must nail everything down?

These are questions I wish to explore, along with offering some practical suggestions for what a truly open-ended sermon might look like (including a sample of such a sermon). But first, the foundational issues.

The Parabolic and Kenotic

In 1965, Frank Kermode delivered a series of lectures later published as *The Sense of an Ending*. He noted the tendency in every age to see the current situation as more dire than any other, and thus, as the end times. He cited as historical example the approach of the year 1000 and the accompanying frenzy. Today we might substitute the year 2000 and all the Y2K computer fears. According to Kermode, this preoccupation with the end of time as we know it, along with our self-centeredness, drives our need for everything to have an ending, even our stories.[17] In his later work, *The Genesis of Secrecy*, Kermode charges humanity with being "pleromatists," those with a tenacious conviction "that somehow, in some occult fashion, if we could only detect it, everything will be found to hang together." This conviction, he notes, resides with the evangelists of the New Testament as well as with us interpreters. We want our endings to wrap things up.[18]

He's right of course; we might as well come clean. We are guilty as charged, pleromatists. The Greek word from which his idiom is drawn means "fullness." We crave completion. We may like our movies and novels with complicated twists and turns, but not in the end. But what if this desire for neat endings belies a sinister side? What if it suggests an insatiable quest to be in control of everything? Perhaps our ancient ancestors conspired together in the garden, imagining that they could eat the forbidden fruit and still not die, even if that was how God said it would turn out. What if this craving for completion in our narratives is a desire to be like God—and even God is not willing to control the ending but is a self-emptying deity?

As students of Greek will recall, the antonym of *pleroma* (fullness) in the New Testament is *kenos* (empty). Ministers recognize the verbal form of *kenos* as the term Paul employs in his Christ hymn, testifying about the one who "*emptied* himself, / taking the form of a slave, / being born in human likeness" (Phil. 2:7, emphasis added).

But this kenotic approach has rarely been the church's first impulse in preaching and teaching. Not hardly. In *Confessing the Faith*, Douglas John Hall notes the church's tendency through the ages to defend itself from the pulpit, a tendency that goes against the example of the church's head, the Christ who forgave even enemies while upon the cross. Hall later adds that while preachers need a certain level of *confidence* (from the Latin, "with faith"), they do not need *certitude* (defined in the dictionary as "freedom from doubt"), which "in preachers is more destructive than in most people, for it gives a falsely secure image of the life of faith and understanding."[19]

Similarly, homiletician David Lose distinguishes between *confession*, a theological enterprise, and *persuasion*, a rhetorical undertaking. It may be, concedes Lose, that our sermons seek to persuade to some degree or another, but in a confessional understanding the end or goal is not nearly so crucial as the impetus—bearing witness to truth.[20] Lose draws on the feminist perspectives of Sonja Floss and Cindy Griffin, and their notion of "an invitational rhetoric." They observe that the traditional aim of persuasion is changing others by exercising control over them, a "rhetoric of patriarchy." An invitational rhetoric, however, seeks not to conquer but to share: "In this mode, then, a story is not told as a means of supporting or achieving some other end but as an end in itself—simply offering the perspective the story represents."[21]

Lose quotes Walter Brueggemann's description of preaching, which includes adjectives typically associated with the parables of Jesus: "playful, open, teasing, inviting, and capable of voicing the kind of unsure tentativeness and ambiguity [Lowry's favorite term] that exiles must always entertain, if they are to maintain freedom of imagination outside of the hegemony."[22] For Lose, the resulting rhetoric is kenotic, a cruciform approach to preaching in which the content, shape, and style of our sermons are more inviting than dominating. And yet, this playful, emptying approach to preaching is at the same time "bold and tentative, both assertive and vulnerable," because in the cross God's power is made manifest. This strength is made known in weakness.[23]

Reading the homiletical work of Lose and others, I think of Parker Palmer's *The Courage to Teach*, which depicts this same dynamic in the classroom.[24] Namely, that it takes great courage to teach, especially if we realize the vulnerability that comes with it. If the teacher (insert "preacher") decides not to be the center of attention but lets the subject instead be the primary focus, then the teacher's role is not only diminished but she/he becomes dependent upon learners to participate more fully. In a classroom students actually join the conversation. In a sermon, perhaps the dialogue that accompanies all good preaching, albeit silently in most places, will continue after the benediction is pronounced.[25]

What would it mean to preach the open-ended parables of Jesus in kenotic fashion, to announce gospel but to leave room for listeners to figure some things out themselves?

Practical Advice for Parabolic Preaching

For years, the late New Testament scholar Donald Juel devoted himself to a study of the ending of Mark's gospel, which in the most reliable Greek manuscripts is hardly an ending at all: "So they went out and fled from the tomb, for terror and amazement had seized them; and they said nothing to anyone, for they were afraid" (Mk. 16:8). The Greek construction is even more shocking: "They said nothing to anyone, they were afraid for…" The end. Juel believed the first gospel's open-endedness was more than technique; it was essential, in fact, to Mark's theology and rhetorical prowess. Juel loved to tell the story of his student, David Rhoads, who performed the entire gospel of Mark for live audiences. Others had done the same, the most famous being Alec McGowan. But McGowan worked from the *King James Version* of Mark's gospel, which ends quite differently. Drawing from a different set of ancient manuscripts, the *King James* ending is all wrapped up, concluding: "And they went forth, and preached everywhere, the Lord working with them, and confirming the word with signs following. Amen." (Mk. 16:20, KJV).

Since Rhoads worked from the shortest manuscripts that stop at verse eight, he had a problem: how do you end a performance with a non-ending? The first time he performed it, the moment simply felt too awkward. The audience sat uncomfortably in the silence that seemed to last forever. Clumsily, against his own scholarly instincts, Rhoads added "Amen." Everyone loved it. Applause. Yes, they seemed to say, this is how gospels should end. But the next time Rhoads did not concede. He left it hanging, the listeners too. He simply walked off stage. The audience knew that if the gospel of Mark was to continue, it would be up to them.[26]

This story serves as vivid reminder of the restraint necessary if we preachers attempt truly open-ended parabolic preaching. It is not easy to leave things hanging. Our instinct is to fill in the narrative gaps. I once read a sermon by a narrative homiletician whose own work in the field has been cutting-edge, but who chose to close an open-ended parabolic sermon with a prayer that brought complete closure. By way of contrast, I've heard Gene Lowry play scales on the piano for a group of preachers, only to omit the final note. You can sing it and accomplish the same dynamic: *do re me fa so la ti*…When Lowry does it, the lack of completion drives listeners crazy. I suspect it's not easy for Lowry either.

How often is such open-ended preaching in order, and when? In the spring of 2006, several weeks prior to Easter Sunday, Barbara Brown Taylor wrote an article for the *Journal for Preachers*. She noted how preachers in workshops love to share sermons that are not yet finished, to preach partial segments and then gleefully announce, "And that's as far as I've gotten." She admitted she's never tried it on a Sunday, so she decided to do it in her article, to share about her Easter sermon in progress. Her initial question caught my attention, "Wouldn't it be wonderful to do that one Sunday?"[27]

I believe there are times in the life of the local church when a series on the open-ended parables of Jesus just might work, although Easter would not be such a time. In all three years of the Revised Common Lectionary cycle, the parables surface mostly during the summer months of Ordinary Time. What if ministers were to experiment with a series of open-ended parables for three or four Sundays? Not every summer, but every once in a while. In the summer of 2006 I did that in my home church while my pastor was on a much-deserved sabbatical leave.

Experimenting in the Church

Since the folks at Saint Andrew Christian Church and I know each other, I decided to see what it would be like for sermons to begin in ambiguity and to end there as well. Saint Andrew is a relatively young Disciples of Christ church started in 1991 by Rev. Holly McKissick, who is still its pastor. Architecture and liturgy blend the transcendent and immanent beautifully, and the service typically reaches its climax in the eucharist. The sermon, midway through the service, is the other pillar of the church's worship. Following the sermon, parishioners observe a brief time of silence before responding in song and partaking of the eucharist. More than five hundred persons attend one of three Sunday morning services every week. The people of Saint Andrew are open-minded, progressive believers. They are the kind of folks who listen regularly to National Public Radio and are committed to social justice. I figured that folks who listen to the Sunday morning puzzle with Will Shorts en route to church might be intrigued by the riddles of Jesus. It seemed the ideal place to try open-ended parabolic sermons.

I decided to limit the series to four weeks. Two sermons came from Matthew—one week from a pair of parables about the hidden treasure and the pearl of great value (13:44–46), and another week from the one about talents (25:14–30). In Mark's gospel, we looked at the parable about a seed growing (4:26–29), and in Luke, the so-called good Samaritan (10:25–37). We promoted the series ahead of time, even printing the modern-day riddle about the two roads in the forest.

Preparing the sermons proved challenging. As ministers know, the parables are deceptively simple on the surface and notoriously difficult at their core. I had studied and preached from parables before, always appreciating the mystery of it all. What preacher doesn't find some kind of perverse pleasure in interpreting a text in which the commentaries begin, "Who knows what this one means?" I have always loved the challenge, and this time was no exception. What was difficult this time was the real possibility that, in my exegetical preparation, I might not arrive at any level of certainty regarding interpretation. Truth be told, we preachers rarely achieve ultimate certainty, but we are quite good at faking it. We study a text the way Jacob wrestled in the night and, like Jacob, we hope a blessing will come. After all, we eventually have to declare something the focus of our message. But with these riddles I entertained the notion that there might be weeks when my uncertainty in the pulpit was not a rhetorical technique but God's honest truth. As R.E.C. Browne wrote years ago, the minister "is not one who has all the answers (or who knows all the relevant questions), [the minister] is one who has the way of answering that leads to further questions."[28] More than once during those four weeks, I said while preaching, "Who's to say what this parable really means? After all, it's a riddle."

Another challenge was respecting the riddle-like nature right through until Sunday and beyond. Lowry, like Craddock, knows how easy it is for preachers who have wrestled with Scripture all week to give it away in the first few moments of a sermon. Lowry suggests that a preacher's focus statement for any given sermon be expressed more in terms of *itch* than *scratch* to keep the sermonic search alive.[29] As a preacher drawn to inductive and narrative styles, I have usually been able to resist the temptation of giving away the sermon's thesis too early. I know the value of an up-front "Ugh," and delaying "Aha." I was accustomed to building suspense into the sermon, but I was also accustomed to giving it away near the end of the sermon, moving more or less through Lowry's stages. Now, however, I would not only need to figure out what the sermon was about but determine how to leave Lowry's loop unfinished. I am more of a "pleromatist" than I care to admit, even if I'm an inductive version of one.

Space does not allow me to say something about each of the four sermons and the learning experiences, for both the congregation and me. But since the idea of an open-ended sermon can remain just that, let me share one of the sermons. Years ago I had been asked to write an exegetical essay on the so-called good Samaritan parable for a journal.[30] At the time I didn't see much point in rehashing what so many others have said about this well-known and well-loved text. Instead, after stumbling upon an alternative reading that I found compelling, I wrote the article exploring that approach. But I never preached from it, never drew upon the alternative interpretation. With this series on the riddles of Jesus, it seemed a good occasion.

An Open-Ended Sample
"What Do You See?"

Luke 10:23–37

Someone has said that flipping through the pages of Luke's gospel is like walking through an art gallery, so many images to see. Oh sure, all the gospels are full of images, but Luke's impact on art is well-known. Or maybe the gospel of Luke is more like a slide show. Can you picture this first-century evangelist, sandaled-feet, with a remote in hand? I don't mean a PowerPoint display; this is an ancient writing, after all. I'm thinking more of those older carousels with the slides you put in, the kind your parents and grandparents had for sharing scenes from summer vacation. Those actually date back to Luke's time. So Luke clicks the remote and says, "Yeah, now this one is the story of a woman who lost a coin and had to sweep around the house until she found it." Then he clicks—on to the next picture.

In today's reading, there are two images on the screen. Not exactly a split screen, but close. Two stories—the frame story and the picture story. The frame story is the one Luke tells about Jesus and the lawyer; it's the context for the second one. The picture story is the parable Jesus tells inside the frame story, the one he tells the lawyer. As for the frame story, this is how it goes: An expert in the law is looking to test Jesus. So he asks, "What must I do to inherit eternal life?" Jesus knows the answer. So does the man. It's a test though, in how to read the law. Sounding like a modern-day law professor, Jesus turns the quiz back on the expert: "What's written in the law? How do you interpret it?" And sounding like a brilliant law student, the man recites a passage from Deuteronomy and one from Leviticus, never missing a beat: "You shall love the Lord your God with all your heart, with all your soul [in other words, your whole being]…; and your neighbor as yourself" (10:27). Jesus gives the man an A for his answer and says, "Do this and you will live." End of class.

But it's probably not what the expert in the law had in mind, his being quizzed and it being over so quickly. Besides, there was this tricky little loophole in Jewish law about the definition of neighbor. You know—Is my neighbor the woman across the street who never mows her grass? Are the citizens of Baghdad my neighbors? What about the man in front of Barnes and Noble, the one with a cup of spare change? Is my neighbor the person in church who really gets on my nerves? Who is my neighbor? So wanting not to lose face, the man asks one more question, "And who is my neighbor?" That's when the frame story gives way to the picture story, the parable Jesus goes on to tell.

It seems that a traveler was going down from Jerusalem to Jericho, a most dangerous route. People could have warned him this would happen. I remember a few years ago traveling to San Francisco with colleagues from the seminary. We stayed in a really nice hotel there in downtown, not far from Fisherman's Wharf. The first night we asked if it was safe to walk in that neighborhood. They said it was perfectly safe to walk even at night, except not to go left out the front doors. We could walk across the street. We could turn right. Just don't turn left, they said. In Jesus' day, the route from Jerusalem to Jericho was like a left turn out of the hotel. Dangerous.

Well, true to the area's reputation, Jesus describes this traveler as being jumped by thieves, who take his belongings, beat him up, and leave him for dead in a ditch on the side of the road. The poor guy doesn't seem to stand a chance of surviving, but Jesus introduces some characters who come upon the man. The first is a priest, but he passes by, perhaps not wanting to defile himself. Jewish law in Jesus' day was pretty clear on that. Can you see the expert smiling at this point? The second passerby is a Levite, but he too steers clear so as to remain pure. The third traveler feels compassion, bandages the man's wounds, puts him on a donkey, takes him to an inn, and cares for him—before leaving his credit card in case the bill should add up to something. And Jesus, who gets to make up all the details in his story, says this man was a Samaritan, the despised half-breeds of first-century Judaism. Somehow, I don't think the lawyer was smiling at this point, although Luke's community may have been some fifty years later when they first heard it.

What a shocking end to Jesus' story, a Samaritan as hero; but it's not the end of Luke's frame story. Jesus turns to the expert in Jewish law and says, "You wanted to know who your neighbor is. Well, which one of these three travelers do you think was a neighbor to the stranger?" Suddenly, this polished law student stammers a bit, "Well, uh, the uh, (he can't bring himself to say the word *Samaritan*), the uh, the one who showed mercy." "That's right," says Jesus. "Go and do likewise."

That's the last line of the story, "Go and do likewise." Maybe those are red letters of Jesus, or maybe the black letters of Luke, but either way it says, "Go and do likewise." And you thought studying the Bible was hard work. There's no need to sit around in Sunday school class and debate this passage. "Go and do likewise." I don't know why we even need Bible studies. The moral is clear enough, "Go and do likewise." Well, I guess we could sit around and debate who the Samaritans are in our day, you know, the despised of our times, but once we've figured that out, it's, "Go and do likewise."

Most of us like morals to our stories. They help us order our lives. We don't like to leave the theater scratching our heads, muttering amongst ourselves, "So what do you think that was about?" We like morals with our stories. You remember those Aesop's Fables, don't you? The persistent tortoise and that frivolous hare, but look who wins. The moral of the story is, "Go and do likewise." And here it is in the Bible, "Go and do likewise." Build hospitals and name them Good Samaritan. Fund halfway houses and food pantries, and name them Good Samaritan. Put laws in the books about helping folks in need, Good Samaritan laws. "Go and do likewise."

There's only one problem. Do you see it? It's a question John Dominic Crossan asked of this parable more than thirty years ago. Namely, why are we still trying to figure out who the Samaritans are that we need to help if it's the Samaritan in the story who plays the hero? If this were a fable on being neighborly to "those kind of people," shouldn't the man in the ditch have been a Samaritan?

Have you ever heard of the Nora Fragment? It's one of the oldest pieces of writing in the world. It's housed in a museum on the Mediterranean island of Sardinia. It's just a fragment, with only a few markings inscribed on it, but tourists come from all over the world to see it. Scholars, too, trying to decipher it. A few years ago one of those scholars wrote a note to the curator, "I don't want to offend anyone, but the fragment is upside down." All these years they had it upside down.

Do you think we've had this parable upside down? I don't mean to make you dizzy, but is it possible we've misread it? All those years in Sunday school debating who our Samaritans are, when it may have been our approach to parables that needed attention. The parables of Jesus are riddles. They're not like the rules posted at public swimming pools: "No running. No horseplay. No glass containers. No having fun." The parables of Jesus are riddles, not rules. Interpreting the parables of Jesus is like trying to nail Jell-O to the wall. They're slippery, evasive. They require keen vision. In fact, one scholar has suggested that when it comes to parables, the idea is not so much to interpret them, but to let them interpret us.

So what do you see? The reason I ask it that way is because of Luke's stress on seeing, both in this parable and its context. In the parable seeing is key. The priest *sees* the man and crosses to the other side. The Levite *sees* the man, too, but crosses to the other side. The Samaritan, however, when he *sees* the man, has compassion. There appears to be a different kind of seeing going on. So we have this picture story in the context of a frame story, all of which occurs in a larger context, which is to say that prior to this passage Jesus says to his disciples in 10:23, "Blessed are the eyes that see what you see!" If it helps, imagine that verse inscribed on a brass plate next to these pictures from Luke's art gallery. "Blessed are the eyes that see."

So what do you see? If this were a parable on being neighborly to outcasts, why does an outcast serve as hero to the man in the ditch? What kind of parable is this, outcasts that see better than us religious folks? Every time I go to Country Club Plaza, whether it's to the Nelson Art Gallery or to eat with my family, there's always this one man in front of Barnes and Noble. Maybe you've seen him. You have to look. It's easy to miss him. He usually sits on a bucket turned upside down. He has a cup with some change in it. He doesn't ask for handouts, just sits there quietly waiting for mercy. And the times when I or the kids have obliged, he says the same thing. I've heard other people on the streets say it as well. I've even heard people in the churches say it, but it sounds different on the streets. He says, "God bless you." That's what he says. "God bless you." Now who is he to be blessing me in the name of God?

David May, my New Testament colleague at the seminary, was telling me that he uses slides in his classes from time to time—you know, as a way to teach the Bible, Luke's gospel, or what have you. Maybe a picture of the kind of coin that woman might have lost. Or some archaeological find. A map of ancient Palestine. That sort of thing. He said every once in a while during a lecture, one of the slides is upside down. If you know anything about slide projectors, there's nothing you can do right away to fix it. David usually laughs, then says, "If you turn your head like this... If you'll just cock your head, try to..." Imagine that, asking people to turn upside down to see.

Turns out, that's what the gospel demands if we're really going to see. Only, in this parable it may well be that the key to this riddle in Luke's gospel is not just the identity of the helper, a Samaritan; but the identity of the man in the ditch. I know, it just says "a man." "A man was going down from Jerusalem to Jericho..." I know, but listen to how he is described: he falls among thieves; he is stripped; they take his garment; he is beaten; he is rejected by the religious establishment; and he is ministered to by outcasts. Who is that man in the ditch, and what's he doing there?

Concluding Reflections

Several parishioners commented on an interpretation that ran counter to any they had ever heard. Some were shocked, some confused, some delighted. As for the issue of the sermon's open-ended nature, so far as I know, only one gentleman didn't pick up on the subtleties. He asked, "Okay, I don't get it. Who was the man in the ditch?" I had wondered if the ending had been too obvious, giving away the riddle. Evidently not. I said to him, "What if the man in the ditch was Jesus himself?" His eyes lit up and he went away clearly intrigued.

Of course the parables of Jesus are intriguing by their very nature. For weeks after the series was over people were discussing the parables. Like riddles themselves, they create interest. Remember the one about the two roads in the forest? More than a month after the series was over people were still wrestling with it. Here it is again: A road in the forest comes to a fork, with one path leading to death and the other to life. Twin boys guard the paths. One of them always tells the truth and the other always lies. You don't know who is who, and you don't know which boy is guarding which path. You can only ask one question. What question do you ask, and based on the boy's answer, which road do you then take?

13

Convoking Spirit-ed Conversation

Narrative Preaching, Epistolary Literature, and Moral Discernment

DAVID J. SCHLAFER

My faculty colleague was the quintessential contrarian. In his classes (always conducted Socratically), the devil never wanted for an advocate. He took his predilections into the seminary chapel pulpit, where (not unpredictably) he had "issues" with the very notion of preaching at the eucharist. "I'm always under pressure 'to preach to the Table,'" he complained. "Everyone expects that whatever questions a sermon raises, they must all be resolved prior to the eucharistic prayer. I want to pose—and the church needs to deal with—complex matters of faith and practice that can't be settled by the end of a sermon so that it can 'point' toward a celebration of communion."

Richard Lischer's searching early critique of narrative preaching as "telling the story" deeply resonates with my colleague's concern: "[A] story is a plot whose episodes and complications are directed toward a conclusion, usually a resolution... Such a shape does not always reflect the way things are but mercifully—or arrogantly— imposes a pattern on the disorder and anarchy of life as it is."[1]

Lischer advances a further implication of this claim: "Theology lives by story, but without more precise modes of conceptualizing and interpreting, theology is reduced to repetition or recital and loses its power and flexibility to address new situations."[2]

Then, challenging the assumption he finds latent in a simplistic understanding of narrative preaching—that "one size fits all," he arrives at a provocative conclusion: "It can be argued that story does not provide the resources for implementing ethical growth or socio-political change. Stories may be the inspiration for change and set the tone or historical background for change, but they are not equipped to make the kinds of discriminations necessary for informed ethical decisions."[3] (It may not surprise you to learn that my faculty colleague was a moral theologian.)

What place does narrative preaching have in one of the most challenging tasks that preachers face: fostering moral discernment from the pulpit? If "three points and a poem" will not suffice here (any more than in other sermons); neither will "make them laugh, make them cry, make them feel religious" by means of compelling stories depicting surprising advents of "amazing grace." Salvation may come, as the apostle Paul claims, by grace through faith rather than via law and works; but how does the Christian community "work out" this salvation "with fear and trembling" (as he also says)—particularly when it must continually address complex, conflicted, and urgent moral issues?

However preachers negotiate their way through the theological issues of law and grace, faith and works (or the text of Galatians in relation to that of James), the bottom line of their "Christian moral responsibility" sermons often comes down to some variation on, or combination of the following:

- Edicts–*"This we must do!"* (statements of necessary moral stance or action)
- Rebukes–*"Shame on us!"* (censures for lapses and transgressions)
- Sentences–*"We are toast!"* (pronouncements of impending punishment)
- Analyses –*"The problem involves…"* (examinations, theological and empirical)
- Exhortations–*"By God, we CAN!"* (infusions of motivating inspiration)

- Platitudes–"*If only we would...*" (expressions of lofty ideals)
- Big Pictures–"*God is acting to...*" (claims regarding ultimate perspective)

To characterize these seven approaches so summarily (almost as cartoons) is not to disparage a single one. There are biblical illustrations aplenty of each; and all of these preaching forms, appropriately shaped, in the proper setting, have a valid place in Christian preaching.

Edicts, for instance, are appropriate when decisive intervention is urgent. Rebukes are called for when repentance is in order. Sentences, alas, as Jeremiah discovered to his anguish, are occasionally essential as preludes to moral restoration. Analyses are required in the midst of complex issues, conflicting data, and contentious disagreements. Exhortations have great value when moral resolve is lacking. Platitudes, even pious abstractions, sometimes help remind a community of its identity. Big Pictures are essential for grounding difficult, even tragic choices and actions in the sustaining context of God's enduring covenant love.

Storytelling can be employed strategically in any of these preaching projects—as can inductive preaching methods generally. Careful attention to the importance of narrative plotting, in every case, can make the difference between a preacher's doing time and *doing time* in the pulpit (as Eugene Lowry's title says so nicely).[4] Yet all these sermon forms have a significant common factor—whatever the moral work involved in preparing and delivering them, whether this involves deploying moral reasoning (Analysis), for example, or announcing moral conclusions (Edict), or encouraging moral action (Exhortation)—the preacher does the work for, or on behalf of, the congregation. The results of a preacher's effort need not be dictatorially deposited; the preacher may neither intend to issue an unexceptionable authoritarian word, nor be perceived as attempting such. Yet the authority and responsibility of the pulpit (to say nothing of the social givens of preaching in a worship setting) seem to suggest, however subtly, that the preacher will function as moral community spokesperson (certainly), mentor (probably), perhaps even as adjudicator ("The Decider") for a community of faith.

By expressing appreciation (or disapproval) to the preacher's face (or behind the preacher's back), by voting with their feet (either by following where the preacher's words lead, or by walking off in the opposite direction) the congregation is making its "response" to the preaching event. In none of the sermon types noted above, however, are listeners regularly, if ever, provided generous space, generative nurture, and vocational challenge to make, on their own (as Lischer says), "the kinds of discriminations necessary for informed ethical decisions."

Yet the work of moral discernment, particularly in settings of moral crisis and moral quandary, cannot be done to or for a community—any more than an orchestra conductor can "do" a symphony, or an athletic coach can play "for" a team in a competitive sporting contest. No preaching act or sermon series, regardless of how effective, can produce the practice of community moral discernment; communities must do it. And while they can be mentored in the midst of it, they can only "learn by doing." How can narrative preaching, with or without stories, foster a community in such a journey? Moral crisis—moral quandary—what are these, exactly?[5]

The most common connotation of "crisis," in American culture, anyway, is (as the *Merriam-Webster Dictionary* puts it): "a paroxysmal attack of pain, distress, or disordered function." (9/11 was nothing if not such a "crisis.") Yet this definition masks a more fundamental meaning of crisis: "a vitally important or decisive stage in the progress of anything, a turning point" (as the *Oxford English Dictionary* puts it)—roads diverging, one of which must, of necessity, be chosen.[6] Such choices, made reactively in the wake of 9/11, have shown, particularly in retrospect, that the crisis involved in the terrorist attacks was far deeper than the initial shocks of pain and loss of pride it produced.

A quandary is a dilemma—one wherein whatever choice we make comes with an inevitable high cost. The "lesser of evils" is still evil; the "greater good" involves the sacrifice of other goods that are precious indeed. A moral crisis involving a moral quandary, this is a decision from which, as individuals and communities, we instinctively shrink back, and yet to no avail, for sooner or later to refrain from choosing is to have chosen. Instinctively and by long conditioning, we want our preachers to tell us what we should do in the midst of moral crises and quandaries—if only so that we can disagree with them.

How can preaching, particularly narrative preaching, support the community of faith in making hard choices having no unambiguously "right" answers? Choices concerning the protection of civil liberty in the face of terrorist threats, choices about how to protect the environment in the midst of economic development necessary for eradicating desperate poverty, choices over allocation of limited resources for health care and medical research, choices involved in caring for the elderly and the unborn, choices concerning political and ecclesiastical policy in hotly contested debates over deeply held convictions regarding sexuality? In such crises and quandaries, none of the "Christian moral responsibility" sermon categories named above can provide clear answers, let alone assistance to communities involved in making (to invoke Lischer's line once more) "the kinds of discriminations necessary for informed ethical decisions."

Narrative preaching is drawn to, and explicitly honors, the notion of "salvation history"—the record of "those mighty acts by which [God] has given us life and immortality,"[7] a record in which God is continually represented as "on the move" in effecting the world's redemption. If the gospel is set forth in preaching as a series of static propositions, then the "New Homiletic" correctly claims that the medium and the message are at variance. Narrative preaching theorists (of whom Lowry is a stellar example) insist, therefore, that to be true to the gospel, the sermon event must embody the journey—the high drama of salvation history, deployed across the sweep of scripture: from bondage to freedom, from darkness to light, from death to life.

So far, so good. From the garden of Eden to the New Jerusalem, God keeps making the hard choice of reaching out in saving love, no matter what (however theologically construed), to refashion the created order so that, in time, the reign of righteous peace will come "on earth, as it is in heaven." But how do preachers move from that, by some route other than the standard "moral responsibility" sermon strategies cited, to mentoring the hard choices mere mortals need to make?

A case can be made for another kind of narrative in play throughout scripture and Christian tradition. In addition to "salvation history" narratives, there also are what we might term "narratives of communal discernment," stories of our faith family ancestors who wrestle with moral crises and quandaries. In these narratives they attempt thereby to earth the narrative of salvation history in their struggles to discern, with "fear and trembling," how the reign of God can effectively unfold in the life of communities who seek to be faithful, and who know, in the midst of their fumbling attempts to get it right, that "God is not finished with them yet." Sometimes these communal discernment narratives are presented directly as stories—the midwives' disobeying the Pharaoh's order to slay the infant sons of Hebrew women (Ex. 1), Samuel's anointing of David as king of Israel (1 Sam. 16), Solomon's adjudicating the contradictory claims to motherhood of two women (1 Kings 3), Ruth and Naomi's weighing of conflicting mores in different cultures, Esther's discerning—with Mordecai's help—how to protect her kindred.[8]

The book of Acts is replete with communal discernment stories, some told in detail. Each involves accounts of those involved making difficult discriminations and "hard calls":

- The donating of possessions by Barnabas and by Ananias and Sapphira (4:32—5:11)
- The dispute over food distribution to Hellenistic widows, and its resolution in appointing "The Seven" (6:1–7)
- The baptism of the Ethiopian eunuch by Philip—without apostolic warrant (8:26–40)
- The engaging of Saul (persecutor presenting as convert) by another Ananias, Barnabas, and the believers in Damascus (9:10–31)
- The noonday vision of Peter, his visit with Cornelius, and his defense in Jerusalem about eating with uncircumcised Romans (10:1—11:18)
- The deliberations of the Jerusalem Council over whether Gentiles were to be welcomed into the body of Christ without first becoming Jews (15:1–41)
- The sermons of Paul at Phillipi, Athens, Jerusalem, and Caesarea (chapters 16, 17, 21—22, and 24, respectively), in which he does not tell his listeners off, but invites them into reflective dialogue through an orderly interaction between the conditions he finds and the claims of the gospel)

The parables and teaching of Jesus in the gospels, in the wider, more firmly established paradigm of salvation history, are often treated as images, stories with "morals," or as straightforward moral exhortations, or injunctions. Yet, assuming that these accounts of the life of Jesus are, in the voices of their writers, sermons of a sort, it is possible to hear these words of Jesus as evocative invitations, in light of the oncoming reign of God, to patient, carefully discriminating communal moral judgments. (Matthew 13 is an excellent case in point.)[9]

What, then, of epistolary literature? From the vantage point of narrative preaching (particularly the kind Lischer calls into question), it tends, as a genre, to be regarded (with the faintest of enthusiasm) as the setting forth of "points" concerning Christian belief and practice, rather than as the kind of engaging, bewildering, open-ended adventures found in the stories of salvation that fill the gospels and punctuate the Old Testament.[10] While the historical context of these letters is acknowledged as important (insofar as it can be critically established), that is usually employed only as "background" for sermons on epistle texts—mentioned in the sermon, if at all, merely as a frame of reference. Best to find a story that *embodies* the point abstractly stated if one has to preach from an epistle text!

But what if the epistles could be read as "narratives of communal discernment"—as attempts not necessarily or exclusively to present edicts, exhortations, or big pictures, but to convoke Spirit-ed conversations among communities faced with moral crises and quandaries? This is not to imply that reading the epistles through such a lens is the only or even the preferred reading, but that fostering moral discernment is an essential element in epistle literature. The New Testament letters are not simply treatises on "salvation by grace through faith," "kenosis," or "logos christology"—with moral exhortations attached. If this alternative can be entertained, then what might contemporary preachers—even narrative preachers—learn from their elder preaching colleagues? After all:

- Romans *is* about "salvation by grace through faith" and "presenting [our] bodies as a living sacrifice." Yet it is also Paul's attempt to help a community negotiate its way toward a corporate vocation when the respective theological and moral credentials of Jew and of Gentile are guardedly regarded, each by the other.

- The Corinthian correspondence *is* about "love," "resurrection," "many members in one body," and "apostolic authority." It also seeks, however, to bring a vision of corporate Christian living to bear on patterns of power politics, economic inequity, and social discrimination.
- Galatians is a ringing call to freedom in Christ—a kind of freedom fostered by disciplined moral formation cultivating "the fruit of the Spirit."
- Philippians is about a self-emptying Christ whom God has exalted and about the possibility of joy in the face of adversity; it also concerns faithful folk who have had a serious falling out.
- Ephesians and Colossians are about "high christology" and citizenship in heaven; they also seek to bear responsible witness in a first-century social order.
- Hebrews paints a panoramic vision of a Great High Priest who is nonetheless able to sympathize with human weaknesses; it also labors to foster practical strategies of mutual love, many specifically addressed to the needs of those who themselves suffer "outside the camp."
- The pastoral epistles depict the Christian vocation as "God's own people" called to "proclaim the mighty acts of him who called [them] out of darkness into his marvelous light" (1 Pet. 2.9); they also press the early church to deal with details both of forming Christian households and exercising citizenship in civil society.

Part of the difficulty in accessing the energy of epistolary texts involves how they appear in various lectionaries (or don't). The adventure in discernment on which epistle authors seek to lead their listeners often spans much of, if not the entire, letter. Oral reading of extended sections requires inordinate service time in regular worship—far exceeding the attention spans of most listeners. On Sundays, therefore, congregations hear what lectionary framers deem a letter's "high points" of doctrine or exhortation. If, however, epistles *are* narratives of communal discernment—sermonic attempts to *mentor* moral discernment by *mirroring* it—then brief epistle excerpts inevitably leave out most of the discernment fostering journey that unfolds across the argument of the entire epistle.

While sermon series on the epistles are sometimes presented, especially by preachers in traditions that do not use lectionaries, the effect is often of didactic summation—hardly an enacting of the discernment fostering narrative itself. Furthermore, few preachers can count on a congregation consistently present and "tracking" week after week for the duration of a sermon series. Thus it is important for preachers to steep themselves in the discernment drama unfolding across the entire piece of correspondence; and, in individual sermons, to "play," as appropriate to each particular sermon plot, what is at issue and at stake for listeners, both original and contemporary. What might that look like? Here is one illustration of a possible direction.

The irony (and often the tragedy) in the work of reconciliation is that calls for reconciling sound irrelevant until they are urgently needed, and then they seldom work. Even the notion of convening a fruitful conversation on reconciliation is problematic. Genuine conversation tends to shut down when fault lines develop within communities, each side holding fast to a "truth" deemed incompatible with the other's "truth," each resolving the quandary in a way that contradicts the other's. Paul faces such a situation in the congregation at Philippi. A rift has developed. Two prominent participants have fallen out (each probably surrounded by supporters).

Paul addresses the conflict in Philippi by means of indirection, confronting it without being confrontational, weaving words of healing grace back and forth across a broader theological tapestry, slowly but deftly bringing everyone on board, painstakingly marking out the common ground on which all stand—even though they seem oblivious to the fact.

- "I am confident of this, that the one who began a good work among you will bring it to completion by the day of Jesus Christ" (Phil. 1:6), Paul says in an opening doxology, having noted how the community has been continually "sharing in the gospel."
- Sketching the challenges he faces, Paul expresses his desire to visit them, encouraging them (as a seeming aside) to live lives "worthy of the gospel" so that, even if he only gets reports secondhand, he will know they are "standing firm in one spirit, striving side by side with one mind for the faith of the gospel" (1:27).

- Warming to his theme (and playing several variations), he sings a song of high and humble christology—their *same* mind will be engendered by letting *this* mind be in them which was in Christ Jesus (2:1–10).
- This saving mindset, he continues, is a treasure they must steward "with fear and trembling"—not because they are under threat, but because they have been touched where they live with power from on high (2:12–16).
- *Via* spiritual autobiography, Paul illustrates what is entailed in Christlike humility, its costs and its challenges (chapter 3).
- Naming the primary parties in conflict, he urges them to be "of the same mind," invoking the aid of the community in the work of reconciliation (4:1–3).
- "Finally" (having signaled its importance before), Paul sweeps the community into sheer rejoicing, then gives some practical advice about staying centered in doxology: look for, and name in each other, whatever is true, honorable, just, pure, pleasing, commendable, excellent, and worthy of praise (4:4–9).
- He thanks them for their generosity and registers his trust that God will provide for their needs (4:19).

What might preachers appropriate from Paul about convening conversations concerning reconciliation when the issue cannot be swept under the rug just by "making nice" or asking rhetorically, "Can't we all just get along?" How, in other words, can the community be preserved so that its difficult discernment process can continue—both unbounded and unsquelched by a single worship service (or even those conducted over weeks, months, even years)? Here are some strategic possibilities:

- Identify—fissures notwithstanding—what are common values and commitments.
- Depict an undergirding theological frame of reference—preferably in ways that "sing" rather than expound—ways that engender imagination, that call forth prayer and worship as the necessary spiritual context for moral discussion and debate.
- Remind all concerned that hard questions must be "worked out with fear and trembling," since what is at stake in how

the issue is addressed is of greater concern than the issue itself.

- Make liberal use of engaging case studies in spiritual cost, conflict, and challenge.
- Address specifics evenhandedly, nonjudgmentally, communally.
- Provide focus for continuing interchange, through appreciative truth-telling rather than polemical mud-slinging.
- Affirm the centrality of prayer and worship as a wellspring of spiritual energy for the work of reconciliation.

Paul does not toss out these strategies indiscriminately. He carefully plots them. (He had, after all, read Eugene Lowry's most recent books.) Contemporary preachers cannot simply mimic Paul's outline or method, but they can creatively emulate it. In other words, Paul's preaching *form* may be as, or more, relevant in preaching toward discernment as his *content*—especially because we are not even told what the conflict in the church at Philippi entailed.

The challenge of preaching reconciliation involves proclaiming and evoking the larger purposes we share, the mind of Christ. It is also entails bearing one another's burdens and coming together to rejoice in the life of faith. All these are important, but reconciliation requires more. Needed reconciliation presupposes a persistent rift. It does not always mean coming to agreement—an impossibility when consciences are deeply divided. The divide over moral judgments about homosexuality in mainline Protestant churches, for instance, is a given. The quandary is not what to do, but what reconciliation might mean in the face of intractable division.

What if we applied some of Paul's theological and homiletical insights to the sharp divisions Christians currently encounter regarding homosexual orientation, focused through an understanding of what is involved in seeking reconciliation? Here is one way (summarized not as an outline of points, but as a sketch of plot moves in sequence).

1. Have you ever found yourself trying to referee a long-standing disagreement between folks whose opposing convictions were sincerely and firmly held? Not a spat between greedy grandchildren fighting over who inherits what, but a battle between self-sacrificing patriots, each with political philosophies

so alien as to envision the demise of the nation at the adoption of the other? Talking doesn't help; ignoring the issue doesn't make it go away; mediation seems impossible; and a stand off on the issue could bring the nation to a standstill. That's Paul trying to talk to the Philippians.

2. Such disagreements, especially when acted out destructively, seem so pointless. But not if you are one of the disputants. So much is at stake, and it is virtually impossible "not to take it personally." What if we lived in Philippi, your name was Euodia, mine was Syntyche; and we had been trying to dance our way around whatever it was for years and years?

3. Names and places change; issues do as well. Conflict dynamics don't. What if Paul found himself trying to referee our deep divisions with regard to same-sex marriages—each side quoting scripture at the other, each praying that the other side would come to understand that "thy will be done" means "*my* will be done." What might Paul suggest we do when what is essential for some folks is not an option for others?

4. We gather together (on opposite sides of the room) hoping he will set the other side straight, or that he will introduce considerations none of us have previously considered (after all, we're open-minded). Or maybe we are resigned to hear from him what preachers tend to do—shame all sides into silent submission.

5. But—what's this? He's starting to sing. And he can barely manage to carry a tune. This is embarrassing. And irrelevant. This is what we already deeply know (an utterly lovingly, condescending Christ), and what we long to be (standing side by side in partnership with the gospel). But to what good? It is theology that does not touch our conflict.

6. Paul nods in recognition to our objection but seems to disregard it. Instead, he motions us to join in singing—first about a humble and exalted Christ, but then about one another. He's signaling us out, one after another, for solo parts—but parts in which we are required to sing the virtues of those with whom we disagree.

7. Paul probably *won't* show up in person to host a parish sing-a-long. But suppose that, before we sat down to debate the issue one last time, to take a vote about who, if we split, will end up with what…suppose we were not allowed to begin that

meeting before we were all locked up in the church—every last one of us—and not allowed to leave, or even say another word, until we had sung together for a solid hour?

8. And once we have sung—not "sung our hearts out," but sung our way *into* our hearts and closer to the Heart of the Self-Emptying One—what then will we want, and need, to ask ourselves? Perhaps questions like these:

- How and where have we stood shoulder to shoulder in service of the gospel? What has that taught us about what we have in common—and where we differ?
- How have we each found challenge and borne cost in bearing witness to the gospel through our respective understanding of sexuality as gift and discipline?
- Where, in our own attempts to work out our own salvation through advocating and defending, are there reasonable grounds for "fear and trembling"?
- If we separate from one another for the sake of witness to the gospel or if we stay together for the sake of the gospel, how will we be with one another? Can we respect each other in our differences? What can and should we still do together?
- Each of us in this conflict appeals to certain biblical texts as a basis for, or justification of, its stance regarding the moral crisis and quandary created by our divided mind over homosexuality. How do our "proof texts" appear in light of Paul's "doxological theology"?

This fixes nothing, because it seeks something else—to foster a process in the face of crisis and quandary, rather than to finalize, and perhaps *fossilize,* a fragile human interpretation of "God's will."

Let's look at one more example, drawing on familiar passages in the epistles that seem to speak clearly regarding Christian responsibility in the political order. The author of 1 Peter takes what is often regarded as an authoritarian approach to social arrangements at several levels: citizens, submit to the emperor; slaves, submit to masters; wives, submit to husbands. Taken out of context as abstract injunctions, each of these can be highly problematic. These moral injunctions sound different, however, when set in the context of the narrative of discernment unfolded across the letter and in conversation with the whole of the New Testament.[11]

The challenge of engaging both those within the household of faith and those beyond its doorway is framed in the context of being "a chosen race, a royal priesthood, a holy nation, God's own people, in order that you may proclaim the mighty acts of him who called you out of darkness into his marvelous light" (1 Pet. 2:9). Membership in such a realm inevitably involves being "aliens and exiles" (1 Pet. 1:17, 2:11) in relationship to the powers that be. This requires bearing clear witness to another way of being—a different kind of household, the household of God. Such witness will inevitably lead to suffering—suffering inflicted by those who do not understand and are threatened by a radically different set of allegiances.

"Suffer you will, but don't die on the wrong hills," this author seems to say. Meet these strangers at the threshold of your household. By giving no occasion for unnecessary misunderstanding and malicious misrepresentation, you will demonstrate to your unbelieving neighbors where the *real* boundaries are between *The One* realm and all others.

In other words, *discernment,* again. And for us, perhaps the continuing dialogue can best be conducted by accepting the premise and questioning the behavioral implications—what does membership in "a holy nation" involve in relation to a nation where the political right claims authoritarian prerogatives as an all but divine right? How much, and what kind of "submission" and "suffering" are appropriate "trouble" to undertake in our attempts to be hospitable to the stranger?

The letter to the Romans can be similarly heard. If we take Romans 13:1–7 as a stand-alone piece, the requirements of Christian citizenship seem clear: do whatever the government tells you. Set within the larger discernment narrative, however (even if restricted to Romans 12—13), the answer becomes more complex. There is an intriguing tension between the apparent political imperatives of 13:1–5 and the requirements of becoming a "living sacrifice" (12:1): "Do not be conformed to this world, but be transformed by the renewing of your minds, so that you may discern what is the will of God" (12:2). Employing these two chapters in such a way as to justify a "two swords" theory of citizenship and political responsibility carves this material up altogether too neatly.

Granted the earnest exhortations to radical discipleship on both sides of the "let every one be subject to the governing authorities" passage, a case can be made for reading those "be subject" verses as meaning that "you've got the reign of God to embody—so don't get distracted by merely Roman bureaucracy."

Then there is the conclusion to this "obey the government" section: "Pay to all what is due them—taxes to whom taxes are due, revenue to whom revenue is due, respect to whom respect is due, honor to whom honor is due" (13:7). But what is that, precisely? If it is a flat pronouncement, it is a mere platitude. But what if it is intended rather as a faith community discussion-starter?

How might this approach to Paul's "theology of citizenship" take form in a sermon sketch that seeks to convene a discernment conversation on immigration policy? Here is a possible plotline.

1. "The law is the law." and, "The powers that be are ordained of God." The two phrases are often heard in the same breath, uttered by God-fearing, law-abiding folks. Those who take church seriously may not be above exceeding the speed limit on occasion, but they pay their fines when they get caught (and feel good about it.).
2. "This is not about discrimination, it's about illegal behavior." One often heard that in the Deep South not so many years ago. "Civil rights protestors are criminals." Both phrases, again, spoken by those who went to church—the very folks who uttered the other phrases.
3. How do those sentiments relate to what is often termed "the problem of illegal immigration"? All of a sudden it isn't so clear, because the nation is divided now, and not simply along party lines (or even ethnic lines). If "the State" has spoken and we must obey, it's hard to know just what to do; the state sends all sorts of conflicting signals.
4. It is pretty clear that Paul has a respectful view for government, in its proper place. Just what that place might be, however, is not entirely clear. Paul sends conflicting signals as well. He has just been talking to citizens of Rome about the need to "present your bodies as a living sacrifice"—the first manifestation

of which is not "to be conformed to this world, but to be transformed by the renewing of your minds." What does such transformation look like on the ground?

5. In ancient Israel strangers were welcomed, and slaves were to be released from slavery, but only on the Jubilee, on the Sabbath of Sabbaths, on the fiftieth year. You can't have an economy if there are no terms of exchange. You can't have a nation without boundaries. And yet, illegal immigrants are *resident* aliens. They are already members of our community just like the indentured servants, the slaves, in ancient Israel.

6. As with many thorny social issues our government struggles to address, the presenting problem is the tip of the iceberg. Who we let in, under what conditions, and what we should do with those who haven't followed all the rules—wouldn't it be nice if all we had to do was wait for our Congress to make up its mind and get on with upholding the law. Whatever they manage to come up with, however, is not the voice of God—any more than Caesar's voice was the voice of Paul's Sovereign Lord.

7. How shall we approach those deeper issues? Barbara Brown Taylor recounts an experience that does not give an answer— but helps to pose the question.

Last year, my husband Ed decided that what we needed more than anything was a flock of guinea hens—those unreal-looking salt-and-pepper colored birds with red wattles who make more racket than a pen full of beagles. His first batch of five lasted exactly one day after he let them loose in the yard. We figure that a weasel got them, since all three of the dogs swore that they were innocent. The second batch of five hens also lasted one day, so Ed built a big pen and kept the third batch in it for the better part of a year. The smell was—well, about what you would expect—but the hens survived.

Then a month ago, Ed let them out—and behold, they lived. They quickly took over the five acres around our house, flushing yellow moths from the long grass, and pecking at anything that moved. They also established a pecking order among themselves. Four of them got along fine, but they made life hell for the fifth. They chased her away from the cracked corn Ed pitched to them. They would not let her sit on the fence rail with them. Whatever was wrong with her was invisible to human eyes, but to guinea hen eyes, she was a real leper.

One evening I was down in the garden at dusk, which is when the guinea hens find a low branch to roost on for the night. They picked a young oak that night, right where the clover smell of the pasture meets the deep leaf smell of the woods. One by one, the first four guinea hens took off with a great beating of wings and huddled on the branch. As each one arrived, the others made room. Finally only the fifth one was left on the ground, but every time she rose to join them they beat her back, screaming at her as they rushed at her with their beaks. After six or seven tries she just stood in the wet grass below them and cried.

The next morning, four guinea hens strutted by my kitchen window. I looked everywhere for the fifth, but she was gone for good. I want to believe that she joined the flock down the road, but I don't think she could have made it that far all by herself. The woods around my house are full of predators—not only weasels but also coyotes and wild dogs. A guinea hen's protection is her flock, only her flock would not have her.[12]

8. Paul doesn't give us any policy answers, any more than Taylor's story does. But on both sides of his endorsement of stable government he outlines what such policies would embody: "Live in harmony with one another; do not be haughty, but associate with the lowly; do not claim to be wiser than you are" (12:16).(In a word, no pecking order politics.) "'Love your neighbor as yourself.' Love does no wrong to a neighbor; therefore, love is the fulfilling of the law" (13:9b–10). *That* law *is* the law—and only that has divine authority.

Once again, the intent is not to offer answers *ex cathedra*, but to convoke a continuing Spirit-ed conversation. The story employed toward the end of the sermon plot is compelling—but it opens discussion rather than shutting it down. Thus embedded in this homiletical attempt to plot Paul's mentoring narrative of communal discernment so as to nurture another here and now, Taylor's story *does* work within the ongoing preaching effort to equip Christian communities "to make the kinds of discriminations necessary for informed ethical decisions."

Journeys toward moral discernment, similar to other significant learning processes, have plots—even amid "the disorder and anarchy of life as it is." Effective mentors understand this dynamic well, and incorporate it into their teaching—and their preaching. Eugene Lowry's work is, I think, trivialized when characterized (however nuanced and expounded) as essentially a set of interjections along a trajectory between "Oops!" and "Yeah!" What he has identified, in comprehensible, teachable form, is the dynamic of spiritual discovery, one which preachers do not impose, either on scripture or on listeners, but through which they can move as custodians of the tradition and as colleagues in the community toward the discovery of grace and the discernment of how it can be both embraced and wrestled with in ongoing open-ended moral discernment.

14

Improvisations on the Lowry Loop

New Forms of Narrative Preaching for a Globalized World

THOMAS H. TROEGER

The Interrelationship of Culture and Homiletics

Preachers always preach in a particular cultural setting, and that setting influences the shape and substance of sermons. If we ask what new forms narrative preaching needs to take, we immediately face the question: What is the nature of the culture in which we are preaching, and what are the distinctive characteristics of its public speech? Cultures are so varied that it would be presumptuous to prescribe any single set of forms as if they were universally effective.[1] Each culture has its own rhetorical principles and standards of judgment about what constitutes effective communication by a speaker.

One of Gene Lowry's greatest contributions has been to develop homiletical structures for a media culture that is conditioned to expect surprising twists and turns of plot.[2] He has done this in a sophisticated manner, never reducing "narrative" simply to telling a story, but analyzing the means by which narrative structures create and release tension. The "Lowry loop" has helped dozens of my students to improve their preaching, making them more effective vessels of the Spirit, more engaging witnesses to the lively gospel of Christ. Nevertheless, his loop is culturally conditioned, as I believe Lowry himself would acknowledge, because his loop proposes a particular strategy for the use of language, and because he knows that, "The moment one uses the term *language* we are set in a social context. Surely, the title of Peter Berger and Thomas Luckmann's book *The Social Construction of Reality* of decades past says it all."[3] Lowry's understandings and principles of narrative structure work better for some of my students than for others. The difference is often a function of students coming from a culture with different rhetorical expectations and norms, with different understandings of how language should function in the pulpit, with different social constructions of reality.

Some Implications of Globalization for Homiletics

Having warned about assuming that any one narrative form will work in all cultures, I will risk contradicting myself by making the following broad generalization: increasing globalization is the context for a great deal of contemporary preaching, and when we speak about new forms of narrative preaching, we need to be attentive to this inescapable phenomenon.

"Globalization" is a hotly contested term. Some people denigrate it as a cover up for the spread of aggressive capitalism. Others welcome it as an imperfect but hopeful movement to claim our common humanity. Nayan Chanda, recognizing both the negative and positive values associated with the word, concludes that globalization will continue: "With all its promises and pitfalls, the historical process of reconnecting the human community is here to stay and increasingly visible and increasingly a challenge."[4]

Chanda points out that "globalization," although the term first appeared in 1962, is not new to our era. The process it names has been with us ever since human beings began to migrate: "Just as climate has shaped the environment over the millennia, the interaction among cultures and societies over tens of thousands of years has resulted in the increasing integration of what is becoming the global human community."[5] The difference between those ancient millennia and today is, "The accelerated speed of global interaction has telescoped its impact and the global spread of the media has made it instantly visible—something that in the past happened in slow motion and often out of sight."[6]

It is revealing to note that when Lowry first published *The Homiletical Plot* in 1980, television and cinema were already shaping culture in major ways, but there was not yet the interconnected media world of personal computers, blogs, video games, the World Wide Web, text-messaging, interactive programs, iPods, and the ubiquitous cell phone. As multitasking has become a new way of being and doing for many people, it would be fruitful to ask how it alters the sense of plot on which Lowry's loop is based. I believe that Lowry is already aware of the impact of these modifications because both in his writing and personal conversation he has evinced an increasing interest in episodal preaching. He wonders: "Is it possible that the conversational-episodal sermon is one type of a less linear inductive sermon, which is a certain form of a narrative sermon?"[7] My hunch is that the continuously fragmented experience of multitaskers—answering a cell phone while visiting a favorite Web site and listening to one's down-loaded tunes—may create a new kind consciousness that will be receptive to a "less linear inductive sermon."

Whether or not my hunch is true, Lowry's reflections and Chanda's observation about the "accelerated speed of global interaction" lead me to formulate a question that I believe is central to homiletics now and in the future: How can we nurture new forms of narrative preaching as an effective witness to the gospel in a globalized world? Although there are many ways to respond to the question, I will consider only two: (1) creating improvisations on the Lowry loop and (2) cultivating a theology of imagination.

Improvisations on the Lowry Loop

Put Lowry at a piano and he will begin with some simple tune that we know and love, not infrequently a hymn. But soon those fingers start dancing the edge of mystery as they move up and down the keyboard. There is a syncopation you had not expected, some accidentals creep in, a melisma appears over a half note when it used to sit there all on its own, then there is something strange in the bass that gets repeated in the treble but not repeated exactly as it was in the bass. Lowry is improvising. You can still hear the outlines of the familiar theme, but it is not just the same old tune. Then comes the next improvisation and the next and the next. He is now far away from the beginning key. You can barely make out the original tune, and you are wondering how he will ever get back home to that beloved old melody (and sometimes he is wondering too.).

What Lowry does at the keyboard, he does as well in his homiletical writings: he keeps giving us variations on the loop. See, for example, the "Afterword" in the expanded edition of *The Homiletical Plot* or read his continuing reflections on tension and resolution in *The Sermon: Dancing the Edge of Mystery*. Since Lowry himself plays with his theory, I want to try out a few improvisations that might be useful to nurturing new forms of narrative preaching for a globalized world.

The first improvisation that springs to mind draws upon the accounts of migration and international travel that fill the Bible. Our new forms of narrative preaching would grow from the metaphor of the journey of faith:

- The call
- Setting out
- Challenges and dangers
- Wanderings
- An unmapped turn
- Catching a vision of the promised land
- Coming home.

Another improvisation might be the process of learning the language of the gospel, its parables and paradoxes, its strange new angles on the world that put everything we see in a new light. Our new homiletical forms would grow from the metaphor of becoming fluent in a foreign language:

- Awkwardness
- Mispronunciation and misunderstanding
- Perplexity and befuddlement at new ways of thinking
- Discouragement
- A moment when the language finally clicks in the mind
- Increasing fluency
- An ability to communicate with those whose speech used to mean nothing to us
- Thinking and dreaming in the new language.

Yet another variation might resonate with the arguments in Corinth and Galatia as the gospel drew together people of different backgrounds and cultures. Our forms would schematize the strenuous work of cross-cultural understanding:

- Initial pleasantries to establish a relationship
- Growing courage to discuss differences
- Deep conflicts and disagreements
- The relationship nearly breaking down
- Receiving grace ample enough to keep together
- A profounder sense of our common humanity.

All these play around with the Lowry loop: they involve a process of increasing complication disrupted by a sudden twist that unfolds toward a surprising resolution. They are variations on Lowry's unforgettable theme as we adapt his insights to an increasingly globalized world of international travel, learning new languages, and striving for cross-cultural understanding. My intention in suggesting them is not to push any single improvisation, but rather to model a way of imaginative homiletical thinking. I believe such creativity is one of the things that has made Lowry's work so energizing for preachers.

Cultivating a Theology of Imagination

Lowry is confident about using his imagination, and it is the kind of confidence that preachers need: not arrogance, but vigorously claiming the God-given gifts of inventiveness and play. For new forms of narrative preaching do not work when preachers are themselves suspicious of using their imaginations and being creative.

Some of Lowry's work reveals that he is well-acquainted with the imaginative reserve of preachers, and how it often arises from simplistic polarities between imagination and scholarship:

I hope we do not need to choose between dull, scholarly, instructive lecture-sermons and snappy, creative sound bites. So I say, let the imagination run loose for a while. But now as we are about to begin actually shaping the sermon, it is time for closure—born of both creativity and scholarship. One great result of significant imaginative preparation time is that when we then turn to our scholarly work, our minds are ready with questions born of actual confusion, and wonderments waiting expectantly for birthing resolution. Such work is heady in more senses than one.[8]

The opening sentences in the passage resonate with my experience of teaching seasoned pastors and beginning preachers. Many are timid about using their imaginative powers. A theological fear of the power of the imagination restrains their creativity, a fear that has deep roots in the history of the church. Therefore, if we are going to nurture new forms of narrative preaching for a globalized world, we need to provide a positive theology of the imagination, one that celebrates it as a gift from God that is to be used like any other holy gift—in a spirit of gratitude, delight, and faithfulness. We need to be able to give a theological account of human creativity that nurtures preachers' imaginations so they can develop sermonic forms that are congruent with their unique "voice" as preachers,[9] appropriate for the local setting where they preach, and relevant to globalization as experienced by their people. More important than any one narrative form is the preacher's ability to create new forms for a globalized world that will allow the light of God to shine into the deepest shadows of human life. We need a theology that supports the use of the imagination as a way of being faithful to God.

In a recent multi-authored study of theological education, developing "the pastoral imagination" is a recurring motif. The pastoral imagination is described as "'a way of seeing into and interpreting the world' that in turn, 'shapes everything a pastor thinks and does.'"[10] The study goes on to affirm the need for "finding ways to cultivate the pastoral, priestly, or rabbinic imaginations of [theological] students as cultural representatives and builders of their religious traditions in the midst of these global and local movements."[11]

The study covers the full range of ministerial practice and not homiletics alone. It thus places our search for a theology that will nurture new forms of narrative preaching in a much larger framework. We are doing something far more profound than tinkering with better methods of communication. We are helping preachers in their most consistently visible public role "to be both representatives of the cultures of their religious traditions and agents or builders of those cultures in the changing dynamics of globalization in the modern world."[12]

My goal, then, is to develop a theology that can nurture the narrative creativity of preachers who are working at the intersection of local theology and globalization, a theology that helps them understand their creativity as a way of being faithful to God, a theology that will embolden them to present the gospel through new forms of narrative preaching.

Created to Create

I take as a starting point for this theology the priestly account of the creation of us human creatures: "God created humankind in his image, / in the image of God he created them; / male and female he created them" (Gen. 1:27). "The image of God" is one of those deep, rich phrases from the Bible that has awakened a wide span of interpretations:

> The imago has been understood in primarily cognitive terms as referring to a particular created capacity, whether that be reason [as in Thomas Aquinas] freedom [as in Gregory of Nyssa] the capacity for self-transcendence [as in Reinhold Niebuhr] or even an intrinsic orientation to God [as in Emil Brunner].[13]

But for our purpose of developing a theology that nurtures the use of the imagination to create new forms of imaginative preaching, I will focus on only one interpretation. It is an interpretation that emerges from a poetic reading of the text. I would never suggest this is the only interpretation. The richest passages of the Bible awaken a multiplicity of meanings, and the "image of God" text is no exception. But for now I will explore how being made "in the image of God" means that we are created to create.

The first image of God that appears in the Bible is no image at all: "In the beginning when God created the heavens and the earth, the earth was a formless void and darkness covered the face of the deep, while a wind from God swept over the face of the waters" (Gen. 1:1–2). There is no picture of what God looks like in these verses. There is, however, a vivid portrayal of what God does: God creates. God sends a wind over the waters. This imageless image of God as creator is the only image of God that has yet appeared in the Bible when we read twenty-four verses later: "Then God, said, 'Let us make humankind in our image, according to our likeness'" (Gen. 1:26a). As the biblical witness continues to unfold, we will encounter God as redeemer, God as shepherd, God as fortress, and a multitude of other images. But at this point, in the first chapter of the first book of the Bible, the first image of God we have encountered is the imageless image of God the creator.

Therefore, to be made in the image of God is to be created to create. We honor that image whenever we bring into being works of language, music, science and art that are in harmony with the One who has made all that is. Notice exactly how I put this: it is not everything we create that honors the image of the Creator. We human beings create a lot of things that desecrate the image of God. We create prejudice, injustice, diatribes, manifestos of hate, systems of injustice and oppression, weapons, and instruments of torture. There is a long list of things soaked in blood that we human beings have created. When we create them we distort and disfigure the image of God in ourselves. Perhaps this is why the biblical writers reserve a particular Hebrew word—*bara*—to describe the creative work that belongs exclusively to God: they are eager for us not to hallow our destructive creativity by appealing to the name of God. And perhaps it is this same awareness that makes preachers reticent about being creative, about using their imaginations. They have enough self-awareness to realize that preachers can fashion sermons that are as lethal as any weapon designed by human intelligence and forged by human hands:

> Too often, God, your name is used
> to sanction hate and fear
> so love and justice are refused
> to people you hold dear.
> O never let us use your name
> to harm or hurt or kill
> or consecrate a vicious aim
> as your almighty will.[14]

If we disavow using the gift of the imagination because of its potential for misuse, then we will have to disavow all other gifts as well because we have the capacity to abuse all of them. We engage our imaginations as preachers in order to remind our congregations and ourselves that we are created to create in ways that reflect rather than distort the image of God. I do not mean every sermon will be on this topic, but rather over time our preaching is a witness to the Creating Spirit that swept over the waters and that blows anew upon our congregations through the sermons we create. When we use our imaginations to create new forms of narrative preaching, we are not abandoning tradition; we are carrying on the process that started with, "In the beginning God created…"

That was a great risk on God's part, since the potential for our misusing the creative imagination is always with us. In the case of preachers, there is always the temptation to fashion a sermonic form that is merely entertaining or trendy or cute, or worse yet, to appeal to the vicious character of human nature. But there is also the possibility that we will create something that is connected to the deepest structures of experience and faith, which opens us to the transforming power of Holy Wind and Flame.

The poet Linda Pastan reflects on how God might have played it much safer. She imagines God taking a break after creating all the plants.

> If God had stopped work after the third day
> With Eden full of vegetables and fruits,
> If oak and lilac held exclusive sway
> Over a kingdom made of stems and roots,
> If landscape were the genius of creation
> And neither man nor serpent played a role
> And God must look to wind for lamentation
> And not to picture postcards of the soul,
> Would he have rested on his bank of cloud
> With nothing in the universe to lose,
> Or would he hunger for a human crowd?
> Which would a wise and just creator choose:
> the green hosannas of a budding leaf
> or the strict contract between love and grief?[15]

The poet keeps us from reading too quickly through Genesis 1. She compels us to come to terms with the imaginative audacity of God, with God's willingness to take a vast risk by bringing forth creatures who are created to create. God has no guarantee they will maintain the harmony of creation. In creating us, God risks that we will use our creative powers to set up another order of existence, one in which even the gift of love becomes rigidly affixed to grief.

As things have turned out, it is clear that God indeed took a very great risk in creating us to create. Sometimes when we are overwhelmed by the brutality and bloodiness of human behavior, we may find ourselves at the precipice of despair, wondering if a wise and just Creator might not have more prudently stopped with the plants and settled for receiving "the green hosannas of a budding leaf." We hear the swish of the wind-blown trees and hunger to be in harmony with the One who "swept over the face of the waters." This hunger reaches down to the deep wells from which our holiest imaginings spring. Before there is the sermon, there is the Spirit moving through the heart in sighs too deep for words, sighs that become sound that become notes that become rhythm, melody, harmony, music.

Listening to the Wordless Depths before We Speak

Lowry's writing gives witness to a keen awareness of how his homiletic has been fed by making and listening to music. I kept track of all his musical references in *The Sermon: Dancing the Edge of Mystery*. By my count there are no fewer than eight significant passages about music, and they often bear the weight of his homiletical argument. This may at first seem irrelevant to our developing a positive theology of the imagination to encourage preachers in the creation of new narrative forms; but it is essential to the process. A homiletic that limits the genesis of a preacher's imaginings purely to language ignores that the Spirit may move outside of language before finding articulation in words. One of the ways to encourage the homiletical imagination and the creation of new narrative preaching is for preachers to be as attentive to music as Gene Lowry is. He writes:

> Although by analogy Craddock drew the principle of anticipation from biblical exegetical work, my connection surely came implicitly from music. Stephen Crites is right that "the rhythm and melody lines of music are inherently temporal," which by means of a "succession of pulses and pitched vibrations" provide the listener with a "unity through time."[16]

For Lowry preaching is itself musical in character: "One could speak of the basic *musicality* of any sermon. Music, after all, is also an event-in-time art form, with melody, harmony, and rhythm coming, sequentially. No one *builds* a song; it is shaped and performed."[17]

When Lowry is explaining what he means by "complication," he again flows naturally into observations about music:

We are accustomed to this basic movement of plot as it happens in other art forms. Often such movement brings real pleasure. Mozart is quietly playing a pleasant and simple rendition of "Twinkle, Twinkle, Little Star"—and then the music shifts modality. Numerous variations lure us successively into the light-hearted and intimate dance, the slow minor key walk, and the heavy-handed stately march. Very clever. Quite interesting.[18]

Quite interesting indeed. So interesting that as Lowry eschews simplistic sermonizing he returns again to music, this time jazz, as he quotes Leroy Ostransky:

"Poor and mediocre jazzmen will impose problems on themselves, problems of resolution whose answers are already evident in the resolutions they set up." The key, he says, is not the resolution "however elaborate," but the "inherent intricacy of the irresolution."[19]

And when Lowry wants to show us how narrative sermons "tend to use the glue of single-thread connectors to make the jump toward new and unfamiliar territory," we find ourselves in a concert hall listening to a symphony:

One movement is coming to an end. The listeners expect dead silence. But when the conductor grandly sweeps the arms of conclusion, one oboe holds out with a single note—the fifth tone of the concluding chord, which by musical magic also just happens to be the third tone of the key of the next moment. The move to greater and fresh complication hangs on the thread of a single oboe tone. (Translation: never make transitions by means of broad conclusions, but with the strength of a powerfully thin note of ambiguity.)[20]

Note how he puts the linguistic translation in parentheses, as if it were an afterthought, not really needed if you hear the oboe.

To explain what he means by the "sudden shift" in a sermon, Lowry draws on "the A-A-B-A musical sequence of a typical ballad" and "the moment between B and A, when after a shift of key, of melodic line, and of verse motif (called the bridge), the music restates the theme another time—a theme transformed by the route it has just traveled."[21]

Bringing the sermon to completion, Lowry returns to the jazz moment at the end of the big band presentation; when someone calls out "one more time," he will ever so deftly, lightly, and suggestively repeat a phrase from that earlier articulation of the good news. This reprise quickly places the message graciously in the lap of the listeners—note, not with imperative claim, but with indicative promise.[22]

And from whence comes this homiletic that pulses and sings with music? Lowry says:

> If you can imagine sermon preparation as a kind of improvisational jazz piece, you will get the sense of how important it is to allow the music to get sideways, conflicted, pulled away from its simple mooring. It sometimes feels as though the musicians either have forgotten what piece they are playing or have lost their way. But then comes the turn toward home with a quiet celebratory sense of release visible in the eyes of the musicians—and concluding, then, with a simple reprise. What a trip.[23]

Yes, what a trip, but Lowry would not get there without his music. Take the music out of Lowry and you take away the vitalizing energy. Not all preachers have the musical talent and knowledge that Lowry has, but that is no reason for ignoring what this analysis of the music in his homiletic implies: namely, the importance of being open to those wordless sighs of the Spirit praying for us, sighs whose echoes we so often hear in music. Even if we do not play or sing, we can still be listeners. Listening is itself a kind of performance in which we make our ears, our minds, and our hearts accompanists to the one creating and producing the music.

I do not know what new narrative forms for preaching will arise out of our tending to the depths of music with the same affection and passion as Lowry, but I do know from my own experience that, after preaching and preaching and preaching, after words and words and words, my language is spent. Then I pick up my flute and, pouring music through that silver pipe, I am reconnected to yearnings, longings, dreamings, stirrings, beauty, and glory that dance on the edge of mystery. In that Spirit-filled moment I begin to read more precisely and understand more thoroughly Genesis 1 and what it means to be created in the image of God.

Most of the interpretations of Genesis 1 that I have encountered through books and sermons focus on how God's word brings forth light and land, plants and animals.

"God *said,* 'Let there be light'; and there was light." "God *said,* 'Let the earth put forth vegetation…' And it was so." "God *said,* 'Let the earth bring forth living creatures of every kind…' And it was so."

In focusing on what God said, we may fail to observe that before God spoke a word, God did something else to set the whole process in motion: "a wind from God swept over the face of the waters." First the sound of wind, then the sound of waves as their white caps break and slide down the slopes of the turbulent sea. God blows and creates the music of the sea before God speaks. First: sound; then: speech. First: music; then: word. The word arises out of the sound, out of the song, out of the music of wind and wave.

As I acknowledged earlier, I am offering a highly poetic reading of the opening of Genesis, but the passage itself is highly poetic, it sings to us with the sounds of wind and water. I would also point out that the development of speech in children replicates the pattern of creation: a child's first word arises out of breath, out of sound, out of the music of early cries and laughter. In our globalized world, while we speak many languages, all of us go through that generative process. We are sisters and brothers by virtue of the breath and the music of our first cries and laughter. To remember this is to remember the One who breathed that breath into us, and one of the major callings of the preacher is to keep that memory alive.

To breathe, to make music, to listen to music, to create: all are essential ways that we reclaim our creatureliness and our awareness of being made in the image of God. To allow for these things in our daily formation as well as in our creation of sermons is to claim more faithfully what God has always intended us to be.

The Narrative Line of God's Grace and Compassion

Gene Lowry has had the faith to allow the primeval pattern of sighing, listening, music making, and speaking to shape him and his sermons. Out of it has come his rich ministry and creative scholarship that help us preach in ever-deeper ways the gospel of Jesus Christ. If we are as attentive as Lowry has been to the Spirit, we will find the new narrative forms for preaching that can engage the globalized community. Attending to the immense pain and suffering of that community, we will understand that our search for new narrative forms is nothing less than an act of discipleship: we want to preach sermons that give witness to the narrative line of God's grace and compassion as it unfolds through the twists and turnings of history.

Listen, then, for the Spirit praying through this wounded and broken world in sighs too deep for words. Listen to the music that gathers in your own heart. If you find it difficult to move from the sigh to the word, from the music to the sermon, then start with the Lowry loop and try improvising. Let some of your improvisations be brooding and bluesy, as sad as the world at its saddest, and let others be filled with the playful, imaginative mind that God has given to you as a source of visionary power and delight.

> The Archangel Michael cried,
> "Oops!"
> put down his baton,
> and frowned with displeasure
> at the whole host of heaven.
> The angelic choristers,
> stopped in the middle of their Gloria
> thinking they were to be chastised
> for missing a note.
> But Michael by now had his back to them.
> He had glimpsed something
> out of the corner of his eye
> and was staring down
> over the edge of mystery
> into Kansas.
> "What's wrong?"
> cried the heavenly host,
> their beatific voices

cracking with concern for the choirmaster.
Archangel Michael responded:
"Ugh! Gene Lowry's retiring.
I fear the homileticians will become less musical,
and stuff the air with words alone
to set up a deadly, unmusical homiletical drone
instead of the roller coaster
of the Lowry loop
that makes the heart
sing and dance and whoop."
One of the angel choristers patted
Michael on the shoulder and said:
"This is indeed a grave complication."
Archangel Michael went over to the piano
and absent-mindedly picked out
the melody of the Gloria they had been rehearsing,
repeating it twice,
then transposing it down a step and a half.
The joyful acclamation
turned bluesy.
Soon one of the angels
picked up a trombone
and another a clarinet
and another started plucking a double bass,
while tears filled the eyes
of the rest of the choristers.
But then all of a sudden
Archangel Michael's left hand
found a note he had not expected
and he exclaimed aloud,
"Aha!"
and he began a syncopated version
of the opening tune
till heaven filled
with a foot-stomping,
hand-clapping,
body-swaying Gloria:
Glo – ri – *a!* Glo – ri – *a!* Glo – ri – *a!*
The angels who were not jamming
started to dance,

moving their feet and flapping their wings
and tossing their haloes
like Frisbees
one to another.
The dance grew and grew
till it was a surging sea
of wing and nimbus and radiance,
and the dancers joined in the music
with glad shouts of "Whee!"
When it ended
Archangel Michael rose from the piano
with a big, glad smile
because he realized
that although Gene had retired,
he had left behind
an unforgettable tune,
and there would be new generations
coming along
to add their own improvisations.
Michael told his choristers
that Gene had discovered
the truth sounding in every Gloria:
that the gospel of Jesus Christ
is music in the heart.
Gene's playing and preaching,
his writing and teaching
have been his way of singing
his own holy part.
And with one voice,
the whole host of heaven said:
"Yeah!"

Notes

Introduction

[1]See Richard L. Eslinger, *A New Hearing: Living Options in Homiletic Method* (Nashville: Abingdon, 1987), 65. Although Eslinger uses the term in his chapter on Lowry, in Gene's own words it better applies to Craddock. See Eugene L. Lowry, "The Revolution of Sermonic Shape," in *Listening to the Word: Studies in Honor of Fred B. Craddock*, ed. Gail R. O'Day and Thomas G. Long(Nashville: Abingdon, 1993), 93.

[2]Lowry, "The Revolution of Sermonic Shape," 94.

Chapter 1: A More-or-Less Historical Account of the Fairly Recent History of Narrative Preaching

[1]See the work of Perry Miller, especially *The New England Mind* (Boston: Beacon, 1961).

[2]Henry Steele Commager, with S.A. Morison, *The Growth of the American Republic* (New York: Oxford, 1962).

[3]Harry Emerson Fosdick, *The Modern Use of the Bible* (New York: MacMillan, 1924).

[4]A successor to Fosdick at The Riverside Church, Ernest T. Campbell followed the same practice. His small publication *Campbell's Notebook,* is a good example of this gathering of stories, dialogue, and image.

[5]See Frederick Buechner's sermon, "The Annunciation," in *The Magnificent Defeat* (New York: Seabury Press, 1966).

[6]For a thoroughgoing account of this effort and the scholars who have advanced it—a good many of whom are beyond the range of this chapter—see Richard L. Eslinger's works: *A New Hearing: Living Options in Homiletic Method* (Nashville: Abingdon Press, 1987), and *The Web of Preaching* (Nashville: Abingdon Press, 2002).

[7]Amos Wilder, *The New Voice: Religion, Literature, and Hermeneutics* (New York: Herder and Herder, 1969).

[8]Ibid., 51.

[9]Ibid., 52.

[10]Amos Wilder, *Early Christian Rhetoric: The Language of the Gospel* (Cambridge: Harvard University Press, 1964).

[11]Ibid., 119, 120.

[12]Amos Wilder, *Theopoetic* (Philadelphia: Fortress Press, 1976), 91–92.

[13]Ibid., 2, 6, 8.

[14]Ibid., 16.

[15]Ibid., 20.

[16]Ibid., 21.

[17]Ibid., 35.

[18]Ibid., 37.

[19]Ibid., 49.

[20]Ibid., 59.

[21]Ibid., 85, 86.

[22]Ibid., 56–58.

[23]Ibid., 97.

[24]Ibid., 124, 126.

[25]Letter of Edward Stanley, August 9, 1955.

[26]Edmund A. Steimle, Morris Niedenthal, and Charles Rice, *Preaching the Story* (Philadelphia: Fortress Press, 1980), ix.

[27]Ibid., 9, 12.

[28]H.H. Farmer, *The Servant of the Word* (New York: Scribner's, 1942).

[29]H.H. Farmer, "The Historical Understanding," *History and Theory* 3 (1963–64): 149–202.

[30]Steimle, Niedenthal, and Rice, *Preaching the Story*, 146.

[31]Charles Rice, "The Expressive Style in Preaching," *Princeton Seminary Bulletin*, 54 (March 1971): 30–42.

[32]See here Steimle's essay, "The Fabric of the Sermon," in *Preaching the Story*.

[33]Charles Rice, "The Preacher as Storyteller," *Union Seminary Quarterly Review*, 31 (Spring 1976): 182–97.

[34]Ibid., 185; see Harvey Cox, *The Seduction of the Spirit: The Use and Misuse of People's Religion* (New York: Simon and Schuster, 1973).

[35]See here the work of another Lutheran, Richard Thulin, *The I of Preaching* (Minneapolis: Fortress Press, 1989).

[36]Frederick Buechner, *The Magnificent Defeat* (New York: Seabury Press, 1966), 144.

[37]Ibid., 58–59.

[38]Ibid., 87.

[39]See James Robinson and John Cobb, eds., *New Frontiers in Theology: Volume II, The New Hermeneutic* (New York: Harper and Row, 1964), especially the essays of Ernst Fuchs and of Gerhard Ebeling.

[40]Frederick Buechner, *The Alphabet of Grace* (New York: Seabury Press, 1970).

[41]Paul Scott Wilson, *Imagination of the Heart* (Nashville: Abingdon, 1988), especially chapter one. See here also the work of the imaginative and literary Methodist preacher, Robert Raines: *Creative Brooding* (New York: MacMillan, 1966) and *Sounding* (Waco: Word Books, 1970).

[42]Charles L. Rice, *Interpretation and Imagination: The Preacher and Contemporary Literature* (Philadelphia: Fortress Press, 1970).

[43]Paul Tillich, *Theology of Culture* (New York: Oxford, 1959).

[44]Frederick Herzog, *Understanding God* (New York: Scribner, 1966).

[45]Rice, *Interpretation and Imagination*, 18. The male pronoun reference to the preacher is reprinted from Buechner's original quotation that predates the regular presence of women in the pulpit.

[46]Edmund A. Steimle, The James A. Gray Lectures, Duke University, November 1966.

[47]See here another book that influenced Edmund Steimle—Joseph Sittler, *The Anguish of Preaching* (Philadelphia: Fortress Press, 1966), especially chapter 1, "The Role of the Seminary in the Formation of the Preacher."

[48]Fred Craddock, *As One Without Authority: Essays on Inductive Preaching* (Enid, Okla.: Phillips University Press, 1971), vii.

[49]Ibid., 13. As does Buechner's, in the earlier quotation, Craddock's use of the male pronoun for preacher reflects the general experience of the early 1970s.

[50]Ibid., 21.

[51]Ibid., 53.

[52]Ibid., 54.

[53]Ibid., 54.

[54]Ibid., 57.

[55]Ibid., 57.

[56]Ibid., 60.

[57]Barbara Brown Taylor, *Mixed Blessings*, 2d ed. (Cambridge, Mass.: Cowley, 1998).

[58]Ibid., 37.

[59]Lucy Atkinson Rose, *Sharing the Word* (Louisville: Westminster John Knox Press, 1997).

[60]Leonora Tubbs Tisdale, *Preaching as Local Theology and Folk Art* (Minneapolis: Fortress Press, 1997).

[61]Jana Childers, *Performing the Word: Preaching as Theater* (Nashville: Abingdon Press, 1998).

[62]Martin Luther King Jr., *The Strength to Love* (Philadelphia: Fortress Press, 1963).

[63]See Richard Lischer, *The Preacher King* (New York: Oxford Press, 1995).

[64]Henry Mitchell, "African American Preaching," in *Concise Encyclopedia of Preaching*, ed. William Willimon and Richard Lischer (Louisville: Westminster John Knox Press, 1995), 3.

[65]Henry H. Mitchell, *Black Preaching: The Recovery of a Powerful Art* (Nashville: Abingdon Press, 1990).

⁶⁶Richard L. Eslinger, *The Web of Preaching: New Options in Homiletic Method* (Nashville: Abingdon Press, 2002), 46.

⁶⁷John Knox, *The Integrity of Preaching* (New York: Abingdon, 1957), 12. Knox's use of the generic "man" in this quotation, while it was still widespread at the time of its writing, is obviously anachronistic now.

⁶⁸See Paul Scott Wilson, *Imagination of the Heart: New Understandings in Preaching* (Nashville: Abingdon, 1988), chapter 4.

⁶⁹Ibid., 19.

⁷⁰Ibid., 19–23.

Chapter 2: Theology Undergirding Narrative Preaching

¹For a significant discussion of options, see Eugene L. Lowry, *The Sermon: Dancing the Edge of Mystery* (Nashville: Abingdon Press, 1997), 22–23; cf. Eugene L. Lowry, *How to Preach a Parable: Designs for Narrative Sermons* (Nashville: Abingdon Press, 1989), and John S. McClure, "Narrative Preaching: Sorting It All Out," *Journal for Preachers* 15 (1991): 24–29.

²Lowry, *The Sermon*, 22, 25–28. A quintessential expression of this viewpoint is Lowry's classic *The Homiletical Plot: The Sermon as Narrative Art Form*, exp. ed. (Louisville: Westminster John Knox Press, 2001).

³E.g., C.S. Song, *The Believing Heart: An Invitation to Story Theology* (Minneapolis: Fortress Press, 1999); idem, *Tell Us Our Names: Story Theology from an Asian Perspective* (Salem, Oreg.: Wipf and Stock, 2005).

⁴E.g., Hans W. Frei, *The Eclipse of Biblical Narrative: A Study in Eighteenth and Nineteenth Century Hermeneutics* (New Haven: Yale University Press, 1974); George W. Lindbeck, *Religion and Theology in a Postliberal Age* (Philadelphia: Westminster Press, 1984); Ronald F. Thiemann, *Revelation and Theology: The Gospel as Narrated Promise* (Notre Dame: University of Notre Dame Press, 1985); Stanley Hauerwas and L. Gregory Jones, eds., *Why Narrative? Readings in Narrative Theology* (Grand Rapids: Eerdmans, 1989); Joe R. Jones, *A Grammar of Christian Faith: Systematic Explorations in Christian Faith and Doctrine* (Lanham, Md.: Rowman and Littlefield, 2002). As in all theological movements, different authors in this general stream differ with one another on various points.

⁵For an overview of contemporary theological families and preaching characteristic of those families, see Ronald J. Allen, *Thinking Theologically: The Preacher as Theologian*, (Minneapolis: Fortress Press, 2007).

⁶Stephen Crites, "The Narrative Quality of Experience," *Journal of the American Academy of Religion* 39 (1971): 291.

⁷For a summary of scholarship on this point, see Ronald J Allen, "Shaping the Sermon by the Language of the Text," in *Preaching Biblically: Creating Sermons in the Shape of Scripture*, ed. Don M. Wardlaw (Philadelphia: Westminster Press, 1983), 11–29.

⁸To be sure, the distinction between these two uses of language can be artificial. Language that is ordinarily primary in character can be used in secondary ways. And I frequently have the experience of secondary language (e.g., in a book of systematic theology) stirring deep and intense primary experience. Nevertheless, this distinction has some value for thinking generally about patterns of the function of language.

⁹Susanne K. Langer, *Philosophy in a New Key: A Study in the Symbolism of Reason, Rite and Art*, 3rd ed. (Cambridge: Harvard University Press, 1957;o.p. 1941), 201.

¹⁰I borrow the language of "more" from Bernard E. Meland, *Fallible Forms and Symbols: Discourses on Method in a Theology of Culture* (Philadelphia: Fortress Press, 1976), xiii, 43, 48. Meland, however, often uses the expression to speak of the divine presence in every situation (a "More" than we casually and typically perceive).

¹¹Crites, "The Narrative Quality of Experience," 297.

¹²Susanne K. Langer, *Feeling and Form: A Theory of Art Developed from Philosophy in a New Key* (New York: Charles Scribner's Sons, 1953), 292.

¹³Crites, "Narrative Quality of Experience," 295.

¹⁴The same general points are true of Judaism, though with nuances appropriate to the Torah, Prophets, and Writings, and later Jewish developments.

¹⁵Richard Lischer, "The Interrupted Sermon," *Interpretation* 50 (1996): 178.

[16]Allen, "Shaping the Sermon," 30–34.

[17]The following observations are generally true of the Protestant, Roman Catholic, and Orthodox versions of the Bible.

[18]Ironically, narrative theologians seldom actually do theology in the narrative mode. They typically reflect in conventional analytic forms on primary Christian narrative. For an example of a narrative theologian who tries to keep the narrative structure close to the form of theology itself, see Gabriel Fackre, *The Christian Story: A Narrative Interpretation of Basic Christian Doctrine*, rev. ed. (Grand Rapids: Eerdmans, 1984); idem, *The Doctrine of Revelation: A Narrative Interpretation*, Edinburgh Studies in Constructive Theology (Edinburgh: Edinburgh University Press, 1997).

[19]Jaroslav Pelikan, *Credo: Historical and Theological Guide to Creeds and Confessions of Faith in the Christian Tradition* (New Haven: Yale University Press, 2003), gives attention to the historical circumstances that generated the creeds.

[20]For a reconstruction of Christian history that gives particular attention to the relationship between historical circumstance and doctrine, see Jaroslav Pelikan, *The Christian Tradition: A History of the Development of Doctrine* (New Haven: Yale University Press, 1975, 1977, 1980, 1985, 1991), vols. 1, 2, 3, 4, 5. More concisely, we find a similar approach (with greater emphasis on marginalized groups) in Justo González, *The Story of Christianity* (Nashville: Abingdon Press, 1984, 1985), vols. 1 and 2, and idem, *A History of Christian Thought* (Nashville: Abingdon Press, 1987), 3 vols.

[21]Ronald J. Allen, *Preaching Is Believing: The Sermon as Theological Reflection* (Louisville: Westminster John Knox Press, 2002), 86–87.

[22]For representative critical reflections on narrative preaching, see Lischer, "The Interrupted Sermon"; idem, "The Limits of Story," *Interpretation* 38 (1984): 26–38; David L. Bartlett, "Story and History: Narratives and Claims," *Interpretation* 45 (1991): 229–40; and Richard L. Eslinger, *The Web of Preaching: New Options in Homiletical Method* (Nashville: Abingdon Press, 2002), 46–52, 93–98, 141–45, 193–97, 234–40.

[23]Clifford Geertz, *The Interpretation of Cultures* (New York: Basic Books, 1973), 3-31.

[24]For a summary of supporting data, see Joseph R. Jeter Jr. and Ronald J. Allen, *One Gospel, Many Ears: Preaching for Different Listeners in the Congregation* (St. Louis: Chalice Press, 2002), 49–78.

[25]See Leander E. Keck, *The Bible in the Pulpit: The Renewal of Biblical Preaching* (Nashville: Abingdon Press, 1978), 100.

[26]Ernest T. Campbell, "Every Battle Isn't Armageddon," in *To God Be the Glory: Sermons in Honor of George Arthur Buttrick*, ed. Theodore A. Gill (Nashville: Abingdon Press, 1973), 145.

[27]See further, Allen, *Preaching Is Believing*, 132–33; for an example of these difficulties at work, see Clark M. Williamson, *A Guest in the House of Israel: Post-Holocaust Church Theology* (Louisville: Westminster John Knox Press, 1993), 16–17.

[28]From a personal conversation with Van Seters.

Chapter 3: A Match Made in Heaven

[1]Eugene L. Lowry, *The Sermon: Dancing the Edge of Mystery* (Nashville: Abingdon Press, 1997), 20.

[2]See Mark Chaves, *Ordaining Women: Culture and Conflict in Religious Organizations* (Cambridge, Mass.: Harvard University Press, 1997), 1.

[3]Maxine Walaskay, "Gender and Preaching," *The Christian Ministry* 13 (January 1982): 8.

[4]Edwina Hunter, "Weaving Life's Experiences into Women's Preaching," *The Christian Ministry* 18 (September-October 1987): 16.

[5]Ibid., 16, 14.

[6]Christine M. Smith, *Weaving the Sermon: Preaching in a Feminist Perspective* (Louisville: Westminster John Knox Press, 1989), 15.

[7]Ibid., 14–15.

[8]Mary Catherine Hilkert, "Women Preaching the Gospel," in *Women in the Church I*, ed. Madonna Kolbenschlag (Washington: Pastoral, 1987), 86–87.

⁹Elaine J. Lawless, "Weaving Narrative Texts: The Artistry of Women's Sermons," *Journal of Folklore Research* 34 (1997): 22.

¹⁰Hilkert, "Women Preaching the Gospel," 86, 87.

¹¹Hunter, "Weaving Life's Experiences," 16.

¹²Ibid.

¹³Edwina Hunter, "Finally Said: Women Must Preach Differently Than Men," in *Preaching on the Brink: The Future of Homiletics,* ed. Martha J. Simmons (Nashville: Abingdon Press, 1996), 146.

¹⁴Ibid., 152.

¹⁵Cleophus J. LaRue, "Two Ships Passing in the Night," in *What's the Matter with Preaching Today?* ed. Mike Graves (Louisville: Westminster John Knox Press, 2004), 138.

¹⁶Ibid., 139.

¹⁷Lowry, *The Sermon,* 27.

¹⁸See Carol Gilligan, *In a Different Voice: Psychological Theory and Women's Development* (Cambridge, Mass.: Harvard University Press, 1982); Mary Field Belenky, et al., *Women's Ways of Knowing: The Development of Self, Voice and Mind* (New York: Basic Books, 1986); and Deborah Tannen, *You Just Don't Understand: Women and Men in Conversation* (New York: Ballantine Books, 1990).

¹⁹Smith, *Weaving the Sermon,* 14.

²⁰Carol M. Norén, *The Woman in the Pulpit* (Nashville: Abingdon Press, 1991), 130.

²¹Roxanne Mountford, *The Gendered Pulpit: Preaching in American Protestant Spaces* (Carbondale, Ill.: Southern Illinois University Press, 2003), 156.

²²Charles D. Hackett, ed., *Women of the Word: Contemporary Sermons by Women Clergy* (Atlanta: Susan Hunter Publishing, 1985), 16.

²³Smith, *Weaving the Sermon,* 55.

²⁴Ibid., 14.

²⁵Lawless, "Weaving Narrative Texts," 32.

²⁶Ibid., 27.

²⁷Nelle Morton, "Preaching the Word," in *Sexist Religion and Women in the Church: No More Silence!* ed. Alice L. Hageman (New York: Association Press, 1974), 39.

²⁸Lawless, "Weaving Narrative Texts," 21.

²⁹Leonora Tubbs Tisdale, "Women's Ways of Communicating: A New Blessing for Preaching," in *Women, Gender, and Christian Community,* ed. Jane Dempsey Douglass and James F. Kay (Louisville: Westminster John Knox Press, 1997), 114.

³⁰See studies of early American preaching women such as Catherine A. Brekus, *Strangers and Pilgrims: Female Preaching in America, 1740–1845* (Chapel Hill: The University of North Carolina Press, 1998); Bettye Collier-Thomas, *Daughters of Thunder: Black Women Preachers and Their Sermons, 1850–1979* (San Francisco: Jossey-Bass, 1998); and Beverly Zink-Sawyer, *From Preachers to Suffragists: Woman's Rights and Religious Conviction in the Lives of Three Nineteenth-Century American Clergywomen* (Louisville: Westminster John Knox Press, 2003).

³¹Elaine J. Lawless, *Women Preaching Revolution: Calling for Connection in a Disconnected Time* (Philadelphia: University of Pennsylvania Press, 1996), 97.

³²Hunter, "Weaving Life's Experiences," 16.

³³Lawless, "Weaving Narrative Texts," 22.

³⁴Hilkert, "Women Preaching the Gospel," 87.

Chapter 4: African American Contexts of Narrative Preaching

¹Barack Obama, *The Audacity of Hope: Thoughts on Reclaiming the American Dream* (New York: Crown, 2006), 195–ff. The title of the book is taken from a sermon delivered by the outstanding African American preacher and pastor of Trinity, Dr. Jeremiah Wright Jr. Wright stands squarely in the African American preaching tradition as did his father before him.

²A phrase often used by Henry H. Mitchell, who pioneered scholarship on African American preaching in his *Black Preaching* (Philadelphia: Lippincott, 1970) and *Black Preaching: The Recovery of a Powerful Art* (Nashville: Abingdon Press, 1990).

³See C. Eric Lincoln, *Coming Through the Fire: Surviving Race and Place in America* (Durham: Duke University Press, 1996).

⁴Howard Thurman, *Jesus and the Disinherited* (Nashville: Abingdon Press, 1949) is a classic work by Thurman. Martin Luther King Jr. was said to have always carried a copy of Thurman's book along with his Bible in his briefcase at all times.

⁵John C. Holbert, *Preaching Old Testament: Proclamation and Narrative in the Hebrew Bible* (Nashville: Abingdon Press, 1991), 9–10. Italics added.

⁶Benjamin Elijah Mays, *The Negro's God as Reflected in His Literature* (Boston: Chapman and Grimes/Mount Vernon Press, 1938), 21–24.

⁷James Weldon Johnson, *God's Trombones: Seven Negro Sermons in Verse* (New York: Vikings Press, reprinted in 1955, originally 1927), 1.

⁸See Thomas Spann, "An Interpretation of an African-American Prayer," *The Journal of Religious Thought* 51 (Winter 1994–Spring 1995): 95–110.

⁹Krister Stendahl, "The Bible as a Classic and the Bible as Holy Scripture," *Journal of Biblical Literature* 103 (March 1984): 3.

¹⁰W.E.B. DuBois, *The Souls of Black Folk* (New York: Avon Books, 1965), 338. This work was first published in 1903 when DuBois was still a professor at the author's alma mater, Clark Atlanta University, Atlanta, Georgia.

¹¹Ibid., 442. Quoted by James H. Harris, *Preaching Liberation* (Minneapolis: Fortress Press, 1995), 49.

¹²Cf. Gayraud Wilmore, *Black Religion and Black Radicalism*, 2d ed., rev. and enlarged (Maryknoll, N. Y.: Orbis Books, 1983), 1–28; also 53–ff.

¹³Quoted in Albert J. Raboteau, *Slave Religion: The "Invisible Institution" in the Antebellum South* (Oxford: Oxford University Press, 1978), 235.

¹⁴Henry H. Mitchell, "Preaching and the Preacher in African American Religions," in *Encyclopedia of African American Religions*, ed. Larry G. Murphy, et al. (New York: Garland, 1993), 608.

¹⁵Evans E. Crawford, "Sound On: New Riffs for God's Trombones" (reprint of lecture given at Howard University Divinity School in 2005), 2.

¹⁶Evans E. Crawford, *The Hum: Call and Response in African American Preaching* (Nashville: Abingdon Press, 1995).

¹⁷Obama, *Audacity of Hope,* 208.

Chapter 5: Tracking the Homiletical Plot

¹Eugene Lowry usually reserves the use of the term "episodic" to refer to a distinctive subset of sermons that employ a series of "apparently unrelated vignettes successively accumulating until a final ideational *gestalt* unites the whole." However, the stages of a Lowry loop are certainly episodes in the process, though intending much more connectedness along the way. Eugene L. Lowry, "The Revolution in Sermon Shape," in *Listening to the Word: Studies in Honor of Fred B. Craddock,* ed. Gail R. O'Day and Thomas G. Long (Nashville: Abingdon Press, 1993), 99. Also see Eugene Lowry, *The Sermon: Dancing the Edge of Mystery* (Nashville: Abingdon Press, 1997), 26–28.

²Eugene L. Lowry, *The Homiletical Plot: The Sermon as Narrative Art Form,* exp. ed. (Louisville: Westminster John Knox Press, 2001), 118. (Hereafter, *Homiletical Plot,* exp. ed.)

³Eugene L. Lowry, "What Progress?" in *What's the Matter with Preaching Today?* ed. Mike Graves (Louisville: Westminster John Knox Press, 2004), 162. This collection of excellent essays seeks to explore the question Harry Emerson Fosdick raised in his famous 1928 article. Lowry mentions that Fosdick, too, was disturbed by this "begin-with-answers" approach to preaching (162).

⁴Ibid., 163.

⁵Ibid., 162–63.

⁶The "Lowry loop" of five distinct stages was presented first in Eugene L. Lowry, *The Homiletical Plot: The Sermon as Narrative Art Form* (Atlanta: John Knox Press, 1980). (Hereafter, *Homiletical Plot,* 1980.) More recently, a four-stage version of the homiletical plot was proposed in Lowry, *The Sermon.* See Richard L. Eslinger, *The Web of Preaching:*

New Options in Homiletic Method (Nashville: Abingdon Press, 2002), 33–56, for an analysis of both the five- and four-stage approaches to Lowry's loop.

[7]See Lowry, *Homiletical Plot,* exp. ed., 118–20.

[8]Ibid., 118.

[9]In Lowry, *Homiletical Plot,* exp. ed., the fourth stage, "Good News," is construed as more mobile than the other stages, at times being merged with the third stage and at others being folded into the "Unfolding." See 117–21. Lowry also devotes attention to this mobility of the good news stage in Lowry, *The Sermon,* 81–85.

[10]Page numbers from Lowry, *The Sermon,* are cited in the text.

[11]Lowry, "What Progress?" 164–65. (In the spirit of full disclosure, it should be noted that this writer was a member of one of those "lectionary selection committee[s].")

[12]Lowry, *Homiletical Plot,* 33.

[13]Lowry, "What Progress?" 164.

[14]David Buttrick, *Homiletic: Moves and Structures* (Philadelphia: Fortress Press, 1987), 374.

[15]Lowry, *Homiletical Plot,* 1980, 36.

[16]Ibid., 42.

[17]See Lowry, *The Sermon,* 70—74, for examples of complication derived from this differing contexts.

[18]See Richard L. Eslinger, "Fwd., Fwd., Fwd.: Mega-Story in an Untaught Homiletic," *Journal of Theology* 106 (Summer 2002): 3–22.

[19]Lowry, *Homiletical Plot,* exp. ed., xii.

[20]See Buttrick, *Homiletic,* 141—43, on first-person sermon illustrations.

[21]Lowry, *Homiletical Plot,* 1980, 48.

[22]Ibid., 50.

[23]Eugene L. Lowry, *Doing Time in the Pulpit: The Relationship Between Narrative and Preaching* (Nashville: Abingdon Press, 1985), 74. Quoted in Lowry, *The Sermon,* 75.

[24]Paul Scott Wilson, *Preaching and Homiletical Theory* (St. Louis: Chalice Press, 2004), 90.

[25]Ibid.

[26]Ibid., 89.

[27]Ibid.

[28]Paul Scott Wilson, *Imagination of the Heart* (Nashville: Abingdon Press, 1988), 108.

[29]Paul Scott Wilson, *The Four Pages of the Sermon: A Guide to Biblical Preaching* (Nashville: Abingdon Press, 1999), 269, n. 5. See Richard L. Eslinger, *Web of Preaching,* 236–38, for a further discussion of this issue between Wilson and Lowry.

[30]See Mary Catherine Hilkert, *Naming Grace: Preaching and the Sacramental Imagination* (New York: Continuum, 1999).

[31]See Buttrick, *Homiletic,* 217–21, for an analysis of this concrete language of preaching. Also see Wilson, *Four Pages of the Sermon,* 50–56.

[32]Lowry, *Homiletical Plot,* exp. ed., 120.

[33]Ibid.

[34]Walter Brueggemann, *Finally Comes the Poet* (Minneapolis: Fortress Press, 1988), 4.

[35]See William Willimon, *Peculiar Speech: Preaching to the Baptized* (Grand Rapids: Eerdmans, 1992).

[36]Frank A. Thomas, *They Like to Never Quit Praisin' God: The Role of Celebration in Preaching* (Cleveland: United Church of Christ Press, 1997), 96.

[37]Lowry, "What Progress?" 163.

[38]Ibid.

[39]Ibid.

[40]See, for example, Dan Kimball, Ivy Beckwith, Renee N. Altson, *The Emerging Church: Vintage Christianity for New Generations* (Grand Rapids: Zondervan, 2003).

[41]Charles L. Campbell, *Preaching Jesus: New Directions for Homiletics in Hans Frei's Postliberal Theology* (Grand Rapids: Eerdmans, 1997). (Hereafter cited in the text.)

[42]Lowry, *Homiletical Plot,* 66.

[43]Charles Campbell, *Preaching Jesus,* faults Lowry for the title of this volume, especially when only one of the four sermons analyzed in it is based on a parable. This

leads Campbell to charge, "Implicit in this title is the equation of narrative and parable for the purposes of preaching" (174). Campbell, however, will need to argue this claim on other grounds. As sent to the publisher, Lowry's manuscript was titled "*Designs for Narrative Sermons*," seeking to evoke and honor the contribution of Grady Davis's *Design for Preaching*. The publisher changed the title to the one Campbell critiques.

[44]William C. Placher, *Unapologetic Theology* (Louisville: Westminster John Knox Press, 1989).

[45]Ibid., 134, quoted as part of a larger quote used from Lowry, *The Sermon*, 51.

[46]Ibid., 91.

[47]Campbell, *Preaching Jesus*, 144.

[48]P.T. Forsyth, *Positive Preaching and the Modern Mind* (Grand Rapids: Eerdmans, 1979), 53. Quoted in Lowry, *The Sermon*, 40.

[49]Lowry, *Homiletical Plot*, exp. ed., 127.

[50]Ibid., 122.

[51]Campbell, *Preaching Jesus*, 162.

[52]Ibid.

[53]Ibid., 163.

[54]Ibid., 236–37, 240.

[55]Ibid., 172.

[56]Lowry, "What Progress?" 159.

[57]Wilson, *Preaching and Homiletical Theory*, 94.

[58]Lowry, *Homiletical Plot*, exp. ed., 131.

[59]Campbell, *Preaching Jesus*, 138.

Chapter 6: Story, Narrative, and Metanarrative

[1]Two examples among many: M. Eugene Boring, *1 Peter*, Abingdon N.T. Commentaries (Nashville: Abingdon Press, 1999), appendix 1; Norman Petersen, *Rediscovering Paul: Philemon and the Sociology of Paul's Narrative World* (Philadelphia: Fortress Press, 1985).

[2]Udo Schnelle, *Apostle Paul*, trans. M.E. Boring (Grand Rapids: Baker, 2003), 523, esp. footnotes 110, 111.

[3]"Othering" is the process by which a person or a group are labeled as "Other" by the Imperial discourse. Therefore, "it is a political process, originally connected to the colonial era and, therefore, to Modernity." See the article titled "othering" in *Key Concepts in Post-Colonial Studies*, ed. Bill Ashcroft, Gareth Griffiths and Helen Tiffin (London: Routledge, 1998), 171–73.

[4]For the discussion of postmodernity and skepticism about metanarrative, I am indebted to Paul Lakeland, *Postmodernity: Christian Identity in a Fragmented Age* (Minneapolis: Fortress Press, 1997).

[5]Umberto Eco, *Six Walks in the Fictional Woods* (Cambridge, Mass: Harvard University Press, 1994), 139–140.

[6]This is the position of Jean-François Lyotard, who defines the "postmodern" as "incredulity toward metanarratives" in *The Postmodern Condition: A Report on Knowledge* (Minneapolis: University of Minnesota Press,1984), xxiv.

Chapter 7: Story and Symbol, the Stuff of Preaching

[1]Edmund A. Steimle, Morris J. Niedenthal, and Charles L. Rice, *Preaching the Story* (Philadelphia: Fortress Press, 1980).

[2]The phrase the "the mighty acts of God" deliberately echoes the title of an influential work by George Ernest Wright and Reginald Fuller, *The Book of the Acts of God: Contemporary Scholarship Interprets the Bible* (Garden City, N.Y., Doubleday, 1960).

[3]H. Richard Niebuhr, *The Meaning of Revelation* (New York: Macmillan, 1946), 60.

[4]Hans W. Frei, *The Eclipse of Biblical Narrative: A Study in Eighteenth and Nineteenth Century Hermeneutics* (New Haven: Yale University Press, 1974).

[5]For example, Mark Ellingsen, *The Integrity of Biblical Narrative: Story in Theology and Proclamation* (Eugene, Oreg.: Wipf and Stock, 1990); Gabriel Fackre, *The Christian Story:*

A Narrative Interpretation of Basic Christian Doctrine (Grand Rapids: Eerdmans, 1996); Michael Goldberg, *Theology and Narrative: A Critical Introduction* (Eugene, Oreg.: Wipf and Stock, 1981); Gerhard Laughlin, *Telling God's Story: Bible, Church and Narrative Theology* (Grand Rapids: Eerdmans, 1995); Stanley M. Hauerwas and L. Gregory Jones, eds., *Why Narrative? Readings in Narrative Theology* (Grand Rapids: Eerdmans, 1999); William Placher, *Narratives of a Vulnerable God* (Louisville: Westminster John Knox Press, 1994); George Stroup, *The Promise of Narrative Theology* (Eugene, Oreg., Wipf and Stock, 1997).

[6]Will churches in the Reformed Tradition ever let go of Barth? Doubtful. Maybe for Presbyterians and other Reformed types, Barth will shine on for centuries like Aquinas has in the conservative Catholic tradition.

[7]James Barr, *Semantics of Biblical Language* (London: SCM Press, 1961), and also Barr's *Old and New in Interpretation* (London: SCM Press, 1966); and see Barr's influential lecture, "Revelation Through History in the Old Testament and in Modern Theology," *Princeton Seminary Bulletin* 56 (1963): 4–14.

[8]Langdon Gilkey, "Cosmology, Ontology, and the Travail of Biblical Language," *Journal of Religion* 61 (1961): 194–205. But also see his subsequent major works, Langdon Gilkey, *Naming the Whirlwind: The Renewal of God-Language* (Indianapolis: Bobbs-Merrill, 1969), and idem, *Reaping the Whirlwind: A Christian Interpretation of History* (New York: Seabury Press, 1976).

[9]Brevard Childs, *Biblical Theology in Crisis* (Philadelphia: Westminster Press, 1970).

[10]Brevard Childs, "Interpreting the Bible Amid Cultural Change," *Theology Today* 54 (July, 1997): 200–211.

[11]Thomas G. Long, "What Happened to Narrative Preaching?" *Journal for Preachers* 28 (Pentecost, 2005): 9–14.

[12]Hans Frei, as quoted by Childs in a personal reminiscence, Childs, "Interpreting the Bible Amid Cultural Change," 201.

[13]For a fine introduction to the postliberal position, see Gary Dorrien, "The Origins of Postliberalism," *The Christian Century* (July 4–11, 2001): 16–21.

[14]See George A. Lindbeck, *The Nature of Doctrine: Religion and Theology in a Postliberal Age* (Philadelphia: Westminster Press, 1984), and also *The Church in a Postliberal Age*, ed. James Buckley (Grand Rapids: Eerdmans, 2003).

[15]Paul Ricoeur, *Time and Narrative*, vol. 1, trans. Kathleen McLaughlin and David Pellauer (Chicago: University of Chicago Press, 1984), ix.

[16]A concern discussed in Richard L. Eslinger, *Narrative and Imagination* (Minneapolis: Fortress Press, 1995).

[17]I have dealt with Jesus as a "Living Symbol" of God before; see David Buttrick, *Preaching Jesus Christ* (Eugene, Oreg.: Wipf and Stock, 2002 [1988]), chapter 5; also idem, *Homiletic: Moves and Structures* (Philadelphia: Fortress, 1987), chapter 1.

[18]Eric Auerbach, *Mimesis: The Representation of Reality in Western Culture*, trans. William Trask (Princeton: Princeton University Press, 2003 [1953]).

[19]Eugene L. Lowry, *The Sermon: Dancing the Edge of Mystery* (Nashville: Abingdon Press, 1997), 11.

[20]Fred B. Craddock, *As One Without Authority: Essays on Inductive Preaching* (Enid, Okla.: Phillips University Press, 1971), and idem, *Overhearing the Gospel: Preaching and Teaching the Faith to Persons Who Have Heard It All Before* (Nashville: Abingdon Press, 1978).

[21]David J. Randolph, *The Renewal of Preaching* (Philadelphia: Fortress Press, 1969); Henry H. Mitchell, *Black Preaching* (Philadelphia: Lippincott, 1970), and idem, *The Recovery of Preaching* (San Francisco: Harper & Row, 1977); Eugene L. Lowry, *The Homiletical Plot: The Sermon as Narrative Art Form* (Atlanta: John Knox Press, 1980); Ronald J. Allen, *Contemporary Biblical Interpretation for Preaching* (Valley Forge: Judson Press, 1984); Buttrick, *Homiletic: Moves and Structures*; Thomas G. Long, *The Senses of Preaching* (Atlanta: John Knox Press, 1988), and idem, *The Witness of Preaching* (Louisville: Westminster John Knox Press, 1989); and Paul Scott Wilson, *Imagination of the Heart: New Understandings in Preaching* (Nashville: Abingdon Press, 1988).

[22]In the first section of Karl Barth, *Homiletik: Wesen und Vorbereitung der Predigt* (Zurich: EVZ-Verlag, 1966), he notes the work of homileticians. Clearly he is critical of

rhetorical wisdom. In Dietrich Ritschl, *A Theology of Proclamation* (Richmond, Va.: John Knox Press, 1960), Ritschl, then a Barthian devotee, expresses similar disdain, arguing that Scripture alone is a proper instructional guide for preaching.

[23]Marshall McLuhan, *Understanding Media: The Extensions of Man*, 2d ed. (New York: McGraw-Hill, 1964); Walter J. Ong, *The Presence of the Word: Some Prolegomena for Cultural and Religious History* (New Haven: Yale University Press, 1967), notes that visual media tend to disunify, its effect forming in individual subjectivity, whereas being addressed unifies an audience. More, spoken words tend to relate to structures of verbal understanding and, thus, singularly to faith formation.

Chapter 8: Out of the Loop

[1]Eugene L. Lowry, *The Homiletical Plot: The Sermon as Narrative Art Form*, exp. ed. (Louisville: Westminster John Knox Press, 2001), 20.

[2]Ibid., 25.

[3]Ibid., 26.

[4]Ibid., 23.

[5]See Eugene L. Lowry, *Doing Time in the Pulpit: The Relationship Between Narrative and Preaching* (Nashville: Abingdon Press, 1985), especially chapter 4; idem, *How to Preach a Parable: Designs for Narrative Sermons* (Nashville: Abingdon Press, 1989), especially 23–26; idem, *The Sermon: Dancing the Edge of Mystery* (Nashville: Abingdon Press, 1997), especially chapter 4.

[6]Fred B. Craddock, "Foreword," in Lowry, *The Homiletical Plot*, exp. ed., xvii.

[7]Edmund Steimle, Morris J. Niedenthal, and Charles L. Rice, *Preaching the Story* (Philadelphia: Fortress Press, 1980), 12–13.

[8]Laurens Van Der Post as quoted in Eugene L. Lowry, *Doing Time in the Pulpit*, 39–40.

[9]Barbara Hardy as quoted in ibid., 39.

[10]Charles Taylor, *Sources of the Self* (Cambridge: Cambridge University Press, 1989), 47.

[11]Galen Strawson, "Against Narrativity," *Ratio* (new series) 17, no. 4 (December 2004): 428–52.

[12]Ibid., 428.

[13]Ibid., 430.

[14]Ibid., 434.

[15]Ibid., 433.

[16]Ibid., 447.

[17]Ibid.

[18]Ibid., 437.

[19]Michael Frayn, *Spies* (New York: Picador, 2002), 10, as quoted in James Phelan, "Editor's Column: Who's Here? Thoughts on Narrative Identity and Narrative Imperialism," *Narrative* 13, no. 3 (October 2005): 207.

[20]Strawson, "Against Narrativity," 437.

[21]Oliver Sacks, *The Man Who Mistook His Wife for a Hat and Other Clinical Tales* (New York: Harper, 1987), 110.

[22]Strawson, "Against Narrativity," 437.

[23]Ibid., 449.

[24]James L. Battersby, "Narrativity, Self, and Self-Presentation," *Narrative* 14, no. 1 (January, 2006): 37.

[25]Neil Postman, *Amusing Ourselves to Death: Public Discourse in the Age of Show Business* (New York: Penguin, 1986), chapter 7.

[26]See Thomas G. Long, "What Happened to Narrative Preaching?" *Journal for Preachers* 28, no. 4 (Pentecost, 2005): 9–14.

[27]Adam Hamilton, *Unleashing the Word: Preaching with Relevance, Purpose, and Passion* (Nashville: Abingdon Press, 2003), 43.

[28]Ibid., 44.

[29]Ibid., 83.

[30]Battersby, "Narrativity, Self, and Self-Presentation," 43.

Chapter 9: Jazz Me, Gene

[1]Eugene L. Lowry, *The Sermon: Dancing the Edge of Mystery* (Nashville: Abingdon Press, 1997), 39.

[2]See Fred Craddock, *Overhearing the Gospel :Preaching and Teaching the Faith to Persons Who Have Heard It All Before* (Nashville: Abingdon Press, 1978).

[3]David James Randolph, *The Renewal of Preaching* (Philadelphia: Fortress Press, 1969), 19.

[4]See Richard F. Ward, "Performance Turns in Homiletics," *Reformed Liturgy and Music* 30 (1996).

[5]Lowry, *The Sermon*, 15.

[6]Ibid., 19.

[7]Thomas H. Troeger, *Imagining a Sermon* (Nashville: Abingdon Press, 1990), 67.

[8]Lowry, *The Sermon*, 57.

[9]See Eugene Lowry, "Whither the New Homiletic" in *Homiletic E-Forum*, Fall 2006, online at www.homiletics.org.

[10]See Scott Gibson's "Critique of the New Homiletic: Examining the Link between the New Homiletic and the New Hermeneutic" online at www.preachingtoday.com.

[11]Craddock, *As One Without Authority*, 70–71.

[12]David Buttrick, "On Doing Homiletics Today," in *Intersections: Post-Critical Studies in Preaching*, ed. Richard L. Eslinger (Grand Rapids: Eerdmans, 1994), 101.

[13]John E. Skoglund, "Towards a New Homiletic," *Princeton Seminary Bulletin* 60 (Fall 1967): 57.

[14]Anthony C. Thiselton, "The New Hermeneutic," in *A Guide to Contemporary Hermeneutics*, ed. Donald K. McKim (Grand Rapids: Eerdmans, 1986), 78.

[15]Gibson, "Critique of the New Homiletic," 4.

[16]Thomas G. Long, "And How Shall They Hear?" in *Listening to the Word: Studies in Honor of Fred B. Craddock*, ed. Gail R. O'Day and Thomas Long (Nashville: Abingdon Press, 1993), 170.

[17]Robin R. Meyers, *With Ears to Hear: Preaching as Self-Persuasion* (Cleveland: Pilgrim Press, 1993), 6.

[18]Comments heard, transcribed, and paraphrased from *Jazz and Christianity*, a lecture and concert given by Gene Lowry, accompanied by Milt Abel, and recorded live at the Association of Unity Churches, Unity Village, Mo., 1995.

[19]Ibid.

[20]Ibid.

Chapter 10: Making Music with What You Have Left

[1]Valentino Lassiter, *Martin Luther King in the African American Preaching Tradition* (Cleveland: Pilgrim Press, 2001), 8.

[2]Jerome Groopman, *The Anatomy of Hope: How People Prevail in the Face of Illness* (New York: Random House, 2004).

[3]Ibid., 193.

[4]Ibid.

[5]Ibid.

[6]Martin Luther King Jr., *A Time to Break Silence* (New York: Riverside Press, 1967).

[7]Martin Luther King Jr., as quoted in James M. Washington, *A Testament of Hope: The Essential Writings of Martin Luther King, Jr.* (San Francisco: Harper & Row, 1986), 233.

[8]Ibid., 234.

[9]Ibid., 242.

[10]Ibid., 240.

[11]Ibid.

[12]Ibid.

[13]Groopman, *Anatomy of Hope*, 193.

[14]Ibid.

[15]Henry H. Mitchell, *Celebration and Experience in Preaching* (Nashville: Abingdon Press, 1990), 21–32.

[16]Ibid., 39.

[17]Groopman, *Anatomy of Hope,* 201.

[18]Davidson, as quoted in ibid., 203.

[19]In ibid., 204

[20]In ibid., 205.

[21]This story appeared in the *Houston Chronicle* on Feb. 10, 2001. The author, Rabbi Jack Riemer, has given permission for its use here. However, Rabbi Riemer also indicated that subsequent to the 2001 article, he heard that his source material may have been more "urban legend" than fact.

[22]William R. Bradbury and Edward Mote, "The Solid Rock," in *The New National Baptist Hymnal* 15th printing (Nashville: National Baptist Publishing Board, 1983), 223.

Chapter 11: Gasping for Breath

[1]A sampling of feminist biblical texts written in the last twenty-five years includes: Elisabeth Schussler Fiorenza, *In Memory of Her: A Feminist Theological Reconstruction of Christian Origins* (New York: Herder and Herder, 1983); idem, *Bread Not Stone: The Challenge of Feminist Biblical Interpretation* (Boston: Beacon, 1984); Adele Berlin, *Poetics and Interpretation of Biblical Narrative* (Sheffield: Sheffield, 1983); Phyllis Trible, *Texts of Terror: Literary-Feminist Readings of Biblical Narratives* (Philadelphia: Fortress Press, 1984); Phyllis Trible and Gene M. Tucker, eds., *Rhetorical Criticism: Context, Method and the Book of Jonah* (Philadelphia: Augsburg Fortress Press, 1985); Letty Russell, ed., *Feminist Interpretation of the Bible* (Philadelphia: Westminster Press, 1985); Adele Yarbro Collins, ed., *Feminist Perspectives on Biblical Scholarship* (Chico, Calif., Scholars Press, 1985); J. Cheryl Exum and Johanna W.H. Bos, eds., *Reasoning with the Foxes: Female Wit in a World of Male Power, Semeia* 42 (1988); Carol A. Newsom and Sharon H. Ringe, eds., *The Women's Bible Commentary* (Louisville: Westminster John Knox Press, 1992); J. Cheryl Exum, *Tragedy and Biblical Narrative: Arrows of the Almighty* (Cambridge: Cambridge University Press, 1992); idem, *Fragmented Women: Feminist (Sub)versions of Biblical Narratives* (Sheffield: Sheffield Academic Press, 1993); and too many others to list here.

[2]Delores Williams, *Sisters in the Wilderness: The Challenge of Womanist God-Talk* (Maryknoll, N.Y.: Orbis Books, 1993), 33.

[3]Alfred B. Smith, "Singspiration," copyright, 1941. Text and music printed as Hymn 156 in *Youth's Favorite Songs* (Minneapolis: Augustana Luther League, 1962).

[4]L. Susan Bond, *Trouble with Jesus: Women, Christology, and Preaching* (St. Louis: Chalice Press, 1999), 11.

[5]Patricinio Schweikart, "Reading Ourselves: Toward a Feminist Theory of Reading" in *Gender and Reading: Essays on Readers, Texts and Contexts,* ed. E.A. Flynn and P. Schweickart (Baltimore and London: Johns Hopkins, 1986), 42.

[6]Mordechai Cogan and Hayim Tadmor, *II Kings: Anchor Bible Commentary* (New York: Doubleday, 1988), 57.

[7]Bruce M. Metzger and Roland E. Murphy, eds., *The New Oxford Annotated Bible with Apocryphal/Deuterocanonical Books* (New York: Oxford University Press, 1991), 468.

[8]Danna Nolan Fewell, "Joshua," in *The Women's Bible Commentary,* ed. Carol A. Newsom and Sharon H. Ringe (Louisville: Westminster John Knox Press, 1992), 66.

[9]Jeff Sharlet, "Soldiers of Christ: I. Inside America's most powerful megachurch," *Harpers Magazine* (May 2005): 48.

[10]Trible, *Texts of Terror,* 86.

[11]Ibid., 87.

Chapter 12: Except in Parables of Jesus

[1]Dan Potter, as quoted in *Time* (April 24, 1964). Special thanks to my colleague, Dick Olson, for pointing out the history of this film.

[2]Like a few other terms in the New Testament, the Greek word *parabole* has been transliterated rather than translated. The Hebrew word from which it comes (*mashal*) covers a wide range of meanings—saying, riddle, and proverb being the most popular. This same variety of meanings is evident in the New Testament as well.

[3]C.H. Dodd, *The Parables of the Kingdom* (New York: Charles Scribner's Sons, 1961), 5. Although Dodd's eschatological perspective on the parables has been discredited by many scholars, his description of their rhetorical impact still remains quite valid.

[4]If you seek the solution, it is not to be found in this footnote. Just the fact that you looked may be evidence of the power of riddles. The riddle does appear in many sources, sometimes with the solution as well. For instance, see Dick Francis, *Decider* (New York: G. P. Putnam's Sons, 1993), 142–44.

[5]Flannery O'Connor, as quoted in Doris Betts, "Whispering Hope," in *Shouts and Whispers: Twenty-One Writers Speak About Their Writing and Their Faith*, ed. Jennifer L. Holberg (Grand Rapids: Eerdmans, 2006), 35.

[6]Søren Kierkegaard, as quoted in Fred B. Craddock, *Overhearing the Gospel: Preaching and Teaching the Faith to Persons Who Have Heard It All Before* (Nashville: Abingdon Press, 1978), 9. Emphasis mine.

[7]Paul Scott Wilson, *Preaching and Homiletical Theory* (St. Louis: Chalice Press, 2004), 23.

[8]Fred B. Craddock, *As One Without Authority*, rev. ed. (St. Louis: Chalice Press, 2001), 53, 113.

[9]In addition to Eugene L. Lowry, *The Homiletical Plot: The Sermon as Narrative Art Form* (Atlanta: John Knox Press, 1980), which was revised in 2001, see Richard A. Jensen, *Telling the Story: Variety and Imagination in Preaching* (Minneapolis: Augsburg, 1980); James Earl Massey, *Designing the Sermon: Order and Movement in Preaching* (Nashville: Abingdon Press, 1980); and Edmund A. Steimle, Morris J. Niedenthal, Charles R. Rice, *Preaching the Story* (Philadelphia: Fortress Press, 1980). The use of the term "*modern* narrative movement" is an important distinction, since manifestations have appeared throughout the church's history, and especially in the African American church in the last 150 years.

[10]Eugene L. Lowry, *The Homiletical Plot*, exp. ed. (Louisville: Westminster John Knox Press, 2001), 66–69. Although Lowry acknowledges the narrativity of other portions of Scripture, the parables seem to be the ideal embodiment of narrative ambiguity. See also his *How to Preach a Parable: Designs for Narrative Sermons* (Nashville: Abingdon Press, 1989), 20. It should be noted that, contrary to the title, parables were not his exclusive focus. Perhaps the volume should have been titled *How to Preach Parabolically*.

[11]Lowry, *The Homiletical Plot*, exp. ed., 21, 90.

[12]Ibid., 26. Although he has rethought the loop both in its number of stages and some of its terminology (see his work *The Sermon: Dancing the Edge of Mystery* [Nashville: Abingdon Press, 1997]), ambiguity remains a constant. The sermon moves from ambiguity to resolution.

[13]Lowry, *The Homiletical Plot*, exp. ed., 19.

[14]Ibid., 23.

[15]These colors represent different opinions on the authenticity of sayings attributed to Jesus. Members of the Jesus Seminar used color beads to express their judgments: Red, Jesus undoubtedly said this; Pink, Jesus probably said this; Gray, Jesus did not say this, but it expresses ideas akin to Jesus' message; and Black, Jesus did not say this, represents a later tradition.

[16]David E. Aune, *The New Testament in Its Literary Environment* (Philadelphia: Westminster Press, 1987), 51. Of the sixty-five parables that Aune uses in his calculations, the riddle-like parable (or "parable proper") is only one of four types. Thus, the open-ended parables constitute an even smaller percentage of the teachings of Jesus.

[17]Frank Kermode, *The Sense of an Ending: Studies in the Theory of Fiction* (London: Oxford University Press, 1966). See chapter 4, for instance, "The Modern Apocalypse," 93–124.

[18]Frank Kermode, *The Genesis of Secrecy: On the Interpretation of Narrative* (Cambridge, Mass.: Harvard University Press, 1979), 72.

[19]Douglas John Hall, *Confessing the Faith: Christian Theology in a North American Context* (Minneapolis: Fortress Press, 1996), 12–13, 349. Even the use of the indefinite article in Hall's subtitle is telling for this very reason.

[20]David J. Lose, *Confessing Jesus Christ: Preaching in a Postmodern World* (Grand Rapids: Eerdmans, 2003), 200.

²¹Sonja K. Floss and Cindy L. Griffin, "Beyond Persuasion: A Proposal for an Invitational Rhetoric," *Communication Monographs* 62 (1995): 2–4, 7.

²²Walter Brueggemann, *Cadences of Home: Preaching Among Exiles* (Louisville: Westminster John Knox Press, 1997), 57.

²³Lose, *Confessing Jesus Christ*, 205–6.

²⁴Parker J. Palmer, *The Courage to Teach: Exploring the Inner Landscape of a Teacher's Life* (San Francisco: Jossey-Bass, 1998).

²⁵Among more recent approaches to conversational preaching, see O. Wesley Allen Jr., *The Homiletic of All Believers: A Conversational Approach* (Louisville: Westminster John Knox Press, 2005); John S. McClure, *The Roundtable Pulpit: Where Leadership and Preaching Meet* (Nashville: Abingdon, 1995); and Lucy Atkinson Rose, *Sharing the Word: Preaching in the Roundtable Church* (Louisville: Westminster John Knox Press, 1997).

²⁶See Donald H. Juel, "A Disquieting Silence: The Matter of the Ending," in *The Ending of Mark and the Ends of God: Essays in Memory of Donald Harrisville Juel*, ed. Beverly Roberts Gaventa and Patrick D. Miller (Louisville: Westminster John Knox Press, 2005), 2. The story is expanded upon in Juel's *The Gospel of Mark* in Abingdon's *Interpreting Biblical Texts Series* (Nashville: Abingdon Press, 1999).

²⁷Barbara Brown Taylor, "Preaching Easter," *Journal for Preachers* 29 (Easter 2006): 42.

²⁸R.E.C. Browne, *The Ministry of the Word* (London: SCM Press, 1958), 60. See his fascinating chapter, "The Essential Untidiness," 58–71.

²⁹Lowry, *The Sermon*, 107.

³⁰Mike Graves, "Luke 10:25–37, The Moral of the 'Good Samaritan' Story?" *Review and Expositor* 94 (Spring 1997): 269–75.

Chapter 13: Convoking Spirit-ed Conversation

¹Richard Lischer, "The Limits of Story" *Interpretation* 38 (January 1984): 30.

²Ibid., 34

³Ibid., 35.

⁴Eugene L. Lowry, *Doing Time in the Pulpit* (Nashville: Abingdon Press, 1985). See also his helpful distinction, in the first chapter of *How to Preach a Parable: Designs for Narrative Sermons* (Nashville: Abingdon Press, 1989) regarding the relationship of story and narrative—all stories are narratives, but not all narratives are stories.

⁵Some of the material in this chapter is drawn from David J. Schlafer and Timothy F. Sedgwick, *Preaching What We Practice: Proclamation and Moral Discernment* (Harrisburg, Pa.: Morehouse, 2007), especially chapter 8. Not discussed in this chapter, but addressed throughout that book, is how distinctive Christian moral practices can be employed as lenses for moral discernment, and how techniques of narrative preaching strategy can be focused with specific relevance in the continuing task of preaching toward moral discernment.

⁶In his essay "The Will to Believe," philosopher William James spoke of certain choices as "live, momentous, and forced." See William James, *The Will to Believe and Other Essays in Popular Philosophy* (New York: The Plimpton Press, 1897, subsequently reprinted in many editions).

⁷Collect at the Liturgy of the Palms, *The Book of Common Prayer* (New York: Church Publishing, Inc., 1986), 270.

⁸Discernment is called for not just on the part of characters in biblical stories; it is required of *readers* who must balance the apparently conflicting advice found in different biblical texts, e.g., the promise of prosperity for the virtuous in deuteronomic literature with the suffering of Job, injunctions requiring behaviors both *inclusive* and *exclusive* with respect to those outside the Covenant community.

⁹The parables of the wheat and tares, of the long-sought pearl of great price juxtaposed with that of the treasure stumbled upon in a field, of the fishermen who sort out good fish and bad fish from the net that draws in fish "of every kind"—all of this concluded by Jesus' observation that every scribe trained for the kingdom, like the master of a household, "brings out of his treasure what is new and what is old" (13:52).

[10]The sermon samples that constitute *How to Preach a Parable*, for instance, include one Old Testament narrative, one gospel narrative, one gospel parable, and one epistle passage—which is a recounting by Paul of the story of his conversion.

[11]See Carolyn Osiek and David L. Balch, *Families in the New Testament World: Households and House Churches* (Louisville: Westminster John Knox Press, 1997).

[12]This material is taken from a lecture presented by Barbara Brown Taylor to participants in the Preaching Excellence Program, and has been reprinted in her *Preaching Through the Year of Matthew: Sermons that Work*, vol. 10, ed. Roger Alling and David J. Schlafer (Harrisburg, Pa.: Morehouse, 2001), ix–xi.

Chapter 14: Improvisations on the Lowry Loop

[1]Leonora Tubbs Tisdale, *Preaching as Local Theology and Folk Art* (Minneapolis: Fortress Press, 1997).

[2]Eugene L. Lowry, *The Homiletical Plot: The Sermon as Narrative Art Form*, exp. ed. (Nashville: Abingdon Press, 2001). Note especially how he begins his chapter on "Plot Forms" by drawing on a movie and a television series, 22ff.

[3]Eugene L. Lowry, *The Sermon: Dancing the Edge of Mystery* (Nashville: Abingdon Press, 1997), 40.

[4]Nayan Chanda, "What Is Globalization? Coming Together: Globalization means reconnecting the human community," *Yale Global Online*, (November 19, 2002), at http://yaleglobal.yale.edu/about_essay.jsp .

[5]Ibid.

[6]Ibid.

[7]Lowry, *The Sermon*, 28.

[8]Ibid., 106.

[9]Mary Donovan Turner and Mary Lin Hudson, *Saved from Silence: Finding Women's Voice in Preaching* (St. Louis: Chalice Press, 1999).

[10]Charles R. Foster, Lisa E. Dahill, Lawrence A. Golemon, Barbara Wang Tolentino, *Educating Clergy: Teaching Practices and Pastoral Imagination* (San Francisco: Jossey-Bass, 2006), 22. Quotations within quotations are from C.R. Dykstra, "The Pastoral Imagination" *Initiatives in Religion* (2001): 2–3, 15.

[11]Foster, et al., *Educating Clergy*, 264. The citation refers to R.J. Schreiter, *The New Catholicity: Theology Between the Global and the Local* (Maryknoll, N.Y.: Orbis Books, 1997).

[12]Foster, et al., *Educating Clergy*, 264.

[13]Ian A. McFarland, *The Divine Image: Envisioning the Invisible God* (Minneapolis: Fortress Press, 2005), 2.

[14]Unpublished hymn text by the author.

[15]Linda Pastan, "The Imperfect Paradise," in *The Imperfect Paradise: Poems* (New York: W.W. Norton & Co., 1988), 80.

[16]Lowry, *The Sermon*, 19

[17]Ibid., 55.

[18]Ibid., 66–67.

[19]Ibid., 69.

[20]Ibid., 72.

[21]Ibid., 78.

[22]Ibid., 86.

[23]Ibid., 105.

Contributors

Ronald J. Allen is Nettie Sweeney and Hugh Th. Miller Professor of Preaching and New Testament, Christian Theological Seminary, Indianapolis, Indiana.

David Buttrick is Drucilla Moore Buffington Professor Emeritus of Homiletics and Liturgics, The Divinity School, Vanderbilt University, Nashville, Tennessee.

Fred B. Craddock is Bandy Distinguished Professor Emeritus of Preaching and New Testament, Candler School of Theology, Emory University, Atlanta, Georgia.

Richard L. Eslinger is professor of homiletics and worship, United Theological Seminary, Trotwood, Ohio.

Mike Graves is William K. McElvaney Visiting Professor of Preaching, Saint Paul School of Theology, Kansas City, Missouri, and regional minister of preaching for the Greater Kansas City Christian Church (Disciples of Christ).

Thomas G. Long is Bandy Professor of Preaching, Candler School of Theology, Emory University, Atlanta, Georgia.

Barbara K. Lundblad is Joe R. Engle Associate Professor of Preaching, Union Theological Seminary, New York, New York.

William B. McClain is Mary Elizabeth McGehee Joyce Professor of Preaching, Wesley Theological Seminary, Washington, D.C.

Robin R. Meyers is senior minister of Mayflower Congregational UCC Church and professor of rhetoric at Oklahoma City University, Oklahoma City, Oklahoma.

Charles L. Rice is emeritus professor of homiletics, Drew Theological School, Drew University, Madison, New Jersey and a priest in the Episcopal Diocese of Newark.

David J. Schlafer is an Episcopal priest and homiletician who has taught preaching at Nashotah House, Seabury Western, the University of the South, Virginia Theological Seminary, and the College of Preachers.

Frank A. Thomas is senior pastor, Mississippi Boulevard Christian Church, Memphis, Tennessee, and adjunct professor of preaching, McCormick Theological Seminary, Chicago, Illinois.

Thomas H. Troeger is J. Edward and Ruth Cox Lantz Professor of Christian Communication, Yale Divinity School, Yale University, New Haven, Connecticut.

Beverly Zink-Sawyer is professor of preaching and worship, Union Theological Seminary and Presbyterian School of Christian Education, Richmond, Virginia.